North Carolina Real Estate License Exam Prep

All-in-One Review and Testing to Pass North Carolina's PSI Real Estate Exam

Second Edition

Stephen Mettling
David Cusic
Ryan Mettling

Performance Programs Company
502 S. Fremont Ave., Ste. # 724
Tampa, FL, 33606
www.performanceprogramscompany.com

Material in this book is not intended to represent legal advice and should not be so construed. Readers should consult legal counsel for advice regarding points of law.

© 2017 by Performance Programs Company
502 S. Fremont Ave. Suite #724,Tampa, FL 33606
info@performanceprogramscompany.com
www.performanceprogramscompany.com

ISBN 978-0692767412

Contents

Introduction

Welcome licensee candidates and future real estate professionals!

We know you have worked hard just to get here – you've completed or nearly completed your prelicense curricula, and now all you have to do is pass the state license exam. But easier said than done – and that's where we come in. We know the exam can be tough, and very nerve-wracking to prepare for. That's why we created the North Carolina Real Estate License Exam Prep (NC-RELEP) the way we did. Since we have been managing real estate schools and developing curriculum for forty years, we know how all this works – or fails to work. Let us assure you – you made the right decision buying this publication to prepare for your North Carolina exam. Here's why.

First, NC-RELEP is comprehensive in that it contains both key content review and testing practice. And the text review is NC-specific – not just simplistic national content, but terse, relevant and accurate state laws and regulations presented as a well-organized set of state 'key point reviews' ideal for pre-test memorization. But let's not dismiss the importance of the national content either. NC-RELEP's national key point reviews are a succinct compression of tested national principles and practices that comprise the national portion of state license exams from coast to coast. Our content is drawn from our own national textbook, Principles of Real Estate Practice – one of the most widely used principles textbooks in the country. Finally, our national content, as well as our question selection, is further tailored to the state testing outline promulgated by PSI for North Carolina. Thus the breadth and depth of the law reviews and test questions reflect the topic emphasis of your state's testing service and your NC license exam.

A word about the test questions… NC-RELEP's testing practice section consists of ten national practice tests, three state practice tests, and one state exam sample test. The practice tests are roughly 50 questions in length and the sample test is 105 questions. The test questions are designed to cover the content covered by the law reviews – which reinforces your learning of the total body of information tested by your state exam. The questions are direct, to the point, and designed to test your understanding. When you have completed a given test, you can check your answers against the answer key in the appendix. You may also note that each question's answer is accompanied by a brief explanation, or "rationale" to further reinforce your understanding.

Your particular study and testing practice strategy using NC-RELEP is up to you. But to fully exploit its comprehensive content coverage, you should try to review and memorize the key point reviews as much as possible. Then you should make every effort to take each exam, review your mistakes, and re-read the key point reviews that cover your weaker areas.

In the end, as you know, it's all up to you. Unlike other publications, we are not going to tell you that using this book will guarantee that you pass your state exam. It still takes hard work and study to pass. But we have done our best here to get you ready. Following that, the most we can do is wish you the best of success in taking and passing your state exam. So good luck!!

About the authors

For over forty five years, Stephen Mettling and David Cusic, PhD, have operated Performance Programs Company, one of the nation's most successful training organizations specializing in real estate program development. Mr. Mettling and Dr. Cusic have jointly written over 100 books, courses, and custom programs in all facets of real estate for some of the country's largest real estate schools, associations and organizations.

Mr. Mettling has also served as vice president and author for the country's largest real estate training and publishing organization. Under various capacities, he has managed the acquisition, development, and sale of national real estate textbooks and publications, as well as directed the country's largest affiliated group of real estate schools.

Dr. Cusic, an author and educator with international real estate training experience, has been engaged in vocation-oriented education since 1966. Specializing in real estate training since 1983, he has developed numerous real estate training programs for corporate and institutional clients around the country.

Ryan Mettling, partner and currently publisher of Performance Programs, is an accomplished online curriculum designer, author and course developer. His other principal publication is Real Estate Math Express. Mr. Mettling graduated Valedictorian from the University of Central Florida's College of Business Administration.

Consulting Editor Matt Davies is a North Carolina-licensed Broker-in-Charge whose special passion is helping others obtain real estate licensure. A Business Administration graduate of Bryant University with a concentration in accounting, Matt worked for PricewaterhouseCoopers before entering the real estate profession. Matt has been a licensed broker for 12 years and licensed instructor for 7 years.

Section I: National Principles & Law Key Point Review

Note: in the following pages, salespersons are sometimes distinguished from brokers. For broker-only states, the reader should substitute "broker" for "salesperson" and "managing broker" or similar title for "broker" as appropriate.

Rights

Land / Real Estate / Real Property

Land:	surface, all *natural things* attached to it, subsurface, and air above the surface
Real estate:	land + **manmade** permanent attachments
Real property:	real estate + bundle of rights

Bundle of Rights

"PUTEE":	*P* ossess
	U se
	T ransfer
	E xclude
	E ncumber

Physical Characteristics of Real Estate

Physical characteristics
- Immobility; indestructibility; heterogeneity.

Immobility
- Land cannot be moved from one site to another; its location is forever fixed

Indestructibility
- Land is permanent and cannot be destroyed since by definition it extends below ground and into the sky
- Since land is permanent, it does not depreciate
- Only improvements depreciate and are insurable

Non-homogeneity
- Land is non-homogeneous; no two parcels of land are exactly the same since they have a different location

Physical aspects of real estate

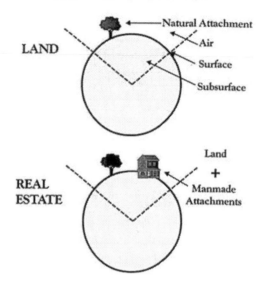

Legal Title v. Equitable title

Legal title

- Full legal ownership of property and the bundle of rights as they apply to it. Contrasts with equitable title.

Equitable title

- An interest that gives a lienholder or buyer the right to acquire legal title to a property if certain contractual conditions occur

---

Riparian / Littoral

Riparian Rights (Rivers and Streams)

- navigable: own land to water's edge
- *not navigable*: own underlying land to midpoint of stream

Littoral Rights (Lakes and Seas)

- own to high water mark

Memory Tip: R : River Riparian   L: Lake Littoral

Real / Personal / Fixture

Real Property:
- land
- fixtures
- attachments

Personal Property:
- chattels
- trade fixtures
- emblements

Differentiation criteria:
- intention; adaptation; functionality; relationship of parties; contract provisions

Conversion:
- real to personal property-- severance personal to real property-- affixing

Emblements:
- plants or crops considered personal property

Trade fixtures:
- personal property items temporarily attached to real estate in order to conduct business

Interests & Estates

Interests

Possession	Non-possession
• Estate	• Encumbrance • Public interest

Estates

Freehold (Own)	Leasehold (Lease)

• Fee simple
  - Absolute
  - Defeasible
 	
• Life Estates
  - Conventional
  - Legal
	• Estate for years
	• Periodic
	• Estate at Will
	• Estate at Sufferance

Freeholds

Fee simple	• *not limited* by one's lifetime • absolute: *highest* form of ownership interest • defeasible: *reverts* to previous owner per conditions
Life estate	• passes *to another* upon death of a named party • remainder: *named party* to receive estate • reversion: *previous owner* to receive estate
Conventional life estate	• *limited* to lifetime of life tenant or named party • pur autre vie: limited to lifetime of another,

9

	passes to remainderman or previous owner

Legal life estate	• created by operation of state law as opposed to a property owner's agreement
	• designed to protect family survivors
	• homestead:
	  • rights to one's **principal residence**
	  • laws protect homestead from creditors
	  • family must occupy the homestead
	  • cannot be conveyed by one spouse
	  • endures over life of head of household
	  • interests extinguished if property destroyed

Leaseholds

Estate for years	• specific, **stated duration**, per lease
Periodic	• lease term **renews automatically** upon acceptance of rent
Estate at Will	• for **indefinite period** subject to rent payment; cancelable with notice
Estate at Sufferance	• tenancy **against landlord's will** and without an agreement

Ownership

Forms of Ownership

Tenancy in severalty	• *sole* ownership
Tenancy in common	• co-tenants individually own undivided interests • **any ownership share possible** • no survivorship • can convey to outside parties
Joint tenancy	• equal undivided interest jointly owned • **survivorship** • requires **four unities** to create: time, title, interest, possession
Tenancy by the entireties	• **husband and wife** own equal undivided interest • Now applies to same-sex couples in some states
Community property	• **joint property ownership** by spouses as opposed to separate property

Joint Tenancy & Four Unities

Unity of ownership	• owners hold single title jointly
Equal ownership	• owners always hold equal shares
Transfer	• may transfer to new owner as a tenancy in common interest with remaining joint tenants
Survivorship	• on death, interests and rights pass to other joint tenants
Creation	• requires "four unities," *PITT*:

1. *P*ossession: acquire same possessory rights
2. *I*nterest: acquire equal, undivided interests
3. *T*ime: acquire interests at same time
4. *T*itle: acquire interests with same deed

Community Property

Separate

- acquired *before marriage*
- acquired by *gift or inheritance*
- acquired with *separate-property funds*
- *income* derived from *separate property*

Community

- all other property earned or acquired during the marriage

Estates in Trust

- *Trustor* gives title, deed, trust agreement to trustee
- *Trustee* renders fiduciary duties to trustor and beneficiary
- *Beneficiary* receives ownership benefits

Condominiums

- ownership of a *unit of airspace* plus an *undivided interes*t in the *common elements* as tenant in common with other owners
- may be sold, encumbered or foreclosed *without affecting other unit owners*
- creation: by developer's declaration

Cooperatives

- ownership of *shares in owning corporation*, plus *proprietary lease* in a unit
- corporation has sole, undivided ownership

Encumbrances & Liens

Easements

Appurtenant
- *attaches* to the estate
- *dominant* tenement's *right to use* or restrict adjacent *servient* tenement
- *by necessity*, to *landlocked* owners
- party wall easement in a shared structure: to not damage or destroy

in Gross
- *does not attach* to the estate
- **Personal**-- not transferrable, ends upon death of easement holder
- **Commercial**-- transferrable, granted to a business

by Prescription
- obtainable through *continuous, open, adverse use* over a period

License
- *personal* right to use a property
- *does not attach*
- *non-transferrable*
- *revocable*

Lien Types

Examples

voluntary / involuntary:
general / specific:
superior / junior:

- mortgage lien / tax lien
- against any & all assets / against car or house
- paid before juniors / paid after superiors by date of recording

Lien vs. Title Theory State

- **lien theory state** -- lender of mortgaged property holds equitable title rather than legal title; borrower holds legal title.

- **title theory state** – lender holds legal title to the mortgaged property until the mortgagor satisfies the terms and obligations of the loan.

Lien Priority

- Order in which liens against a property are satisfied
- The highest priority lien is paid by foreclosure proceeds before any other lien

Superior Liens by rank

- Real estate tax liens
- Special assessment liens

Junior Liens by date of recording

- Federal income tax liens
- Judgment liens

- Federal estate tax liens
- State inheritance tax liens

- Mortgage liens
- Vendor's liens
- Mechanics liens (priority by date work performed)

Foreclosure

Mortgage lien foreclosure:
- liquidation of collateral property by *judicial, non-judicial,* or *strict* foreclosure

Judicial foreclosure:
- lawsuit and court-ordered public sale; *deficiency judgments*, *redemption rights*

Non-judicial foreclosure:
- *"power of sale"* granted to lender; no suit; *no deficiency* judgment; *no redemption* period after sale

Strict foreclosure:
- court orders *legal transfer of title directly to lender* without public sale

Deed in lieu of foreclosure:
- defaulted *borrower deeds property to lender* to avoid foreclosure

Transferring & Recording Title

Notice

Notice:
- how ownership is evidenced to the public

Actual notice:
- *knowledge acquired directly* through demonstrable evidence, e.g., presenting or inspecting a deed, visiting a party in possession

Constructive notice:
- *knowledge one could have obtained*, as presumed by law; imparted by recording in public records "for all to see"

Voluntary / Involuntary

Voluntary transfer

- deed
- will
- public grant

Involuntary transfer

- descent (without will, with heirs)
- escheat (without will nor heirs)
- foreclosure (loan default)
- eminent domain (public good)
- adverse possession (hostile, open use)

Deed Validity

Requirements:
1. grantor
2. grantee
3. in writing
4. legal description
5. granting clause
6. consideration
7. grantor's signature
8. acknowledgement
9. delivery and acceptance

Deed Clauses

Premises:	granting
Habendum:	type of estate
Reddendum:	restrictions
Tenendum:	other property included

Deed Types

Bargain and sale:	"I own but won't defend"
General warranty:	"I own and will defend"
Special warranty:	"I own and warrant myself only"
Quitclaim:	"I may or may not own, and won't defend"
Special purpose deeds:	Used for different purposes, interests conveyed, or by different parties

Deed Restrictions

Deed restriction
- single-property use restriction as stipulated in a deed; may not be discriminatory

- examples: minimum area of a residence; setbacks; limits on other structures; conducting commercial activities

Declaration restriction
- use restriction in multiple-property declarations; enforced by court injunction

Deed condition
- usage restriction that can trigger repossession by a previous owner if violated

Transfer Tax

- **Documentary stamp tax:** tax on conveyance of real property based on price of property conveyed
- Facilitates ad valorem assessment
- Payment evidenced on deed

Testate / Intestate

Order of Title Transfer

Dies testate with heirs:
- first to creditors
- then to homestead
- then **to heirs by will**

Dies intestate with heirs:
- first to creditors
- then to homestead
- then *to heirs by laws of descent*

Dies intestate, no heirs:
- first to creditors
- then **to state by escheat**

Evidence of Title

Forms of evidence to prove marketable title and ownership:

- title insurance
- attorney's opinion of abstract
- title certificates
- Torrens registration

Leases

Estate Types

Gross lease
- landlord pays expenses; tenant pays higher rent than net

Net lease
- tenant pays some or all expenses; rent is less than gross

Percentage lease
- landlord receives rent minimum plus percentage of retailer's sales

Residential lease
- gross lease hybrid; short term; uniform terms reflect landlord-tenant standards

Ground lease
- landlord owns and leases ground but does not own improvements

Proprietary lease
- for cooperative unit owners; indefinite term; assigned to new unit owner on sale

Leasing of rights
- leasehold transfer of rights for limited use; examples: air, mineral, water rights

---

URLTA

Leases:
- clear lease terms
- fair market rent
- cannot waive rights

Deposits:	• limits on amounts • tenant's right to interest • rules and deadlines for returning
Landlord Obligations:	• bargain in good faith • provide maintenance and repairs • comply with building codes • provide safety and access • procedure for delivery of notices
Tenant Obligations:	• maintain condition • abide by rules and regulations • no damage or abuse • abide by approved uses • no disturbance of other tenants

Lease Termination

Causes

- default
- notice
- property destruction
- death

- term expiration
- voluntary agreement
- condemnation
- abandonment under certain conditions

Land Use

Planning and Zoning Definitions

Building code: A standard of construction of an improved property established by local government officials

Certificate of occupancy: A document confirming that a newly constructed or renovated property has fully complied with all building codes and is ready for occupancy

Concurrency: A planning policy that requires developers to correct foreseen negative impacts of a development during the construction period of the project itself rather than afterwards

Condemnation: 1. A decree that a parcel of private property is to be taken for public use under the power of eminent domain. 2. A government order that a is no longer fit for use and must be demolished.

Deed restriction: A provision in a deed that limits or places rules on how the deeded property may be used or improved

Eminent domain: A power of a government entity to force the sale of private property for subsequent public use

Land use control: Regulation of how individual owners use property in a municipality or planning district. Control patterns are in accordance with a master plan

Master plan: An amalgamated land use plan for a municipality, county, or region which incorporates community opinion, the results of intensive research, and the various land use guidelines and regulations of the state. Acts as a blueprint for subsequent zoning ordinances and rulings

Non-conforming use : A legal or illegal land use that is not consistent with the current zoning ordinance

Police power: A government's legal authority to create, regulate, tax, and condemn real property in the interest of the public's health, safety, and welfare

Restriction: A limitation on the use of a property imposed by deed, zoning, state statute, or public regulation

Special exception: A land use in conflict with current zoning that is authorized because of its perceived benefit to the public welfare

Variance: A land use that conflicts with current zoning but is authorized for certain reasons, including undue hardship to comply and minimal negative impact to leave it alone

Zoning ordinance: A municipal land use regulation

Land Use Planning

Goals of land use control
- preserve property values; promote highest and best use; safeguard public health, safety and welfare; control growth; incorporate community consensus
- process: develop plan; create administration; authorize controls

The master plan
- long term growth and usage strategies; often required by state law
- local plans fuse municipal goals and needs with state and regional laws

Planning objectives
- control growth rates: how much growth will occur and at what rate
- control growth patterns: type of growth desired, where it should be located
- accommodate demand for services and infrastructure

Plan development
- research trends and conditions; blend local and state objectives into master plan

Planning management
- commission makes rules, approves permits, codes, and development plans

Public Land Use Controls

Zoning
- "police power" granted by state-level enabling acts; zoning ordinance: creates zones, usage restrictions, regulations, requirements
- Enables urban land managers to create separate land uses that do not conflict with one another nor create incompatible adjacencies

Types of zone
- residential, commercial, industrial, agricultural, public, PUD
- residential zoning regulates *density*, or number of dwellings in an area
- commercial zoning regulates *intensity*, or how much commercial activity is permitted in relation to size of the site

Zoning administration
- Zoning Board of Adjustment oversees rule administration and appeals

Zoning Appeals
- **Nonconforming use:** legal if use existed prior to zone creation, illegal otherwise
- **Variance:** use exception granted based on hardship
- **Special exception:** based on public interest
- **Amendment:** change of zones; rezoning

Eminent Domain
- allows a government entity to purchase a fee or easement interest in privately owned real property for the **public good** and for **public use** in exchange for "just compensation"

Planned Unit Development (PUD)
- PUD zoning designed to regulate use of whole tracts of land with a singular design
- Design purposes are to achieve optimum space efficiency and open space

Subdivision Regulation
- plat of subdivision and relevant requirements must be met and approved; must meet FHA requirements for insured financing
- location, grading, alignment, surfacing, street width, highways
- sewers and water mains
- lot and block dimensions
- building and setback lines
- public use dedications
- utility easements
- ground percolation

Building Codes
- comprehensive onsite and offsite construction and materials standards; must be met to receive certificate of occupancy

Environmental Restrictions
- flood control; solid waste disposal; air quality; water quality; marine protection; noise control; toxic substances controls; lead paint; CERCLA; Superfund

Zoning Appeals

Zoning Board of Adjustment: oversees rule administration and appeals.

Nonconforming use: legal if use existed prior to zone creation, illegal otherwise

Variance: use exception granted based on hardship

Special exception: based on public interest

Amendment: change of zones; rezoning

Environmental Controls

Areas of concern
- air, soil, water quality; ambient health hazards; natural hazards

Major legislation
- limits damage to environment; standards for air, land, water, materials use

Responsibilities & liabilities
- disclosure and information for practitioners; remediation for owners

Environmental Laws

Legislation	Date	Regulated
Solid Waste Disposal Act (later part of RCRA)	1965 (1976, 1999, 2002)	landfills
Air Quality Act, Clean Air Act	1967 (1970)	air quality standards
National Environmental Policy Act (NEPA)	1969 (1970)	created EPA
Flood Control Act	amended 1969	building in flood zones; flood insurance
Resource Recovery Act	1970	solid waste disposal
Water Quality Improvement Act	1970	dumping in navigable waters; wetlands
Water Pollution Control Act amendment	1972	dumping in navigable waters; wetlands
Clean Water Act	1972 (1977)	dumping in navigable waters; wetlands
Lead-based paint ban (US Consumer Product Safety Commission rule)	1978	lead-based paint in residences
PCB ban (EPA rule)	1979	polychlorinated biphenyls
RCRA amendment	1984	underground storage tanks
Comprehensive Environmental Response, Compensation and Liability Act (CERCLA)	1980	hazardous waste disposal
Superfund Amendment and Reauthorization Act	1986	hazardous waste cleanup costs
Asbestos ban (EPA rule)	1989	asbestos in building materials
Residential Lead-based Paint Hazard Reduction Act (EPA and HUD rule)	1992 (1996)	lead-based paint disclosure and treatment
Flood Insurance Reform Act	1994	flood insurance in flood zones
Brownfields legislation	2002	industrial site cleanup

Legal Descriptions

Purpose
- to accurately locate and identify the boundaries of a parcel of real property to a degree acceptable by courts of law in the state where the property is located
- general criterion is that it alone provides sufficient data for a surveyor to locate the parcel

Metes and Bounds Method

- describes perimeter by landmarks, monuments, distances, angles
- usable within rectangular survey system
- starting at point of beginning (POB), follow perimeter, **return to POB**

Lot and Block System
- used to describe properties in residential, commercial, industrial subdivisions
- tracts of land divided into lots, then grouped into blocks

Rectangular Survey System

Meridians:	• north-south lines six miles apart
Parallels:	• east-west lines six miles apart
Range:	• north-south strip between meridians
Tier:	• east-west strip of area between parallels; also called township strip
Township:	• the six-mile by six-mile square at the intersection of a range and a tier
Section of a township:	• a 1 mile x 1 mile square; 1 section = 640 acres; 36 sections per township
Fractions of a section:	• going from the smallest to largest unit, indicate size and location within successively larger quarters or halves of the section: E 1/2 of the NE 1/4 of the NE 1/4 of Section 8

Economics

Supply
- the quantity of a product or service available for sale, lease, or trade at any given time

Demand
- the quantity of a product or service that is desired for purchase, lease, or trade at any given time

Supply / Demand / Price

Real Estate Supply	• property available for sale or lease; measured in dwelling units, square feet, acres
Real Estate Demand	• property buyers and tenants wishing to acquire; measured in households, square feet, acres
Interaction	• if supply increases relative to demand, price decreases; • if demand increases relative to supply, price increases

Supply-Demand Cycle

unmet demand →
    construction adds supply →
        market equilibrium →
            construction adds more supply →
                oversupply →
                    construction stops →
                        market equilibrium →
                            demand absorbs supply →
                              unmet demand →
                                  cycle repeats

Factors Influencing Supply and Demand
- cost, availability of financing
- availability of developable land
- construction costs
- capacity of infrastructure
- governmental regulation and police powers
- changes in the economic base
- in- and out-migrations of major employers
- labor availability
- land availability

Government Influences on the Real Estate Market
- local zoning power
- local control and permitting of new development
- local taxing power
- federal influence on interest rates
- environmental legislation and regulations

Market Indicators
- **Vacancy rates**
  - increases indicate buyer / tenant market & falling prices / rents
  - decreases indicate seller / landlord market & rising prices / rents

- **Building permits** – increases indicate declining vacancy; increasing prices & construction
- **Prices**
  - increases indicate rising demand or declining supply or both
  - decreases indicate falling demand or rising supply or both

Appraisal

Regulation of Appraisal Practice

FIRREA
- Financial Institutions Reform, Recovery and Enforcement Act (**FIRREA**) enacted in 1989 to regulate appraisal practices
- requires that competent individuals whose professional conduct is properly supervised perform all appraisals used in federally-related transactions
- As of January 1, 1993, federally-related appraisals must be performed only by state-certified appraisers
- **USPAP** - Uniform Standards of Professional Appraisal Practice – competency standards established by the **Appraiser Qualifications Board** of the Appraisal Foundation

Concepts and Principles of Value

Supply and demand
- When demand exceeds supply, scarcity exists, values rise.
- When supply exceeds demand, surplus exists, values decline.
- When supply and demand are, the market is in balance, values stabilize.

Utility
- A property's use in the marketplace contributes to the demand for it.

Transferability
- How readily or easily title or rights to real estate can be transferred affects the property's value.

Anticipation
- The benefits a buyer expects to derive from a property over a holding period influence what the buyer is willing to pay for it.

Substitution
- A buyer will pay no more for a property than the buyer would have to pay for an equally desirable and available substitute property

Contribution
- the contribution to value of an improvement is equal to the change in market value that the addition of the improvement causes

Change
- Market conditions affect the benefits that can arise from the property

Highest and best use
- A property achieves its maximum value when it is put to whichever use generates the greatest income and return. The highest and best use must be legally permissible, physically possible, financially feasible, and maximally productive

Conformity
- A property's maximal value is attained when its form and use are consonant with surrounding properties and uses

Progression and regression
- The value of a property is influenced by the values of neighboring properties

Assemblage
- Conjoining adjacent properties can create a combined value in excess of the values of the unassembled properties. This excess value is called **plottage value**

Subdivision
- The division of a single property into smaller properties can result in a higher total value

Types of Value

Market value
- Market value is an estimate of the price at which a property will sell at a particular time. This type of value is the one generally sought in appraisals and used in brokers' estimates of value

Insured value
- Insured value is the face amount a casualty or hazard insurance policy will pay in case a property is rendered unusable

Reproduction value
- Reproduction value is the value based on the cost of constructing a precise duplicate of the subject property's improvements, assuming current construction costs.

Replacement value
- Replacement value is the value based on the cost of constructing a functional equivalent of the subject property's improvements, assuming current construction costs

Salvage value
- Salvage value refers to the nominal value of a property that has reached the end of its economic life. Salvage value is also an estimate of the price at which a structure will sell if it is dismantled and moved.

Assessed value
- Assessed value is the value of a property as estimated by a taxing authority as the basis for ad valorem taxation

Depreciated value
- Depreciated value is a value established by subtracting accumulated depreciation from the purchase price of a property

Book value
- Book value is the value of the property as carried on the accounts of the owner. The value is generally equal to the acquisition price plus capital improvements minus accumulated depreciation.

Investment value
- The value of an income property as indicated by the capitalized value of the cash flow the property generates

Market Value Requirements

The price willing buyer and seller would agree on given:

- a cash transaction
- reasonable market exposure
- parties have market and property use information
- there is no pressure to complete the transaction
- transaction is arm's length: parties are not related
- marketable title
- no hidden influences

Appraisal Process

1. Identify the purpose
2. Assimilate the relevant data
3. Assess the highest and best use
4. Estimate the value of the land
5. Apply the three approaches to value
6. Reconcile the values from the approaches
7. Compile the report

Sales Comparison Approach

1. Identify comparable sales
2. Compare comps to the subject and make adjustments to the comparables
3. Weight values indicated by adjusted comparables for the final value estimate of the subject

Adjusting Comparables

Rules for selecting comparables
- must be physically similar
- in subject's vicinity
- recently sold in arm's length sale

Rules for adjusting comparables
- never adjust the subject!
- deduct from comparable if better than subject
- add to comp if worse than subject
- Remember: ("Subtract if Superior !")

Weighting adjustments
- best indicator has fewest and smallest adjustments and smallest net adjustment from the sale price

Cost Approach

1. Estimate land value
2. Estimate replacement cost of improvements
3. Estimate total depreciation
4. Subtract: (improvements - depreciation)
5. Add: (land value + depreciated improvements)

Depreciation, etc.

Depreciation
- **loss of value** from deterioration, functional obsolescence, or economic obsolescence

Deterioration
- **wear and tear** from use and aging

Functional Obsolescence
- **outmoded** physical or design **features**: curable or incurable

Economic Obsolescence
- loss of value due to adverse **changes in surroundings**: incurable

Curability
- curable: cost to cure is less than resulting

contribution to value

- incurable: cost to cure exceeds contribution to value

Income Approach

- Based on the principle of anticipation: the expected future income stream of a property underlies what an investor will pay for the property
- Also based on the principle of substitution: that an investor will pay no more for a subject property with a certain income stream than the investor would have to pay for another property with a similar income stream.

Steps in the Income Approach

1. Estimate potential gross income
2. Estimate effective gross income (potential - vacancy)
3. Estimate net operating income (NOI) (effective income - expenses)
4. Select and apply capitalization rate (NOI ÷ cap rate)

Gross rent multipliers
- Simplified income-based methods to estimate value
- Method consists of applying a multiplier to the estimated gross rent of the subject
- Multiplier is derived from market data on sale prices and gross rent
- Does not necessarily produce accurate value estimates

Formula
- GRM = price divided by monthly rent
- Value = GRM times monthly rent

Preparing a Comparative Market Analysis

Steps
1. Identify comparables sold, for sale properties, and expired listings
2. Compile comparison data for each comparable: price, sale date, location, age, lot size, site aspects, living area, bedrooms, etc.
3. Complete adjustments for differences; rules:
   a. Never adjust the subject
   b. Add value to the comparable if a feature is inferior to the subject
   c. Subtract value from the comp if a feature is superior to the subject
4. Derive total adjustments for each comparable
5. Reconcile all value-adjusted comps to the subject to identify a value estimate

Finance

Mortgage Transaction

Elements
- promissory note: promise to repay loan
- mortgage: pledge of property as collateral for loan

Mechanics
- borrower gives lender promissory note and mortgage
- lender gives borrower funds and records a lien

Hypothecation
- use of real property as collateral for a mortgage loan

Financial components
- original principal: capital amount borrowed on which interest payments are calculated
- loan balance: remaining unpaid principal at any point in the life of the loan
- interest: charge for the use of money; rate fixed or variable
- Annual Percentage Rate (APR) includes interest and all other finance charges; lender must disclose on residential properties
- point: one percent of the loan amount
- loan origination fee: charged by lender at origination to obtain required return
- term: period of time for repayment of interest and principal
- payment: the periodic payment of interest and/or principal
- down payment: borrower's cash payment applied to the purchase price
- loan-to-value ratio: the loan's share of the total value of the property
- equity: at closing, the borrower's cash invested in the property; thereafter, the difference between the market value and the loan balance

Trust Deed Transaction

Elements
- promissory note: trustor's promise to repay loan
- deed of trust: title to property as collateral for loan

Mechanics
- trust deed conveys title from the borrower/trustor to a third-party trustee
- trustee holds title on behalf of the lender/beneficiary until the debt is repaid

Promissory note
- legal instrument executed by borrower stating debt amount, loan term, method and timing of repayment, interest rate, promise to pay; may repeat other provisions from mortgage document or deed of trust; negotiable instrument assignable to a third party

Mortgage Clauses

Payment of Principal and Interest: Prepayment and Late Charges
- Borrower must make timely payments according to the terms of the note
- Late payments or early payoffs may trigger penalties

Funds for Taxes and Insurance
- Borrower must make monthly payments to cover taxes and hazard insurance

- Borrower may also have to pay flood insurance and mortgage insurance premiums
- **Escrow account**: reserve account for periodic payments of taxes and insurance.
- Real Estate Settlement Procedures Act (RESPA) limits funds the lender can require for this purpose.

PITI

- Borrower's monthly payment for principal and interest is called the P&I payment (principal and interest)
- The amount which includes the escrow payment is called PITI (principal, interest, taxes, insurance).

Charges and Liens

- Borrower is liable for paying any charges, liens, or other expenses that may have priority over the mortgage or trust instrument.

Hazard or Property Insurance

- Borrower must keep property insured as the lender requires.

Occupancy, Preservation, Maintenance and Protection of the Property

- Borrower must take and maintain occupancy as the borrower's principal residence according to requirements
- Borrower must not abuse or neglect the including use for illegal purposes, creating hazardous waste on the property, or destroying the improvements

Protection of Lender's Rights in the Property

- Lender may take actions to protect its rights in the property if the borrower jeopardizes the property's value. The costs of these actions would be charged to the borrower

Mortgage Insurance

- Lender may require private mortgage insurance, or PMI which protects the lender against loss from borrower default
- Applies to loans that are not backed by the Federal Housing Administration (FHA) or Veterans Administration (VA) and that have a down payment of less than 20% of the property value

Inspection

- Lender may inspect the property with reasonable cause to fear damage to the collateral

Condemnation

- If the property is condemned or taken by eminent domain, lender reserves a claim on any resulting proceeds

Transfer of the Property or a Beneficial Interest in Borrower

- If borrower sells the property without the lender's approval, the lender may demand immediate repayment of the loan balance. This alienation clause, aka a due-on-sale clause, allows lender to prevent unapproved loan assumptions
- The requirement to repay the loan before the scheduled due date is called **acceleration**.

Borrower's Right to Reinstate

- If lender holds borrower in default, borrower has the right to reinstatement by performing certain actions, usually paying overdue payments plus expenses the lender
- Clause is called a redemption clause
- Gives the borrower time to satisfy obligations and prevent a forced sale

Release

- Agreement to release the lien obligation when borrower has paid off the loan
- Release clause, aka **defeasance** clause, may require lender to execute a **satisfaction of**

mortgage, aka **release of mortgage**
- If deed of trust, lender directs trustee to execute a **release deed** or **deed of reconveyance** to the borrower as trustor.
- Release deed or satisfaction should be recorded as necessary

Escalation Clause
- Allows lender to increase the loan's interest rate

Types of Mortgages

Conventional mortgages
- Originated by banks and private financial institutions
- No government-related insurance or guarantees as with FHA or VA
- Typically require 20% down payments; smaller down payments may require PMI
- Assumptions require approval

Government loan programs
- **FHA** – federally insured loan programs (see following)
- **VA** – federally guaranteed loan programs (see following)

Amortized fixed-rate v adjustable loans
- **Amortized:** payments include increasing increments of principal which retire loan balance over loan term
- **Fixed rate:** interest rate does not change – can have for amortized or interest-only loans
- **Adjustable loans:** interest rate fluctuates up or down with an index; payments may also vary

---

Adjustable Loan Characteristics

- **Mechanics**: rate adjusts up or down with index; payments may or may not change;
- **Negative amortization**: loan balance increases if payments are less than what is owed given the balance and rate, i.e., unpaid monthly amounts are added to the principal balance
- **Rate and payment caps:** maximum amounts the interest rate or payments can increase in a given adjustment period or over the life of the loan; protects borrower from unaffordable increases
- **Index and margin:** interest rate tied to any number of financial indices. Margin equals a fixed point spread between the index and the interest rate
- **Teaser rates:** to attract borrowers, adjustable loans may have low initial rates which increase over subsequent adjustment periods to a more permanent market level.

Custom Mortgages

- **Partially amortized with a balloon:** payments will not retire principal balance over life of the loan, thus requiring a lump-sum payment, or "balloon" payment at end of term
- **Interest-only loans:** loans where payments are interest only, and the principal balance is retired in full at maturity using a balloon payment
- **Biweekly mortgage:** loan payments are every-two weeks, a device that reduces total interest paid, but also shortens risk period for the lender
- **Package mortgage:** mortgage loans which also finance articles of personal property as part of the purchase transaction
- **Home equity loans:** funds borrowed using the homeowners equity for collateral; funds can be used for any purpose
- **Purchase money mortgage:** a seller-financed loan to the buyer of portions of the purchase price using the property as collateral. Usually accompanied by a senior underlying first mortgage
- **Reverse annuity mortgage:** a financial arrangement where the homeowner pledges equity to a

lender in exchange for periodic payments of the pledged equity. In essence it is the periodic receipt of equity liquidation in exchange for an increase of debt owed on the property.

FHA Loans

Insured loans granted by approved lenders to qualified borrowers.

Loan term:	• 15, 30 years
Qualifying ratios:	• income: 31% • debt: 43%
Minimum downpayment:	• 3%
Mortgage insurance:	• required at 78% LTV or above • premium = one-time 1.75-2.25% of loan am plus annual premium
Points:	• None
Maximum loan amount:	• varies by Metropolitan Statistical Area

VA Loans

Guaranteed loans:	• granted by approved lenders to qualified veterans
Qualifying ratios:	• depends on lender
Minimum downpayment:	• None
Points:	• 1.25 - 3.3, depending on downpayment, type of loan, type of veteran

Loan Qualification

Equal Credit Opportunity Act
- lender must evaluate applicant according to applicant's own income and credit information

Income qualification
- income ratio and debt ratio qualify borrower's income; income ratio applied to gross income determines housing expense maximum; debt ratio takes revolving debt into account
- income ratios: 25-28% conventional; 31% FHA-insured
- debt ratios: 36% conventional; 43% FHA and 41% VA

Cash qualification
- lender verifies applicant's sources of cash for down payment; extra cash enhances income qualification evaluation

Net worth
- extent to which applicant's assets exceed liabilities as a further source of reserves

Credit evaluation
- lender obtains credit reports to evaluate applicant's payment behavior

Loan commitment
- written pledge by lender to grant loan under specific terms; firm, lock-in, conditional, take-out

---

The Mortgage Market

Supply and demand for money
- relationship between supply and demand for money affects interest rates, consumer prices, availability of mortgage money; regulated by Federal Reserve

Federal Reserve control of money supply among banks
- Sells T-bills to reduce money supply and increase interest rates; buys T-bills to increase supply and decrease rates
- Sets the reserve requirement for member banks
  - increase reserves to tighten money and raise interest rates
  - decrease reserves to loosen money and lower interest rates
- sets the discount rate for member banks
  - increase rate to tighten money
  - decrease rate to increase money supply

Federal Home Loan Bank System (FHLBS)
- Counterpart to the Fed for savings and loan associations

Federal Deposit Insurance Corporation (FDIC)
- Insures deposits up to $250,000 per depositor, per insured bank, for each account ownership category

The primary mortgage market
- Originates mortgage loans directly to borrowers;
- Includes savings and loans, commercial banks, mutual savings banks, life insurance companies, mortgage bankers, credit unions

The secondary mortgage market
- Buys existing loans to provide liquidity to primary lenders; Fannie Mae, Ginnie Mae, Freddie Mac, investment firms, life insurance companies, pension funds

Role of FNMA, GNMA, and FHLMC
- FNMA buys conventional, FHA- and VA-backed loans and pooled mortgages; guarantees payment on mortgage-backed securities
- GNMA guarantees payment on certain types of loans
- FHLMC buys and pools mortgages; sells mortgage-backed securities

Mortgage loan originator v. lender/banker v. broker
- Mortgage loan originator: solicits, negotiates mortgage loans; requires MLO license
- Mortgage broker: an intermediary who brings mortgage borrowers and mortgage lenders together, but does not use its own funds to originate mortgages
- Mortgage banker: person or entity who funds or services loans for others and/or who sells mortgages to the secondary market

Investment

Investment Terminology

Appreciation
- An increase in the value of a property owing to economic forces beyond the control of the investor

Asset
- A tangible or intangible item of value

Basis
- A measurement of how much is invested in the property for tax purposes; **adjusted basis** is the original cost of the asset plus capital improvements minus depreciation

Capital gain (or loss)
- The difference between the net sales proceeds of an asset and its adjusted basis

Cash flow
- The remaining positive or negative amount of income an investment produces after subtracting all operating expenses and debt service from gross income

Equity
- That portion of a property's value owned by the legal owner, expressed as the difference between the property's market value and all loan balances outstanding on the property

Leverage
- The relationship between the yield rate of an investment and the interest rate of funds borrowed to finance the investment. If the yield rate is greater than the loan rate, positive leverage results. If the yield rate is less than the loan rate, negative leverage results

Liquidity
- The degree to which an investment is readily marketable, or convertible to another form of asset. If immediately salable, an investment is liquid; the longer it takes to sell, the more illiquid the investment. Real property is relatively illiquid in comparison with other types of investment

Tax shelter
- An investment that produces depreciation or other non-cash losses that a taxpayer can deduct from other income to reduce tax liability

Investment Characteristics

Ownership benefits
- income
- appreciation
- tax shelter: depreciation and interest deductions

Ownership risks
- relatively illiquid
- management intensive
- negative leverage and price movements

Investment Entities

Direct
- investor buys directly and manages personally

General partnership
- all members own and manage

Limited partnership
- general partner manages; limited partners own but do not manage

Real Estate Investment Trust
- investors buy trust certificates; trust invests in real estate assets
- investors share returns per ownership percent

Risk Assessment

Market risk
- Changes in the demand may cause investment to lose value and become illiquid

Business risk
- Changes in the operation of a business impacting the investment may reduce the income and appreciation capacity of the investment

Purchasing power risk
- Changes in the value of money as an exchange medium, such as through inflation, may decrease the practical value of your invested resource

Financial risk
- Changes in financial markets & interest rates may reduce the value of the investment by making it less desirable and more expensive to maintain

Business Brokerage

Licensed activity
- Business brokers must be licensed in real estate
- Involves lease or fee conveyancing or dispositions

Business enterprise v business opportunity brokers
- Business enterprise brokers – engage in corporate transactions to sell or buy businesses that sell goods or services
- Business opportunity brokers – sell or buy small businesses

Comparisons between business and real property brokerage
- Different to real estate brokerage –
  - involves non-real-estate assets
  - business valued differently than real estate
  - may include corporate stock
  - may involve assuming short- and long-term liabilities
  - business market unlimited in geographic scope

- Experience & knowledge needed beyond real estate
  - corporate finance
  - business accounting
  - business valuation
  - business laws

Taxation

Real Property Taxation

Property exemptions
- Immune property: government property
- Exempt property: religious organization and nonprofit facilities
- Partial exemption: homestead exemption

Tax lien enforcement
1. unpaid taxes →
2. tax sale ordered →
3. equitable right of redemption →
4. tax sale to pay taxes, interest, and charges →
5. statutory right of redemption →
6. tax deed to successful bidder or holder of tax certificates

Federal Income Taxes

Principal residence taxation
- Taxpayers can deduct mortgage interest, ad valorem taxes, and fees relating to mortgage loan acquisitions including points
- May also deduct portions of living area used for in-home business, with qualifications

Investment property income taxation
- Tax is payable on net income after mortgage interest, depreciation, and operating expenses
- Owners may not deduct reserves from income, nor loan principal
- Taxable income is payable at ordinary income tax rates
- Annual depreciation allowed is equal to the improvement value divided by the number of years in the depreciation term (established by IRS); cannot depreciate the land portion of total value

Capital gain taxation of income property
- Taxes are charged on the capital gain realized from the sale of income properties
- Capital gain is equal to the amount realized at closing (price – selling costs) minus the adjusted basis of the property (beginning basis + improvements – total depreciation)

Contract Law

Contract defined
- An agreement between two or more parties who have a "meeting of the minds," and have pledged to perform (or refrain from performing) some act.
- A *valid* contract is *legally enforceable* by meeting certain requirements of contract law.
- If a contract does not meet requirements, it is not valid and the parties to it cannot resort to a court of law to enforce its provisions

Contract Status

Valid
- meets all requirements

Valid but unenforceable
- certain oral contracts; if performed, cannot change outcome

Void
- not valid; unenforceable

Voidable
- may be rescinded due to subsequent discoveries: if performed, cannot change outcome

---

Contract validity

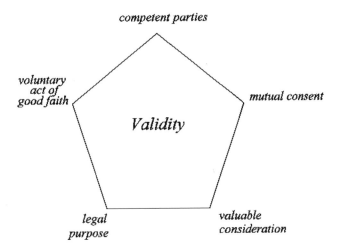

Competent parties
- legal age
- mental competency
- legitimate authority

Mutual consent
- clear and unequivocal **offer and acceptance** with an underlying **meeting of the minds**

Valuable consideration
- two-way exchange of valuable consideration for performance by the other party; not "love and affection"

Legal purpose
- promise, intent and content must be lawful; if illegal, contract is void – cannot contract to break the law

Voluntary, good faith
- no duress, coercion, fraud or misrepresentation

Offer / Counteroffer / Acceptance

Offer
- intention to enter into contract
- must contain all intended terms
- must be in writing
- expires in "reasonable time" or date and time specified

Acceptance
- unequivocal and manifest agreement to offer
- no changes to offer whatsoever
- signed, preferably dated

Completed contract
- communication of acceptance to offeror
- if by mail, offer is communicated upon mailing

Counteroffer
- new or amended terms of a received offer
- original offer is void

Revoking an offer
- may be done at any time prior to offeree's communication of acceptance

Contract Classifications

Oral vs. written
- oral, or parol, contract may not be enforceable

Express vs. implied
- express: all terms expressly agreed to
- implied: unintentional agreement deemed to exist due to terms implied by actions

Bilateral vs. Unilateral
- bilateral: both parties promise to perform
- unilateral: one party performs only if other party performs

Executed vs. Executory
- executed: fully performed
- executory: performance yet to be completed

Termination

Causes

- performance
- infeasibility
- mutual agreement
- cooling-period rescission
- revocation
- abandonment
- lapse of time
- invalidity of contract

Breach & Remedies

Rescission	• cancel contract; return deposits
Forfeiture	• defaulting party gives up something according to contract terms
Liquidated damages	• damages due a damaged party as stated in contract
Suit for damages	• civil suit for money damages not covered by contract
Specific performance	• suit to force party to fulfill contract promises

Agency

Universal / General / Special

Universal	• represent in all matters • can contract for principal
General	• represent in business matters • agent can contract for principal
Special	• represent in single business transaction • normally agent cannot contract for principal • characterizes the brokerage relationship

Termination

Causes

- fulfillment
- expiration
- mutual agreement
- incapacity
- abandonment or destruction of property
- renunciation
- breach
- bankruptcy
- revocation of license

Duties & Obligations

Agent's Fiduciary Duties to Client

Skill, care and diligence	• proactive; competent; act within bounds of expertise

37

Loyalty	• place client interest above customer and self
Obedience	• provided actions, instructions are legal
Confidentiality	• extends beyond listing term indefinitely
Full disclosure	• property condition; customers; material facts
Accounting	• proper handling of monies and documents

Obligations Owed Customers

- honesty and fair dealing
- reasonable care and skill
- proper disclosure

Misrepresentation and Fraud

Puffing – licensee boasting about property's benefits

Fraud
- misstatement or failure to disclose material fact
- knowledge that statement was false or fact should have been disclosed
- party relied on misstatement
- party was damaged by misstatement

Misrepresentation – misstatement or concealment of fact
- intentional misrepresentation: **purposeful misstatement** of material fact
- intentional omission: **purposeful concealment** of material fact
- negligent misrepresentation: **unintended misstatement** that agent should have known
- negligent omission: **unintended concealment** that agent should have known

---

Single / Dual / Sub / No Agency

Single agency	• seller or buyer agency • tenant or landlord representation
Subagency	• outside brokers and agents who help listing agent • listing broker's own agents
Dual agency	• representing both sides • potentially illegal or conflict of interest • must disclose & obtain written consent • voluntary by consent • involuntary by actions of parties (implied agency) • duties: all but full disclosure and loyalty
No agency	• "facilitator" or "transaction broker" • representing neither party in the transaction • duties to both parties: accounting; skill, care and diligence; honesty and fair dealing; disclosures affecting property value

Disclosure Rules

Note: agency disclosure rules vary by state – see State section for laws in your state

Objectives of disclosure
- declare
- explain
- offer choice
- obtain documented consent

Seller agent disclosures to client
- in writing
- on or before listing is executed

Seller agent disclosures to customer
- in writing
- upon first face-to-face contact, or upon substantive communication, depending on state law
- oral disclosure permitted but must have written follow-up

Buyer agent disclosures to seller
- in writing
- upon first contact with listing agent or seller
- substantive contact is assumed

Dual agent disclosures
- "informed, written consent"
- may not disclose price or financing positions or motivations unless authorized

Facilitator disclosures
- on becoming transaction broker or on substantive contact, whichever is first

Listings

Parties / Duties / Contract

Parties	• listing broker-- fiduciary of buyer client or seller client • subagent-- fiduciary of listing broker's client • customer-- non-fiduciary principal in transaction
Fiduciary duties	• to client: loyalty; obedience; disclosure; care; diligence; accounting • to customer: honesty, care and disclosure
Authority	• limited agency agreement • broker may not contract for client unless specifically authorized • clients liable only for broker's acts within scope of authority
Contract law	• unilateral contract • oral listing is valid and enforceable • exclusive listing in some states must be written to be enforceable • personal service contract-- not assignable

Types

Exclusive right-to-sell
- given to one broker
- usually must be written
- must expire
- broker gets commission if property transfers during period

Exclusive agency
- exclusive excepting owner
- oral or written
- must expire
- broker gets commission unless owner sells

Open listing
- non-exclusive
- oral or written
- no stated expiration
- procuring cause gets commission
- no commission if client procures customer

Net listing
- all sale proceeds above a seller's minimum price go to the broker
- discouraged, if not illegal

Multiple listing
- listing placed in MLS
- owners consent to rules and provisions of MLS

Buyer agency agreements
- create a fiduciary relationship with the buyer
- if exclusive, buyer agrees to only work with the buyer representative in procuring a property
- must have an expiration date along with other requirements of a valid listing

Compensation / Termination

Compensation
- negotiated between agent and principal
- where disputed among agents, agent with procuring cause is owed commission
- based on results: find ready willing and able customer

Causes for termination
- performance
- infeasibility
- mutual agreement
- revocation
- abandonment
- breach
- expiration
- invalidity
- incapacitation or death
- involuntary transfer

	• destruction of property
Agent's performance	• may perform only authorized tasks
	• must verify owner and property data
	• may delegate duties to salespeople and other brokers
Revoking a listing	• clients always have power to revoke during period
	• may incur liability for commission or damages

Brokerage

Who May Broker

Varies from state to state

Yes

1. sole proprietorship
2. for-profit corporation
3. general or limited partnership
4. joint venture

No

1. non-profit corporation
2. business trust
3. cooperative association

Broker-Agent Relationship

Legal relationship
- salesperson
  - is agent & fiduciary of broker
  - acts in broker's name
  - is subagent of client

- salesperson may not
  - have two employers
  - be paid by other parties
  - bind clients contractually

Salesperson's employment status
- employee or independent contractor
- defined by agreement

Obligations and responsibilities
- agent to broker:
  - obtain & sell listings
  - follow policies and employment provisions
  - promote ethics and broker's reputation
- broker to agent:
  - provide data, office support, compensation, training
  - uphold ethics, policies, and employment agreement

Agent compensation
- commissions per schedule after splits with cooperating brokers

---

Commingling & Conversion

Not allowed !!

Commingling
- mixing broker's personal or business funds with trust funds
- includes failure to deposit funds in a timely manner

Conversion
- using trust funds for personal or business purposes

Advertising Requirements

- no misleading ads
- ads must contain broker's ID
- broker is responsible for content
- no blind ads (concealed identity)
- must disclose if agent owns property

Anti-Trust Laws

no collusion:
- two or more businesses conspiring to disadvantage a competitor

no price fixing:
- two or more brokers agreeing to fix prices

no market allocation:
- colluding to restrict competition in a market segment in exchange for a competitor's reciprocal agreement

---

Ethics & Fair Housing

Professional Ethics

- apply Golden Rule
- does not have to conflict with profit
- influenced by personal code of behavior
- influenced negatively by employer's or other agents' bad behavior
- not regulated by statute
- support improved professional standards
- act can be legal but unethical
- Code of Ethics and Standards of Practice
  - developed by the National Association of Realtors (NAR)
  - promotes fair dealings with public, clients, and other brokers

Fair Housing Law

Civil Rights Act of 1866
- no discrimination in selling or leasing housing based on race

Executive Order 11063
- no race discrimination involving FHA- or VA-backed loans

Fair Housing Act of 1968 (Title VIII)
- no discrimination based on race, color, religion, national origin

- Exemptions:
  - privately owned home where no broker is used and no discriminatory advertising is used
  - rental of 1-4 unit building where owner is also an occupant; no discriminatory advertising
  - facilities owned by private clubs; leased non-commercially to members
  - facilities owned by religious organizations with non-discriminatory membership requirements

Jones v. Mayer
- no race discrimination, without exception

Housing and Community Development Act of 1974
- no discrimination based on sex

Fair Housing Amendments Act of 1988
- no discrimination based on sex or against the handicapped or familial status

Equal Opportunity Poster
- must be displayed by brokers

Prohibited Acts

Forms of illegal discrimination

discriminatory misrepresentation	• misrepresenting facts in order to discriminate
advertising	• ads that restrict availability
appraising	• may not consider protected classes as a factor adversely affecting value
unequal services	• not rendering same service to all parties
steering	• channeling buyers to or away from neighborhoods
blockbusting	• inducing sale or rent based on incoming minorities that will lower values

| restricting MLS access | • MLS restriction to protected classes |
| redlining | • not making loans in certain areas for discriminatory reasons |

Discriminatory Advertising (HUD)

Race, Color, Origin, Religion	• cannot make limitations or preferences
Sex	• no explicit preference
Familial Status	• no preference or exclusion based on family makeup
Handicap	• no exclusions based on physical capabilities

Violations & Enforcement

- File HUD complaint with Office of Fair Housing and Equal Opportunity
  - within one year
  - HUD investigates
  - attempt to resolve out of court

- May sue in court
  - within two years
  - can get restraining order, damages

- Violators are subject to criminal prosecution

Truth / Reg Z / ECOA / RESPA / Flood

Truth-in-Lending and Regulation Z	• Reg Z implements Truth-in-Lending Act & Consumer Credit Protection Act
	- lender must disclose finance charges and APR prior to closing
	- borrower has limited right of rescission
	- lender must follow advertising disclosure requirements
Equal Credit Opportunity Act	• prohibits discrimination in lending
Real Estate Settlements and Procedures Act	• standardizes settlement practices
	- lender must provide CFPB booklet, "Your Home Loan Toolkit"
	- lender must provide CFPB's H-24 Loan Estimate of settlement costs within three days of application
	- lender must use CFPB's H-25 Closing Disclosure
National Flood Insurance Act	• requires borrowers of "federally-related loans" to obtain flood insurance if property is in designated hazard area

Sale Contracts

Characteristics

- binding, bilateral contract for purchase and sale
- the enforceable "blueprint" for closing
- contract is executory, or to be fulfilled
- expires upon closing
- must be in writing
- for validity, must
  - contain valuable consideration
  - identify property
  - be signed by all

Creation / Deposit / Contingencies

Creation
- created by unqualified acceptance of an offer
- gives buyer equitable title, and power to force specific performance

Deposit, or earnest money escrow
- secures contract validity and buyer's equitable interest
- varies in amount
- deposit controlled by disinterested party who must act according to escrow instructions

Contingencies
- conditions that must be met for the contract to be enforceable
- must be clear
- have expiration date
- require diligence to satisfy

Primary Clauses

- parties
- consideration
- legal description
- price and terms
- loan approval provisions
- earnest money
- escrow
- closing and possession dates
- conveyed interest
- type of deed
- title evidence
- property condition warranty/disclosures
- closing costs
- damage and destruction
- default
- broker's agency disclosure and who pays commission
- seller's representations: property condition, marketable title

Secondary Clauses

- inspections
- owner's association disclosure
- survey
- environmental hazards, compliance with laws
- rental property tenant's rights
- FHA or VA financing condition
- flood plain and flood insurance
- condominium assessments

	• foreign seller withholding
• due-on-sale and seller financing disclosure	• tax-deferred exchange
	• boilerplate: merger of agreements, notices, time of the essence, fax transmission, survival, dispute resolution, addenda

Options

Essentials	• optionor gives option to optionee
	• unilateral contract: seller must perform, buyer need not
	• if option is exercised, option becomes bilateral sale contract
Contract requirements	• non-refundable consideration for the option right
	• price and terms of the sale
	• option period expiration date
	• legal description
	• must be in writing
	• must meet contract validity requirements
Common clause provisions	• how to exercise option
	• terms of option money forfeiture
	• how option money will be applied to purchase price

Contract for Deed

Essentials	• purchase price is paid over time in installments
	• seller retains title, buyer takes possession
	• at end of period, buyer pays balance, gets legal title
Interests and rights	• seller may encumber or assign interest
	• seller remains liable for underlying mortgage
	• buyer may use, possess, or profit
	• buyer must make periodic payments, maintain the property, and purchase at the end of the term
Default and recourse	• buyer may sue for cancellation and damages or specific performance
	• seller may sue for specific performance or damages, or may need to foreclose

Closings

Settlement process
- Identify selling terms & costs
- Determine non-prorated debits and credits
- Complete prorated debits and credits
- Complete closing statement
- Disburse funds

RESPA

Applicability	• for residential property • first or second mortgage • federally-related mortgage, or • assumption modifying loan terms
Information booklet	• lender must provide CFPB booklet, "Your Home Loan Toolkit"
Loan Estimate	• lender must provide CFPB's H-24 Loan Estimate of settlement costs within three days of application
Closing Disclosure	• lender must use CFPB's H-25 Closing Disclosure
Referral fees and kickbacks	• RESPA prohibits payment of referral fees and kickbacks • business relationships between firms involved in the transaction must be disclosed

Debits & Credits

Amount buyer must produce:	excess of ***buyer's debits*** over credits
Amount seller must receive:	excess of ***seller's credits*** over debits

Buyer's credits
- earnest money
- loan amount
- seller's share of prorations buyer will pay

Buyer's debits
- purchase price
- expenses (per agreement or custom)
- buyer's share of prorations prepaid by seller

Seller's credits
- purchase price
- buyer's share of prorated items prepaid by seller

Seller's debits
- expenses (per agreement or custom)
- seller's share of prorated items the buyer will pay
- loan balance and other liens to be paid off

Non-prorated expenses

Buyer usually pays	Seller usually pays
Mortgage recording fees	Stamp tax on deed
Documentary stamp tax	Title insurance
Intangible tax on mortgage	Brokerage fee
Mortgage-related fees: appraisal,	Inspection fees
credit, survey, loan origination	Title-related expenses
Impound reserves: insurance, taxes	Attorney fees
Attorney fees	

Prorated items

	arrears	advance
real estate taxes	X	
insurance premiums		X
mortgage interest	X	
rents received by seller		X
utilities	X	

30-Day 12-Month Proration

Formula:

Monthly Amount = (Annual amount ÷ 12)
Daily Amount = (Monthly amount ÷ 30)
Proration = (Monthly amount x no. of months) + (Daily amount x no. of days)

Example:

An annual tax bill is $1,800. Closing is on April 10. What is the seller's share of the taxes?

1. ($1,800 ÷ 12) = $150 monthly amount
2. ($150 ÷ 30) = $5.00 daily amount
3. ($150 x 3 months) = $450 Jan - Mar; ($5 x 10) = $50 Apr 1 - Apr 10; ($450 + 50) = $500 seller's share

365-Day Method

Formula: Daily amount = Annual amount ÷ 365 days; or
Daily amount = Monthly amount ÷ no. of days in month
Proration = (Daily amount x no. of days)

Example: An annual tax bill is $1,800. Closing is on April 10. What is the seller's share of the taxes?

1. ($1,800 ÷ 365) = $4.93 daily amount
2. Jan 1 thru April 10 = (31 + 28 + 31 + 10) days, or 100 days
3. ($4.93 x 100 days) = $493 seller's share

Truth-in-Lending/RESPA Integrated Disclosures Rule

Forms and Procedures
- effective since October 3, 2015
- mandatory: Your Home Loan Toolkit booklet at loan application
- Loan Estimate form: 3 business days after loan application
- Closing Disclosure: 3 business days before consummation

Good faith
- Loan Estimate costs based on best information available
- Closing Disclosure costs equal estimate costs within certain tolerances

Types of charges
- no limitation on increase over estimate
- 10% tolerance charges
- 0 tolerance charges

Applicable transactions
- most closed-end consumer mortgages, including: construction loans, loans secured by vacant land, loans to trusts
- not covered: home equity loans, reverse mortgages, loans on mobile homes, loans by small lenders (no more than 5 loans per year)

The H-25 form
- 5 pages, variable by loan type

Risk Management

Risk Management Strategies

Avoidance	• refrain from risky activity
Reduction	• reduce probability; share responsibility
Transference	• pass risk by contract; insurance
Retention	• accept risk; self-insurance

Risk Management Procedures

Education	• train in laws, forms and procedures, job performance
Disclosure	• provide information to reduce misunderstanding & lawsuits; agency, property condition, duties, personal interest
Documentation and record keeping	• maintain evidence of compliance; manuals, forms, records, contracts, accounting, other documents
Insurance	• general liability, E & O, fire and hazard, flood, casualty, workers, personal property, consequential loss, surety bond

Primary Areas Of Risk

Agency	• duties to all: honesty, fairness, care, skill, required disclosures; • duties to clients: diligence, loyalty, obedience, confidentiality, accounting, full disclosure • conflicts of interest • confidentiality duty lasts forever
Property disclosures	• property condition, lead-based paint, other conditions
Listing and selling process	• risks: listing agreement accuracy, Comparative Market Analysis results, closing cost estimates, advertising, authorizations and permissions, exceeding expertise
Contracting Process	• contracts for real estate must be in writing • risks: inaccuracy, illegal form, omitted elements, lapsed contingencies, wrong data, unauthorized practice of law
Fair Housing	• may not state preference, limitation or discrimination based on race, color, religion, national origin, sex, handicap, familial status
Antitrust	• Sherman Antitrust Act outlaws restraint of trade; Clayton Act outlaws practices that harm competition; Federal Trade Commission Act outlaws unfair methods of competition
Rules and regulations	• risks: commission of prohibited acts, practicing with an expired license, disclosure failures, earnest money mishandling
Misrepresentation	• unintentional: inaccurate information conveyed unknowingly • intentional: fraud, knowingly conveying false information

Recommending providers	• risks: consumer dissatisfaction, possible vicarious liability, undisclosed business relationship (RESPA violation as well as license violation)
Financing and closing	• risks: fair housing and ECOA violations; failure to monitor contingency period; failure to ensure proper disclosure of closing costs; RESPA violations
Trust fund handling	• risks: mishandling of earnest money deposits; commingling and conversion of trust funds; errors in use of trust accounts

Property Management

Management Functions

Types of manager	• individual, managing properties for multiple owners; building manager, employed to manage a single property; resident, employed to live and manage on site. • may specialize in a property type • manager is a fiduciary of the principal • specific functions determined by management agreement
Reporting	• monthly, quarterly, annually • annual operating budget, cash flow reports, profit and loss statements, budget comparison statements
Budgeting	• operating budget: rental rates, capital expenditures, reserves, salaries and wages; projects income based on past performance and current market • expenses, variable and fixed; capital expenditures: outlays for major renovations and construction; cash reserves set aside for variable expenses
Renting	• keep property rented and tenanted; • select compatible tenants and collect scheduled rents • legal issues: compliance with fair housing laws, Americans with Disabilities Act, and ECOA
Property maintenance	• balance costs of services, owner financial objectives, and tenant needs • routine, preventive, or corrective; staffed in-house or contracted out
Construction	• tenant alterations, renovations, expansion, environmental remediation • legal concerns: Americans with Disabilities Act;
Risk management	• risk ranges from natural disaster to personal injury, terrorism, and employee malfeasance • avoid or remove the source, install protective systems, buy insurance, self-insure

- insurance for rented properties includes casualty, liability, workers' comp, fire and hazard, flood, contents, consequential loss, surety bonds, multi-peril
- handling of trust funds is a major risk area; mishandling carries heavy penalties

---

The Management Agreement

Components	• names; description; lease term; owner's purpose; responsibilities; authority; budget; allocation of costs; reporting; compensation; Equal Opportunity statement
Rights, duties and liabilities	• landlord: receive rent; receive premises in specified condition; enter and inspect; examine books; contract, hire vendors, set rents; pay management fee; comply with laws
	• manager: hire and fire; contract; perform management tasks without interference; maintain financial records, make reports, budget, collect rent, find tenants, maintain property, meet owner goals; liability for trust funds; comply with laws

---

Leasing Considerations

Lease types	• for years, periodic, at will, at sufferance, gross, net, percentage, graduated
Owned and leased inclusions	• items included or excluded in the lease; owner's insurance covers only what is included
Reversionary rights of owners	• all rights of ownership revert to
Landlord rights and responsibilities	• rights: enter premises, receive payment, retake on termination, pursue remedies
	• responsibilities: provide habitable conditions; maintain heating, cooling, electrical, plumbing; keep clean and in repair
Tenant rights and responsibilities	• rights: quiet enjoyment, habitable conditions, right to sue for default
	• responsibilities: pay rent, obey rules, give proper notice, return property in prescribed condition, use only for intended purpose
Evictions	• actual: legal procedure; notice, suit, judgment, taking
	• constructive: tenant vacates on account of landlord failure to maintain premises
Tenant improvements	• ownership and payment according to agreement
Termination of a lease	• expiration, performance, agreement, abandonment, breach, notice, destruction of premises, condemnation, foreclosure, death of either party

	(tenancy at will), death of landlord (life estate)
Security deposit procedures	• determined by law, rules, and agreement
Universal Residential Landlord-Tenant Act	• model law regulating lease language and lease terms; adopted by many states

Section II: Real Estate Math Review

Basic Math

Fractions

Adding and subtracting same denominator:

     Formula: $a / c + b / c = (a + b) \div c$

     Example: $1/2 + 1/2 = (1 + 1) / 2 = 2/2 = 1$

Adding and subtracting different denominators:

     Formula: $a / c + b / d = (ad + bc) / cd$

     Example: $1/2 + 1/3 = (3 + 2) / 6 = 5/6$

Multiplying:

     Formula: $(a / c) \times (b / d) = ab / cd$

     Example: $(2/5) \times (4/6) = 8/30 = 4/15$

Decimals and Percents

Converting decimals to percentages

     Formula: *Decimal number x 100 = Percentage number*

     Example: $.022 \times 100 = 2.2\%$

Converting percentages to decimals

     Formula: *Percent number ÷ 100 = Decimal number*

     Example: $2.2 \div 100 = .022$

Multiplying percents

     Formula: *1. Percent number ÷ 100 = Decimal number*

                          2. Beginning number x Decimal number = Product

     Example: 75% of 256 $(75\% \times 256) = ?$

                 1. $75 \div 100 = .75$

                 2. $256 \times .75 = 192$

Dividing by percents

Formula: 1. *Percent number ÷ 100 = Decimal number*

2. *Beginning number ÷ Decimal = Dividend*

Example: 240 ÷ 75% = ?

1. 75% ÷ 100 = .75

2. 240 ÷ .75 = 320

Decimals, Fractions, and Percentages

Converting fractions to percents

Formula: (1)   a / b or a ÷ b = a divided by b = decimal number

(2)   decimal number x 100 = percent number

Example: (1)   2 / 5 = 2 divided by 5 = 0.4

(2)   .4 x 100 = 40%

Converting a percent to fraction and reducing it

Formula: (1)   X% = X ÷ 100 or X / 100

(2) $\dfrac{X \div a}{100 \div a}$ where a is the largest number that divides evenly into both numerator and denominator

Example: (1)   40% = 40 ÷ 100, or 40 / 100

(2) $\dfrac{40 \div 20}{100 \div 20} = \dfrac{2}{5}$

Converting fractions to decimals and percentages

Formula: *Decimal x 100 = Percent number*

Example: .75 x 100 = 75%

Equations

Additions and Subtractions

Formula: *if* $a = b + c$

then $b = a - c$ *(subtracting c from both sides)*

and $c = a - b$ *(subtracting b from both sides)*

Example: 10   = 6 + 4

$$6 \quad = 10 - 4$$

$$4 \quad = 10 - 6$$

Multiplications and Divisions

Formula: *if* $a = b \times c$

            then $b = a / c$ *(dividing both sides by c)*

            and $c = a / b$ *(dividing both sides by b)*

Example: $10 = 2 \times 5$

            $2 = 10 \div 5$

            $5 = 10 \div 2$

Linear and Perimeter Measurement

Linear measure of rectangles

Formula: *Side A = Area ÷ Side B*

Example: A rectangular house has one side 40' side long and area of 1,200 SF. What is the length of the other side?

            Side A = (1,200' ÷ 40') = 30'

Perimeter measurement

Formula: *Perimeter = Sum of all sides of an object*

Example: A five-sided lot has the following dimensions:

            Side A = 50' Side B = 60'
            Side C= 70' Side D = 100'
            Side E = 30'

            What is the perimeter of the lot?

            P = 50' + 60' + 70' + 100' + 30' = 310'

Area Measurement

Square and rectangle

Formula: *Area = Width x Depth (Horizontal) or Width x Height (Vertical)*

            Width= Depth (Height) ÷ Area

            Depth (Height)= Width ÷ Area

Example: A house is 40' deep and 30' wide. What is its area?

Area = 40' x 30' = 1,200 SF

Triangle

Formula: *Area = (Height x Base) ÷ 2*

Note: Base is also sometimes referred to as "width"

Example: An A-frame house has a front facade measuring 30' across and 20' in height. What is the area of the facade?

Area = (30' x 20') ÷ 2 = 300 Square feet (SF)

Square foot-to-acre conversion

Formula: *Acres = Area SF ÷ 43,560 SF*

Example: How many acres is 196,020 SF?

196,020 SF ÷ 43,560 SF = 4.5 acres

Acre-to-square foot conversion

Formula: *SF = Number of acres x 43,560 SF*

Example: How many square feet is .75 acres?

.75 acres x 43,560 SF = 32,670 SF

Linear and Area Conversion Chart

Linear measures

(cm = centimeter; m = meter; km = kilometer)

1 inch	=	1/12 foot	=	1/36 yard		
1 foot	=	12 inches	=	1/3 yard		
1 yard	=	36 inches	=	3 feet		
1 rod	=	16.5 feet	=	1/320 mile		
1 mile	=	5280 feet	=	1760 yards	=	320 rods
1 centimeter	=	1/100 m				
1 meter	=	100 cm	=	1/1000 km		
1 kilometer	=	1,000 m				

Area measures

1 square inch	=	1/144 sq. foot				
1 square foot	=	1/9 sq. yard	=	144 sq. inches		
1 square yard	=	9 sq. feet	=	1,296 sq. inches		
1 acre	=	1/640 sq. mi	=	43,560 SF	=	208.71 ft x 208.71 ft
1 square mile	=	640 acres	=	1 section	=	1/36 township
1 section	=	1 mi x 1 mi	=	640 acres	=	1/36 township
1 township	=	6 mi x 6 mi	=	36 sq. mi	=	36 sections

57

Metric conversions

(cm = centimeter; m = meter; km = kilometer)

1 inch	=	2.54 cm					
1 foot	=	30.48 cm	=	.3048 m			
1 yard	=	91.44 cm	=	.9144 m			
1 mile	=	1609.3 m	=	1.60 km			
1 centimeter	=	.3937 inch					
1 meter	=	39.37 inches	=	3.28 feet	=	1.094 yards	
1 kilometer	=	3,281.5 feet	=	.621 mile			

Fractions of sections, acres, and linear dimensions

Fraction		# Acres
1 section	=	640 acres
1/2 section	=	320 acres
1/4 section	=	160 acres
1/8 section	=	80 acres
1/16 section	=	40 acres
1/32 section	=	20 acres
1/64 section	=	10 acres

Calculating Area from the Legal Description

Formula:
    (1) *First multiply all the denominators of the fractions in the legal description together.*

    (2) *Then divide 640 by the resulting product.*

Examples:
    How many acres are in the Northern 1/2 of the Southwestern 1/4 of Section 6?

    640 / (2 x 4) = 640 / 8 = 80 acres

    How many acres are in the Western 1/2 of the Northwestern 1/4 of the Northeastern 1/4 of Section 8?

    640 / (2 x 4 x 4) = 640 / 32 = 20 acres

Volume Measurement

Formula:
    Volume = Width x Height x Depth   (assume objects with 90 degree angles)

    Base = (Height x Depth) ÷ Volume

    Height = (Base x Depth) ÷ Volume

    Depth = (Base x Height) ÷ Volume

Example:
    What is the volume of a 40' x 30' x 20' house?

    40' x 30' x 20' = 24,000 cubic feet

Ownership

Condominium Assessment Calculation

Formula: *Monthly assessment = (Total annual building budget x Condo unit % of value) ÷ 12*

Example: Assume a condominium complex with a $300,000 budget and a unit that comprises 1.48% of the total value of the complex. Monthly assessment?

($300,000 x .0148) ÷ 12 = $370 monthly assessment.

Leases

Percentage Lease Rent Calculation

Formula: *Monthly percentage rent = Sales x percent of sales charged*

Example: A store generates $50,000 per month. The lease calls for 1.5% percentage rent. Monthly rent amount?

($50,000 x .015) = $750 / month

Contracts for the Sale of Real Estate

Percentage of Listing Price Calculation

Formula: *Percentage of listing price = Offer ÷ Listing price*

Example: A property listed for $150,000 receives an offer for $120,000. The offer's percentage of listing price is:

$120,000 ÷ $150,000 = 80%

Earnest Money Deposit Calculation

Formula: *Deposit = Offering price x required or market-accepted percentage*

Example: A seller requires a 2% deposit on a property listed for $320,000. The required deposit (assuming a full price offer) is:

$320,000 x 2% = $6,400

Appraisal & Value

Adjusting Comparables

Rules:
1. Never adjust the subject!

2. If the comparable is superior to the subject, subtract value from the

comparable.

3. If the comparable is inferior to the subject, add value to the comparable.

Example: The subject has a $10,000 pool and no porch. A comparable that sold for $250,000 has a porch ($5,000), an extra bathroom ($6,000), and no pool.

Adjustments to comp: $250,000 (+10,000 - 5,000 - 6,000) = $249,000 indicated value of subject

---

Gross Rent Multiplier

Formulas: *Sales price = Monthly rental income x GRM*

Monthly rental income = Sales price / Gross Rent Multiplier

Note: Gross rent multiplier is often abbreviated as GRM.

Examples:
1. What is the value of a fourplex with monthly rent of $2,800 and a GRM of 112?

$2,800 rent x 112 GRM = $313,600

2. What is the GRM of a fourplex with monthly rent of $2,800 and a value of $313,600?

313,600 price ÷ $2,800 rent = 112 GRM

Gross Income Multiplier

Formulas   *Gross Income Multiplier = Sales price ÷ Annual income*

Sales price = Annual income x Gross Income Multiplier

Annual income = Sales price ÷ Gross Income Multiplier

Note: Gross income multiplier is often abbreviated as GIM.

Examples:
1. What is the value of a commercial property with an annual income of $33,600 and a GIM of 9.3?

$33,600 income x 9.3 GIM = $312,480

2. What is the GIM of a commercial property with annual income of $33,600 and a value of $312,480?

$313,600 price ÷ $33,600 = 9.3 GIM

Cost Approach Formula

Formula: *Value = Land value + (Improvements + Capital additions - Depreciation)*

Example: Land value = $50,000; home replacement cost = $150,000; new garage added
                  @ $30,000; total depreciation = $10,000

                  Value = $50,000 + (150,000 + 30,000 - 10,000) = $220,000

Depreciation

Formulas: *Annual depreciation = Beginning depreciable basis ÷ Depreciation term*

                  *Depreciable basis = (Initial property value + Any capital improvements - Land
                  value)*

                  Note: The depreciation term is in number of years.

Example: Property value = $500,000; land value = $110,000; depreciation term = 39 years

                  Step 1: ($500,000 - $110,000) = $390,000 depreciable basis

                  Step 2: ($390,000 ÷ 39 years) = $10,000 annual depreciation

---

Income Capitalization Formula

Formulas: *Value = Annual Net Operating Income ÷ Capitalization rate*

                  Capitalization rate = Annual Net Operating Income ÷ Value

                  Annual Net Operating Income = Value x Capitalization rate

Examples: 1. A property generates $490,000 net income and sells at a 7% cap rate. What
                      is its value?

                      $490,000 ÷ 7% = $7,000,000 value

                  2. A property has a net income of $490,000 and sells for $7,000,000. What is
                      its cap rate?

                      $490,000 ÷ 7,000,000 = .07, or 7%

                  3. A property's value is $7,000,000 and the cap rate is 7%. What is the
                      property's net operating income?

                      $7,000,000 x .07 = $490,000

Net Operating Income (NOI, Net Income)

Formula: *NOI = Potential rent - Vacancy loss + Other income - Operating expenses*

                  Note: NOI does not include debt payments!

Example: A building has 10 office suites generating annual potential rent of $10,000 each.
                  Vacancy = 10% and annual expenses are $35,000. Vending machines yield

$5,000. What is the NOI?

$100,000 rent - 10,000 vacancy + 5,000 other income - 35,000 expenses = $60,000 NOI

Finance

Points

Definition: 1 point = 1% of the loan amount or .01 x loan amount

Formulas: *Points = Fee paid ÷ Loan amount*

Fee paid = Loan amount x Points

Loan amount = Fee paid ÷ Points

Examples:
1. A borrower pays $500 for a $10,000 loan. How many points are paid?

   $500 ÷ 10,000 = .05 = 5 points

2. A borrower pays 5 points on a $10,000 loan. What is the fee paid?

   $10,000 x .05 = $500

3. A borrower pays $500 as 5 points on a loan. What is the loan amount?

   $500 ÷ .05 = $10,000

Rules of
Thumb: 1 point charged raises lender's yield by .125%

8 points charged raises lender's yield by 1%

Example: A lender wants to yield 7% on a 6.5% loan. How many points must he or she charge?

(7% - 6.5%) = .5%

.5% ÷ .125% = 4 points

Interest Rate, Principal and Payment

Caveat!
> Interest rates in mortgage financing apply to the <u>annual </u>interest payment and <u>exclude</u> principal payment. Remember to convert annual payments to monthly or vice versa as the question requires, and to exclude principal payments from your calculations!

Formulas: *Payment = Principal x Rate*

Principal = Payment ÷ Rate

Rate = Payment ÷ Principal

Examples: 1.   A borrower has a $100,000 loan @ 6% interest. What are the annual and monthly payments?

Annual payment = $100,000 x .06 = $6,000
Monthly payment = $6,000 ÷ 12 = $500

2.   A borrower has a $500 monthly payment on a 6% loan. What is the loan principal?

Principal = ($500 x 12) ÷ 6% = ($6,000 ÷ .06) = $100,000

3.   A borrower has a $500 monthly payment on a $100,000 loan. What is the loan rate?

Rate = ($500 x 12) ÷ $100,000 = ($6,000 ÷ 100,000) = .06 = 6%

Total Interest, Interest Rate, and Loan Term

Formulas: *Interest-only loan:*   *Total interest = Loan amount x Rate x Term in years*

Amortized loan: *Total interest = (Monthly PI payment x 12 x term) - Loan amount*

Examples: 1.   A borrower obtains a 10-year interest only loan of $50,000 @ 6%. How much interest will he or she pay?

($50,000 x .06 x 10) = $30,000

2.   A borrower obtains a 10-year amortized loan of $50,000 @ 6% with monthly payments of $555.10. How much interest will he or she pay?

($555.10 x 12 x 10) - $50,000 = $16,612

Amortization Calculation

Formulas: *Month 1:*   *Principal paid = Monthly payment - (Loan amount x Rate ÷ 12)*

Month 2:   *New loan amount = (Previous month principal - Principal paid)*

Principal paid = Monthly payment - (New loan amount x Rate ÷ 12)

Example: A borrower obtains a 30-year $100,000 amortized loan @ 7% with a $665.31 monthly payment. What is the principal paid in the second month?

Month 1:   Principal paid = $665.31 - ($100,000 x 7% ÷ 12) = $665.31 - (583.33 interest paid) = $81.98

Month 2:   New loan amount = $100,000 previous month beginning loan amount - $81.98 principal paid = $99,918.02

Principal paid = $665.31 - ($99,918.02 x 7% ÷ 12) = $665.31 - (582.86 interest paid) = $82.45

Loan Constants

Formulas: *Monthly payment = (Loan amount x Loan constant) / 1000*

      Loan amount = (Monthly payment ÷ Loan constant) x 1000

      Loan constant = (Monthly payment ÷ Loan amount) x 1000

Examples: 1. A borrower obtains a loan for $100,000 with a 6.3207 constant. What is the monthly payment?

       Monthly payment = ($100,000 ÷ 1,000) x 6.3207 = $632.07

     2. A borrower has a monthly payment of $632.07 on a loan with a monthly constant of 6.3207. What is the loan amount?

       Loan amount = ($632.07 ÷ 6.3207) x 1000 = $100,000

     3. A borrower obtains a loan for $100,000 with a monthly payment of $632.07. What is the loan constant?

       Loan constant = ($632.07 ÷ $100,000) x 1,000 = 6.3207

Loan - to - Value Ratio (LTV)

Formulas: *LTV ratio = Loan ÷ Price (Value)*

      Loan = LTV ratio x Price (Value)

      Price (Value) = Loan ÷ LTV ratio

Examples: 1. A borrower can get a $265,600 loan on a $332,000 home. What is her LTV ratio?

       LTV Ratio = $265,600 ÷ 332,000 = 80%

     2. A borrower can get an 80% loan on a $332,000 home. What is the loan amount?

       Loan = $332,000 x .80 = $265,600

     3. A borrower obtained an 80% loan for $265,600. What was the price of the home?

       Price (value) = $265,600 ÷ .80 = $332,000

Financial Qualification

Income ratio qualification

Formula: *Monthly Principal & Interest (PI) payment = Income ratio x Monthly gross income*

Example: A lender uses a 28% income ratio for the PI payment. A borrower grosses $30,000 per year. What monthly PI payment can the borrower afford?

Monthly PI payment = ($30,000 ÷ 12) x .28 = $700

How much can the borrower borrow if the loan constant is 6.3207? (See also-loan constants)

Loan amount = ($700 ÷ 6.3207) x 1,000 = $110,747.22

Debt ratio qualification

Formulas: *Debt ratio = (Housing expense + Other debt payments) ÷ Monthly gross income*

Housing expense = (Monthly gross income x Debt ratio) - Other debt payments

Example: A lender uses a 36% debt ratio. A borrower earns $30,000 / year and has monthly non-housing debt payments of $500. What housing payment can she afford?

Housing expense = ($30,000 ÷ 12 x .36) - 500 = ($900 - 500) = $400

Investment

Appreciation Calculations

Simple appreciation

Formulas: *Total appreciation = Current value - Original price*

Total appreciation rate = Total appreciation ÷ Original price

Average annual appreciation rate = Total appreciation rate ÷ number of years

One year appreciation rate = (Annual appreciation amount) ÷ (Value at beginning of year)

Examples: 1.   A home purchased for $200,000 five years ago is now worth $300,000. What are the total appreciation amount, total appreciation rate, and average appreciation rate?

Total appreciation = ($300,000 - 200,000), or $100,000

Total appreciation rate = ($100,000 ÷ 200,000), or 50%

Average annual appreciation rate = 50% ÷ 5 years = 10%

2.   A home costing $250,000 is worth $268,000 one year later. What is the one-year appreciation rate?

One-year appreciation rate = ($18,000 ÷ 250,000) = 7.2%

65

Compounded appreciation

Formula: *Appreciated value = Beginning value x (1+ annual rate) x (1+ annual rate) ...... for the number of years in question*

Example: A $100,000 property is expected to appreciate 5% each year for the next 3 years. What will be its appreciated value at the end of this period?

Appreciated value = $100,000 x 1.05 x 1.05 x 1.05 = $115,762.50

Rate of Return, Investment Value, Income

Formulas: Where Income = net operating income (NOI); Rate = rate of return, cap rate, or percent yield; and Value = value, price or investment amount:

Rate = Income ÷ Value

Value = Income ÷ Rate

Income = Value x Rate

Examples:

1. An office building has $200,000 net income and sold for $3,200,000. What was the rate of return?

   Rate = ($200,000 NOI ÷ 3,200,000 price) = 6.25%

2. An office building has $200,000 net income and a cap rate of 6.25%. What is its value?

   Value = ($200,000 ÷ 6.25%) = $3,200,000

3. An office building sells for $3,200,000 at a cap rate of 6.25%. What is its NOI?

   Income = $3,200,000 x 6.25% = $200,000

Basis, Adjusted Basis, and Capital Gain

Formulas: *Capital gain = Amount realized - Adjusted basis, where*

Amount realized = Sale price - Selling costs

Adjusted basis = Beginning basis + Capital improvements - Total depreciation

Total depreciation = (Beginning depreciable basis ÷ Depreciation term in years) x Years depreciated

Depreciable basis = Initial property value + Capital improvements - Land value

Example: Tip: work example backwards from last formula to first formula.

An apartment building was purchased for $500,000, with the land value estimated to be $100,000. The owner added a $100,000 parking lot. The

66

property was depreciated on a 40-year schedule (for present purposes!). Three years later the property sold for $700,000, and selling costs were $50,000. What was the capital gain?

1. depreciable basis = $500,000 purchase price + 100,000 parking lot - 100,000 land = $500,000

2. total depreciation = ($500,000 ÷ 40 years) x 3 years = $37,500

3. adjusted basis = $500,000 purchase price + 100,000 parking lot - 37,500 total depreciation = $562,500

4. amount realized = $700,000 sale price - 50,000 selling costs = $650,000

5. capital gain = $650,000 amount realized - 562,500 adjusted basis = $87,500

Depreciation

Formulas: *Annual depreciation = (Beginning depreciable basis) ÷ (Depreciation term in number of years)*

Depreciable basis = (Initial property value + Capital improvements - Land value)

Example: Property value = $500,000; land value = $110,000; depreciation term = 39 years

1. ($500,000 - 110,000) = $390,000 depreciable basis

2. ($390,000 ÷ 39 years) = $10,000 annual depreciation

Equity

Formula: *Equity = Current market value - Current loan balance(s)*

Example: A home that was purchased for $150,000 with a $100,000 loan is now worth $300,000. The current loan balance is $80,000. What is the homeowner's equity?

Equity = $300,000 value - $80,000 debt = $220,000

Net Income

Formula: *NOI = Potential rent - Vacancy loss + Other income - Operating expenses*

Note: NOI does not include debt payments!

Example: A building has 10 office suites generating annual potential rent of $10,000 each. Vacancy = 10% and annual expenses are $35,000. Vending machines yield

$5,000. What is the NOI?

$100,000 rent - 10,000 vacancy + 5,000 other income - 35,000 expenses = $60,000 NOI

Cash Flow

Formula: *Cash flow = (Net Operating Income - Debt service) where debt service is PI payment*

Example: A building generates $100,000 NOI after expenses and has a debt payment of $40,000. What is its cash flow?

Cash flow = $100,000 - 40,000 = $60,000

Investment Property Income Tax Liability

Formula: *Tax liability = (NOI + Reserves - Interest expense - Depreciation) x Tax bracket*

Example: An office building has NOI of $200,000, an annual reserve expense of $20,000, interest expense of $130,000 and annual depreciation of $50,000. Assuming a 28% tax bracket, what is its income tax liability?

Tax liability = ($200,000 + 20,000 - 130,000 - 50,000) x 28% = $11,200

Return on Investment

Formula: *ROI = NOI ÷ Price*

Example: An investment property generates a cash flow of $100,000 and appraises for $1,500,000. What is the owner's return on investment?

ROI = $100,000 ÷ 1,500,000 = 6.67%

Return on Equity

Formula: *ROE = Cash flow ÷ Equity*

Example: An investment property generates a cash flow of $100,000. The owner has $500,000 equity in the property. What is the owner's return on equity?

ROE= $100,000 ÷ 500,000 = 20%

Real Estate Taxation

Converting Mill Rates

Definition: 1 mill = $.001; a mill rate of 1 mill per $1,000 = .1%; a 1% tax rate = 10 mills

Formula: *Tax = (Taxable value ÷ 1000) x Mill rate*

Example: A tax rate on a house with a $200,000 taxable value is 7 mills per thousand dollars of assessed valuation. What is the tax?

Tax = ($200,000 ÷ 1,000) x 7 mills = $1,400

Tax Base

Formula: *Tax base = Assessed valuations – Exemptions*

Example: A town has a total assessed valuation of $20,000,000 and exemptions of $4,000,000. What is the tax base?

$20,000,000 - 4,000,000 = $16,000,000

Tax Rate, Base, and Requirement

Formulas: *Tax rate = Tax requirement ÷ Tax base*

Tax base = Tax requirement ÷ Tax rate

Tax requirement = Tax base x Rate

Example: A town has a tax base of $160,000,000 and a budget of $8,000,000. What is the tax rate?

Tax rate = ($8,000,000 ÷ 160,000,000) = .05, or 5%, or 50 mills

Special Assessments

Formula: *Special assessment = Total special assessment cost x Homeowner's share*

Example: A homeowner owns 100' of an 800' seawall that must be repaired. The total assessment will be $80,000. What is the homeowner's assessment?

1. Homeowner's share = 100' ÷ 800' = .125, or 12.5%

2. Special assessment = $80,000 x 12.5% = $10,000

Commissions

Commission Splits

Formulas: *Total commission = Sale price x Commission rate*

Co-brokerage split = Total commission x Co-brokerage percent

Agent split = Co-brokerage split x Agent percent

Broker split = Co-brokerage split - Agent split

Example: A $300,000 property sells at a 7% commission with a 50-50 co-brokerage split and a 60% agent split with her broker. What are total, co-brokerage, agent's, and broker's commissions?

Total commission = $300,000 x .07 = $21,000

Co-brokerage splits = $300,000 x .07 x .50 = $10,500

Agent split = $10,500 x .60 = $6,300

Agent's broker's split = $10.500 - 6,300 = $4,200

Seller's Net

Formula: *Seller's net = Sale Price - (sale price x commission) - Other closing costs - Loan balance*

Example: A home sells for $260,000 and has a loan balance of $200,000 at closing. The commission is 7% and other closing costs are $2,000. What is the seller's net?

Seller's net = ($260,000 - (260,000 x .07) - 2,000 - 200,000) = $39,800

Price to Net an Amount

Formula: *Sale Price = (Desired net + Closing costs + Loan payoff)) (1 - Commission rate)*

Example: A homeseller wants to net $50,000. The commission is 7%, the loan payoff is $150,000, and closing costs are $4,000. What must the price be?

Sale price = ($50,000 + 4,000 + 150,000) ÷ .93 = $219,355

Closing Costs, Prorations

30-Day 12-Month Method

Formulas: *Monthly amount = Annual amount / 12*

Daily amount = Monthly amount / 30

Proration = (Monthly amount multiplied by the # months) + (Daily amount multiplied by the # days)

Example: An annual tax bill is $1,800. Closing is on April 10. What is the seller's share of the taxes?

1. Monthly amount = ($1,800 ÷ 12) = $150; no. of mounts = 3

2. Daily amount = ($150 ÷ 30) = $5.00; no. of days = 10

3. Proration = ($150 x 3) + ($5 x 10) = ($450 + 50) = $500 seller's share

70

365-Day Method

Formula: *Daily amount = (Annual amount ÷ 365) or (Monthly amount ÷ Length of month)*

Proration = Daily amount multiplied by the # days

Example: An annual tax bill is $1,800. Closing is on April 10. What is the seller's share of the taxes?

1.   Daily amount = ($1,800 ÷ 365) = $4.93

2.   Jan 1 thru April 10 = (31 + 28 + 31 + 10) days, or 100 days

3.   Proration = $4.93 x 100 days = $493 seller's share

Income Received in Advance (Rent)

Logic: *Credit buyer and debit seller for buyer's share*

Example: Seller receives $1,000 rent. The month is ¾ over.

1.   Buyer's share is ($1,000 x 25%) = $250

2.   Credit buyer / debit seller $250.

Expenses paid in Arrears (Tax)

Logic: *Credit buyer and debit seller for seller's share*

Example: Buyer will pay $1,000 taxes. The year is ¾ over.

1.   Buyer's share is ($1,000 x 25%) = $250

2.   Credit buyer / debit seller $750.

Insurance Coverage

Recovery with Co-Insurance Clauses

Formula: Recovery = (Damage claim) x (Percent replacement cost covered ÷ Minimum coverage requirement)

Example: An owner insures a home for $100,000. Replacement cost is $150,000. A co-insurance clause requires coverage of 80% of replacement cost to avoid penalty. Fire destroys the house. What can the owner recover from the insurer?

Claim recovery = $150,000 x (67% cost covered ÷ 80% required) = $125,625

Section III: North Carolina Laws & Regulations

The following outline is a condensation of NC Real Estate License Law as codified in Chapter 93A , Articles 1 and 4, of the general statutes of North Carolina. The Study Guide also includes the provisions of the North Carolina Real Estate Commission's regulations as presented in Title 21, Chapter 58, Subchapters 58A and 58B, Sections A.0100, A.0500, A.1600, A.1700, B.0400, B.0500, and B.0600, as well as its "Trust Account Guidelines" and "License Law and Rule Comments."

Licensing Regulation

Who must be licensed

- Any party transacting real estate for compensation on behalf of another
- May be corporation, partnership, limited liability company (LLC), association

Activities requiring licensure

- Listing
- Selling
- Leasing
- Property management
- Auctioning
- Business brokerage
- Referring if done for compensation
- Licensees may not pay finder's or referral fees to unlicensed parties.

Exemptions from licensure

- Property owners selling own property
- Attorneys-in-fact
- Attorneys at law if in normal course of providing legal services; but attorneys may not broker
- Receivers acting under court order
- Trustees acting under a trust agreement or will
- Certain salaried employees of broker-property managers

Activities permitted to unlicensed employees
- General administrative tasks
- Property management – can show property and use pre-printed lease forms; may not negotiate terms

Real Estate Commission (NCREC)

Purpose

- to protect general public in dealing with licensees

Scope of authority and powers

- License law administration and registering time share projects

- Managing prelicense and CE education
- Educating public and licensees about real estate
- Regulating business activities of licensees
- Disciplining violators of license law
- Cannot regulate compensation, nor does it arbitrate commission disputes

Disciplinary authority

- Can reprimand, censure licensees and suspend or revoke licenses
- Can seek injunctive relief
- Violations of license law or rules are misdemeanors but do not constitute convictions unless pursued in court
- Not permitted to fine licensees unless the infraction is a violation of time share laws

Members and structure

- 9 members: 7 appointed by governor and 2 by General Assembly
- 3 must be licensed brokers; 2 must be public members not involved in real estate or appraisal
- Commissioners serve 3-year terms

License Types

Broker

- may operate as unsupervised independent agent

Provisional Broker

- must be supervised by Broker-in-Charge (BIC)

Real estate firm broker

Limited nonresident commercial broker

- Limited to commercial brokerage
- Must declare an affiliation and cooperation agreement with a resident NC broker
- Must state identity in all advertising; no "blind" ads

Non-resident license

- need not be resident
- can get if state has similar provisions for NC residents and candidate passes state portion of license exam

Broker-in-Charge designation

- licensee must be a broker

License Requirements

- 18 years old
- US citizen, non-citizen national, or qualified alien

- Have Social Security number
- Complete the license application and pay the appropriate fee
- Satisfy education requirement (see below)
- Pass state exam
- Demonstrate moral character

Application procedure

Initial application procedure

- Submit application and fee along with exam fee
- Application cancelled if applicant fails the exam or fails to appear

Examination

- Exams are confidential; violation is grounds for denial of license

Moral character

- Must demonstrate moral character
- If in question, applicant may have a hearing
- Notice of questionable character sent via certified mail
- Applicant has 60 days to respond; if no response, application is deemed denied

Criminal background

- Must submit a criminal records report

Licensing business entities

- Non-proprietorships must apply and obtain a firm license
- If entity changes its business form, it must re-apply and get new license
- Must provide description and data on business, character, license history
- At least one principal of the entity must have active broker's license and serve as qualifying broker
- Entity licensing does not permit unlicensed persons to practice real estate
- Qualifying broker must designate a broker-in-charge (BIC) at each office where brokerage occurs
- Partnership—qualifying principal broker of any partnership must be a general partner
- Corporation-- qualifying broker must be an officer
- LLC-- qualifying broker must be a manager
- Business entities must certify that they are in good standing with the NC Secretary of State at the time their licenses are renewed

License term, expiration

License term

- one year-- **All licenses expire** on June 30th following issuance
- Practicing with expired license subjects one to penalties

Renewal:

- apply within 45 days prior to expiration, pay fee
- upon 2nd renewal, must fulfill CE requirement if renewing active license
- if inactive, licensee not required to complete CE

Education Requirement for Brokers and Brokers-in-Charge

Broker candidate

- pass 75-hour prelicense course within 3 years prior to application as provisional broker and complete the 90-hour post-licensing course within 3 years
- both the 75-hour prelicense course and 90-hour post-licensing course are only available in a live instruction format
- applicants may receive waiver of the 75-hour prelicense course if they completed 75 hours (or more) of salesperson prelicense education in another state
- must complete one 30-hour component of the post-licensing requirement each year by the license anniversary date in order to remain on active status

Broker-in-Charge

- two years' experience or equivalent as full-time broker or provisional broker within previous five years or education equivalent to the experience requirement
- complete the 12 hour broker-in-charge course within 120 days following BIC designation
- complete specially designated broker-in-charge continuing education elective

Initial Licensing Exam

- Administered by PSI
- Has both a national section (100 questions) and state section (40 questions)
- Passing score is 71% for the national section; 72.5% for state section
- If only one section is passed, the applicant will have to retake only the failed section
- Both sections must be passed before the end of the applicant's 180-day examination eligibility period
- An applicant qualifying for licensure based on licensure in another state only has to take and pass the state section of the examination

Out-of-State Candidates and Reciprocity
- North Carolina no longer has license reciprocity agreements with other states
- If the candidate is an active licensee in another state, they are exempt from the national portion of the licensing exam. However, they must pass the North Carolina specific section of the exam
- Brokers who were licensed in North Carolina by reciprocity shall be entitled to retain such license indefinitely as long as they continue to renew their license

Continuing Education Requirements

Initial licensure

- Upon initial licensure, licensees are not required to complete any continuing education during the first partial year of practice.
- Following the first expiration on June 30th, licensees in their first full year of practice must fulfill the continuing education requirement. The CE requirement must be completed by June 10th.
- Initial licensure for CE purposes is defined as including initial issuance, reinstatement of a canceled, revoked, or surrendered license, and any license expired for more than six months

Renewal

- Brokers NOT designated as broker-in-charge or broker-in-charge eligible must have 8 hours of CE, consisting of

- o 4 hours of general update course developed by NCREC
- o 4 hours of approved elective course

- Brokers WHO ARE designated as broker-in-charge or broker-in-charge eligible must have 8 hours of CE, consisting of

  - o 4 hours of the required Broker-in-Charge Update (BICUP) course
  - o 4 hours of approved elective course

- licensee bears responsibility for providing evidence of completion
- Continuing education is not required to renew an inactive license
- Continuing education is required to activate an inactive license (however, members of Congress or the General Assembly are exempt from this requirement)

Continuing education for nonresident licensees

- must complete 8 hours of approved education, but both 4-hour components may be NCREC-approved electives, or one 4-hour course may be the NCREC update course, or
- licensee may complete 8 hours offered in the state of residence or state where course was taken. Licensee in this case must demonstrate that the course was completed as well as approved by the licensing agency in the state where the course was taken

Post-licensing education requirement

- must complete additional 90 hours of postlicense education within 3 years following the date of initial licensure to become broker
- the 90-hour requirement consists of 3 30-hour courses
- at least one 30-hour course must be taken within one year of the date following initial licensure
- upon completion of all three courses, the provisional status of the broker license is removed
- failure to complete the first or second 30-hour course satisfactorily and within the required time frame will result in the provisional broker's license being placed on inactive status
- licensees holding inactive licenses must complete both the post-licensing and continuing education requirements to be eligible for activation
- to reinstate the cancelled license, licensees may be required at NCREC's discretion to satisfy the post-licensing education requirement as well as the requirement for original licensure, including taking the state exam
- time extensions: licensees may obtain extensions of time to satisfy the post-licensing education requirement for any of the first three years following the date of initial licensure as a broker if the licensee provides satisfactory evidence of being unable to obtain the necessary education due to an incapacitating illness or other circumstance which existed for a substantial portion of the year in question and which made compliance with the education requirement impossible or unreasonably burdensome.

License Status: Active and Inactive

All licenses are either active or inactive (unless expired, canceled, revoked, suspended or surrendered)

- Licenses issued to firms or brokers other than provisional brokers are issued as active licenses
- Licensees on inactive status may not practice or earn compensation, including referrals
- Inactive licensees must still renew license prior to expiration

Events triggering inactive status

- Initial licensure for provisional brokers
- Written request by licensee

- No BIC supervision
- Failure to complete CE requirement
- Firm license-- when there is no qualifying broker and/or BIC

Converting inactive to active broker's license

- Apply, confirm CE completion-- broker is active upon delivery or mailing
- If no acknowledgement of receipt by NCREC, agent must cease practicing

Converting inactive to active firm license

- Make application; the principal broker must also be active

License reinstatement

- Expired for 6 months or less
    - apply
    - pay fees
    - prove CE completion
    - have BIC supervision

- Expired for over 6 months but less than 5 years
    - apply
    - pay fees
    - demonstrate moral character
    - may need to retake exam or courses

- Expired for over 5 years
    - treated as a new applicant

Revoked license

- apply
- pay fees
- demonstrate moral character
- complete education

Surrendered

- at the end of term, make application
- pay fees
- demonstrate moral character
- complete education

Suspended

- license is restored at end of suspension if CE is current and licensee has BIC supervision

Violations and Prohibited Actions under License Law

- Misrepresentation or omission of a material fact
    - can be willful or negligent
    - can be about the property or about the principal's ability to complete the transaction
- False promises
- Conflict of interest
- Undisclosed dual agency

- Accepting commissions from party other than broker or BIC
- Failing to account for trust monies
- Unworthiness or incompetence
- Paying a commission in violation of law
- Improper, fraudulent, or dishonest dealing
- Practicing law
- Commingling or failure to deposit trust funds in trust account
- Failure to deliver copy of sale contract to parties
- Failure to deliver closing statement
- Obtaining license using false or fraudulent claims
- Violating State Fair Housing Act
- Violating other NCREC rules

Hearing Procedure for Complaints

- Complaint must

  - be in writing
  - identify the licensee
  - present the facts

- Scope of investigation may go beyond the complaint
- NCREC initiates investigation and sends letter of inquiry to licensee

  - Licensee has 14 days to respond

- Hearing is conducted
- NCREC renders its verdict
- Broker may appeal to superior court
- Broker may be charged with vicarious liability; principal can be liable for agent's malfeasance
- Agents in violation may be exposed to civil and criminal liability

Notification of Changes

- Must report changes of name, firm, and addresses within 10 days to NC Real Estate Commission
- Must report criminal convictions within 60 days

Unfair or Deceptive Trade Practices Act (UDTPA)

- Protects aggrieved consumers against businesses
- If proven history of deception by agent, liable for treble (3x) damages

Regulation of Appraisals

- Individuals in NC performing formal appraisals must be licensed
- Licensed appraisers are regulated by the NC Appraisal Board
- Licensed appraisers need not have a broker or provisional broker license

North Carolina Real Estate Education and Recovery Fund

- pays unsatisfied judgments against North Carolina brokers for acts they committed
- can fund the development of educational books and programs
- the maximum payout is $25,000 per individual per year and $75,000 per individual for their career
- the maximum payout is $50,000 per transaction
- will automatically result in the broker's license being suspended until the Fund is repaid (with interest)

Agency Relationships and Agreements

Permissible relationships

- **3 primary agency relationships**

  - with seller
  - with buyer
  - as property manager

- **Created by listing, buyer representation, or property management agreement**

- **Seller agency**
  - Agreement must be in writing
  - Agreement must have a definite expiration date
  - Agreement must contain the licensee's license number

- **Buyer agency**
  - Agreement may initially be oral but must be written prior to making an offer
  - If the agreement is oral, it must be non-exclusive and open-ended (without expiration)

- **Property management relationship**

  - Created by written management agreement
  - Must be written upon initial relationship formation
  - Unlike other agency agreements, this agreement may be automatically renewable

- **Tenant agency agreements** must be in writing prior to making an offer to lease

Agency Disclosure

- Agents must give buyers and sellers the pamphlet "**Working with Real Estate Agents**" upon first substantial contact or within 3 days following first substantial contact

- First substantial contact = the point at which confidential information is disclosed by the prospective buyer or seller

- **Listing agent's disclosure to buyer**

  - Written disclosure upon first substantial contact

- **Buyer agent's disclosure to seller**

  - Upon initial contact to seller or listing agent
  - Must confirm in writing upon delivery of an offer (may be in offer)

- Agents representing sellers in auctions are exempt

- Buyer agent in auction must disclose upon buyer's contract to purchase

Dual agency

- Agent may not represent second party without written permission

  - Obtain permission at formation of relationship – in writing for listing; may be oral if for buyer agency
  - Subsequent to listing, seller permission may initially be oral if a buyer's agency agreement is oral – but must be in writing before offer
  - When buyer agency is in writing, seller's agreement to dual agency must be in writing
- Firm must disclose dual agency
- Dual agent may not advocate for one party over another

Dual and designated agency

- With prior express approval of both parties, broker-in-charge may designate a seller agent and buyer agent

  - Authority must be in writing

- Broker-in-charge (BIC) cannot be designated agent if a provisional broker is the other designated agent
- Dual agent may not disclose acceptable price, motivation, or other confidential information
- Dual agent's duties can be limited to those specified in contract

Agency agreements

- Buyer agency agreements must be in writing prior to offer; can initially be oral
- Seller listings must be in writing from inception
- Listings must have termination dates that take effect without notice
  - Broker leasing for landlord may have automatic renewals in listing agreement

- Net listings are legal, but are not recommended practice in NC

Implied agency

- Not permitted under NC License Law

Agent's duties to unrepresented parties

- Treat honestly and fairly
- Avoid false promises
- Account for funds
- Act competently
- Deliver contracts
- Disclose referral fees and kickbacks

Types of Agency Agreements

- Exclusive right to sell
- Exclusive agency
- Open
- Transaction broker
- Full service

- Limited service
  - Includes services such as MLS participation, open houses, advertising, showings, negotiations, etc.
  - Agents still owe honesty, fairness, skill, care, disclosure, and accounting duties

Protection Agreements

- Contracts to ensure compensation for procuring buyer; typically used with for-sale-by-owner transactions
- Does not create an agency relationship
- Seller still owed duties of honesty, fair dealing, and material facts disclosure
- The broker must disclose the Working with Agents brochure.

Brokerage Practice, Ethics, Fair Housing

Advertising

- Ads must identify the brokerage name; blind ads are not allowed
- Licensees must file any assumed name with NCREC and the county register of deeds office in each county in which the broker intends to engage in brokerage activity
- Provisional broker ads must have consent of broker and identify broker's firm or name
- Provisional broker may not display sign without broker's consent
- Provisional broker may not use a proprietorship name

Broker-in-Charge/Provisional Broker relationship

Provisional broker

- works on behalf of and represents the broker
- may only practice with active license and BIC supervision
- may be supervised by only one broker-in-charge at a time
- may only receive compensation from the broker
- on association with a firm must, with the broker-in-charge, immediately notify Commission of the BIC who will be supervising

Broker-in-charge

- must immediately notify Commission of the BIC who will be supervising a new provisional broker

  - If provisional broker is inactive, notification must also request activation and state that the provisional broker has completed post-licensing and continuing education requirements
  - the provisional broker may practice real estate upon mailing or delivery of the notice
  - if the notice is not acknowledged by NCREC within 30 days, the provisional broker must cease practice
  - if the provisional broker has not completed the required education, he or she must cease practice until the deficiency is made up and a new notification mailed

- must report that provisional broker has ceased working with the BIC within 10 days of the termination

Broker-in-Charge (BIC)

- Firm must designate a broker to serve as broker-in charge of main and branch offices
- BIC cannot manage more than one office at a time
- Any one office can only have one BIC – multiple offices can have 1 BIC if under the same roof

- Brokers who are sole proprietors must self-designate as BIC if the broker handles trust monies, advertises or has affiliations with one or more other brokers
- BICs must notify NCREC of license status changes within 10 days

BIC responsibilities

- Retain licenses of all brokers in office under his/her supervision
- Notify commission of status changes
- Proper advertising
- Proper trust accounting
- Proper record keeping
- Proper provisional broker supervision
- Proper agency and disclosure practice in office
- NCREC strongly encourages BIC to stipulate what types of agency will be conducted

BIC qualifications

- must be a broker and not a provisional broker
- have 2 years full-time brokerage experience, or equivalent part-time experience within previous 5 years (or an education and experience equivalent approved by NCREC)
- must complete the 12-hour education requirement within 120 days following designation
- If BIC fails the experience test or education requirement, the BIC status is immediately terminated.

BIC termination: BIC status will be immediately terminated if:

- the firm's or broker's license expires or is suspended, revoked or surrendered
- the broker's license becomes inactive for any reason
- the broker fails to complete his/her continuing education requirement
- the broker's firm ceases to engage in business
- the broker ceases to act as the broker-in-charge of the office where the broker was the BIC
- If broker loses BIC status and wishes to regain it, the broker must satisfy all education and experience requirements
- BIC transfer versus termination: a simultaneous move from one office to another is not considered a termination, but a transfer

BIC continuing education

- must complete prescribed 4-hour continuing ed course ("Broker-In-Charge Update Course") each following designation (in addition to another 4-hour elective CE course)
- failure to complete CE requirement results in termination at the end of the license period

BIC status changes

- notify in writing within 10 days

Exemptions from designating a BIC:

- firm is not required to designate a BIC if

    o organized for purpose of receiving compensation through another firm
    o the firm is a Subchapter S corporation
    o has no principal office, and
    o only employs the qualifying broker

Commissions and Compensation

- NCREC may not regulate or stipulate agent fees and salaries
- Agents may not receive kickbacks for expenditures made on behalf of principal without written consent
- No kickbacks for referrals without disclosure to principal; referral fees among licensed brokers are exempt

Handling of Documents

- Agents must provide all parties with copy of any instrument at point of execution or within 5 days
- Broker is held responsible for accuracy and delivery of the closing statement at closing or within 5 days following closing
- Documents must be delivered immediately, but in no event later than five days

Trust Accounts

- BIC is responsible for trust account management
- BIC may delegate maintenance and reconciliation of trust accounts
- Trust accounts required whenever brokerage holds money belonging to a third party
- Only one trust account required when managing property or handling trust funds for transactions
    - Separate accounts are need for each HOA managed or for the broker's personal properties
- All monies received by provisional broker must be delivered to broker immediately
- Broker must get authorization from principal to deposit trust funds in interest-bearing account
- Accounts must bear words "trust account" or "escrow account"
- Funds must be held in an insured institution
- **Earnest money deposits and security deposits**:
    - o Must be deposited the later of 3 banker days following the effective date of the contract, or receipt of the deposit
    - o If the deposit is cash, it must be deposited immediately or no later than 3 days following receipt
- **Cash rent and repair funds:** must be deposited 3 days following receipt

- Trust fund disbursement

    - o May disburse to closing agent or attorney 10 days or less before closing
    - o May not disburse for any other reason without written authorization unless ordered by Court or, with 90 days' notice, transfer to clerk of Court in county where property is located

- **Trust account record keeping** must include:

    - o Bank statements
    - o Cancelled checks
    - o Deposit tickets
    - o Payment record sheet
    - o Separate ledger for each sales transaction
    - o Journal or check stubs with chronology
    - o Copies of contracts
    - o Closing statements
    - o Property management statements
    - o Covenants, by laws, minutes of property owner association
    - o Invoices, bills, and contracts paid

83

- Records must be sufficient to leave an audit trail
- Records must be retained for 3 years following closing or termination of property management agreement
- Disputed trust funds

  o Broker must leave monies in account until given a written release by principals or by court order
  o Broker can provide 90 days' notice to transfer deposited money to the clerk of the court in the county in which the property is located

- Abandoned claim

  o Broker may disburse to other party according to the written agreement

- Conversion of trust funds

  o Broker may not under any circumstances use trust account funds for other purposes
  o Broker cannot 'deficit spend' trust monies, i.e., cannot spend more money than is in the account for a given client for a particular purpose, for example repairs.
  o Broker cannot use security deposit funds until the lease has terminated and the premises has been surrendered
  o Funds in a trust account for a given client may not be spent for expenses incurred by another client

Non-Agency Disclosures

NC Residential Property Disclosure Act

- Every owner must give property condition disclosure to buyer if property is a 1-4 unit residential building for re-sale
- Disclosure must be delivered at or before time of offer
- Buyer may be able to cancel contract if not delivered
- To cancel, buyers must deliver written notice within 3 days after receipt of statement or date of contract, whichever comes first
- Buyer cannot cancel sales contract after closing or occupancy, whichever comes first

Agent's interest in transaction

- **Agent selling a property the agent owns or has an ownership interest**:
  o agent may list but must disclose his/her licensee status
  o agent may not act as a buyer agent in the transaction

Material facts disclosure

- Agents must disclose material facts they know or reasonably should have known
- May relate to the property condition itself
- May concern issues relating to the property or surroundings
- May concern the principal's ability to complete the transaction
- Must disclose material facts even if selling "as is."
- Includes the following environmental issues per NC General Assembly ruling:
  - EIFS; leaking polybutylene pipes; meth labs

Items not considered material facts:

- death; suicide; AIDS; Registered sex offender; property is haunted

Drafting Legal Instruments

- Brokers may not draft legal documents
- Agent should refer client to an attorney; client may draft changes in own handwriting
- Licensees may fill in blanks of preprinted forms when authorized by parties
- Licensees may use electronic forms, but may not alter form
- Agents cannot draft or complete deeds
- Contracts with electronic signatures are fully enforceable

NC Fair Housing Act of 1983

- Prohibits same discriminatory activities as federal fair housing laws
- Private owners selling their home, with or without a broker, are not exempt

Exemptions

- Owners renting room within owner-occupied home
- Rental of a unit in 1-4 unit dwelling if owner or a family member lives in a unit
- Rental of rooms in a single-sex dormitory

Enforcement

- Parties alleging discrimination must file complaint with NC Human Relations Commission (NCHRC)
- NCHRC investigates and tries to resolve out-of-court
- If no resolution, it issues a right-to-sue letter
- Aggrieved parties can then sue in court
- Complainants must sue within 180 days after filing complaint

Preparing Comparative Market Analyses (CMAs)

- Agents may prepare CMAs, but NCREC maintains a standard of competency
- NCREC will discipline licensees who fail to meet the competency standard

Broker Price Opinions (BPOs) – Rules

- Provisional brokers may perform BPOs for others provided there is no related compensation other than the commission for the overall transaction
- Brokers may perform BPOs for a fee
    - Such brokers must have direct access to MLS
    - May not pull tax records; must have data relating to conditions of sale
- Lenders may not use BPOs as underwriting support for originating loans

Property Management, Landlord-Tenant Relations

NC Statute of Frauds

- Leases must be in writing if lease term exceeds 3 years
- NC mineral leases must be in writing regardless of duration

Agency relationship of property managers

- Created by written management agreement
- Must be in writing upon initial relationship formation
- If an agent establishes a tenant relationship, the agreement must be in writing prior to making an offer to lease

Property manager licensing & compensation

- If a property manager is the owner's agent, the manager must have real estate license
- If a property manager is the owner's employee, the employee need not be licensed
- Property manager most often paid a fee based on amount of rent property generates

Residential Rental Agreements Act

- Act governs NC landlord-tenant relations
- Purpose is to ensure all rental units are safe, fit and habitable
- Obligations between landlord and tenant are mutually dependent: if one defaults, the other is relieved of obligations
- Landlord duties
  - Maintain premises as safe, fit and habitable

- Tenant duties
  - Maintain the unit
  - Pay full rent on time

- Landlord default

  - If uninhabitability is not corrected, tenant may self-evict without consequences, but must vacate the premises. (constructive eviction)
  - Tenant may not withhold rent until a court order so allows (unless tenant vacates)
  - If tenant withholds rent and does not vacate, tenant has violated lease
  - Tenant cannot complete repairs and deduct expenses from rent or bill landlord (self-help)

- Tenant default

  - Landlord must obtain a court-ordered eviction (actual eviction / summary ejectment)
  - Landlord may not "self-help", e.g., change locks, cut off utilities, etc.
  - Landlord cannot evict as a retaliatory measure, eg, when tenants request repairs

- Sexual harassment prohibition

  - Landlord may not use sex as a means to collect rent or negotiate leases

- Tenant foreclosure protections

  - Foreclosing parties on property having recorded lease must honor tenancy terms
  - Tenant must receive advance notice; has a right to terminate lease

NC Tenant Security Deposit Act

- Act governs handling and maximum amounts of rental deposits
- Maximum deposits

  - 2 weeks' deposit if week-to-week tenancy
  - One and a half months' deposit if a month-to-month tenancy
  - 2 months' deposit if more than month-to-month

- Landlord must place deposits in a trust account or get a bond as a guarantee

    o If an agent is involved, agent may only deposit in trust account
    o Depository institution must be located in NC and be insured

- Deposit is only usable for unpaid rent, damage, early departure, unpaid bills, or re-renting if evicted

    o Must distinguish damage from normal wear and tear
    o Cannot access funds until lease is terminated and possession is completed

NC Vacation Rental Act

- Stipulates uniform rules for short-term rentals
- Leases must be in writing
- Advance rent payments and deposits must be escrowed
- Rents must be refunded if uninhabitable
- Tenants must maintain units
- Provides for expedited evictions for defaulting tenants
- Agents may pay a travel agent for procuring a tenant provided rules are followed

NC rental notice periods

- Tenants must give 1 week notice for a month-to-month tenancy unless otherwise agreed in writing
- Tenants must give 1 month notice for a year-to-year tenancy

Document handling

- Agents must give owner copies of leases unless they have permission to retain leases
- Agents may prepare leases if using a pre-printed form and making no material changes in terms without owner's permission
- Unlicensed assistants may fill out pre-printed forms – but cannot negotiate terms rates or amount of security deposit

NC Real Estate Contract Law

Contract law & auctions

- Auctioneer must be licensed
- Crier (party conducting the bid announcements) need not be licensed
- With a reserve auction, seller retains right to not sell if bid not achieved
- With a non-reserve auction, seller must sell for highest bid

North Carolina Statute of Frauds

- Leases exceeding three years must be in writing and must be recorded
- Real property conveyances must be in writing to be enforceable

Uniform Electronic Transactions Act (UETA)

- The Uniform Electronic Transactions Act made electronic signatures enforceable, legally binding

NC Conveyance Contracts

Offer to Purchase and Contract

- NCREC sets rules for preprinted contract forms, but does not create or approve forms
- NC Bar Association and NC Association of Realtors have approved a standard "Offer to Purchase and Contract" form (NCAR / NCBA Standard OPC)
- The standard sales contract is OPC Standard Form 2-T
- Legally binding once signed
- If licensees use a pre-printed form, it must contain the following provisions (NCREC Subchapter 58A, Section A.0112)

  o Names of parties
  o Legal description
  o Personal property included
  o Price and payment method
  o Financing amount and terms
  o Assumption; costs, terms
  o Deposit, escrow agent, acknowledgement, criteria for disbursement
  o Buyer's general intended use, and that such use is not prohibited
  o Special assessments and payment responsibility
  o Closing and possession dates
  o Signatures of buyer and seller
  o Date of offer and acceptance
  o Title conveyed as fee simple and marketable by general warranty deed, free of encumbrances, unless otherwise set forth
  o Items to be prorated or adjusted
  o Who pays closing expenses
  o Buyer's right to inspect prior to closing
  o Who pays for repairs if needed
  o Provision that property will be in same condition at closing
  o Identity of each agent and firm and who they represent

- Principals may amend the form or draft their own
- Agents may not insert provisions regarding compensation, forfeiture of earnest money, or disclaimer of liability
- Fixtures : NCAR sales contracts list numerous fixtures that are included free of liens in sale price

  o Criteria is items affixed or attached to property
  o Exceptions to listed fixtures must be written in as exceptions

Leases

- Oral leases for less than 3 years are enforceable.
- Leases exceeding 3 years must be in writing to be enforceable
- Must be in writing to be valid and enforceable

Recording conveyance contracts

- NC has a 'pure race' statute which establishes ownership according to when the conveyance was recorded

Vacation Time Sharing Plans Act

Definition of time share

- an interest in real estate

- right to occupy during 5 or more separate periods over at least 5 years

Project registration requirement

- must be registered with NCREC before shares can be offered for sale

Developer's responsibilities

- must designate a project broker to supervise all licensed provisional brokers and brokers for a project · project broker must be a licensed broker; provisional brokers are not eligible
- must provide public offering statement to purchaser
- must designate a registrar to record the time share instrument
- developer need not be licensed

Project broker's responsibilities

- must maintain records of monies, transactions, and registration
- must deposit purchaser's down payment (or other payments) in escrow account immediately and maintain in escrow for 10 days to allow for cancellation

Agent's license requirements

- must have real estate broker's or provisional broker's license in order to sell
- must have a project broker to supervise transactions

Agent's responsibilities

- must immediately deliver purchaser's deposit to project broker

Purchaser protections

- contract of sale voidable for 5 days after execution
- recorded time share instrument receives same protection as any recorded real estate instrument

Right of Survivorship in Joint Tenancy

- There is no right of survivorship in a NC joint tenancy unless expressly stated

Agricultural Trade Fixtures

- Agricultural trade fixtures are considered real property

Lateral & Subjacent Support

- **Right to lateral support** – property in its natural state entitled to be supported by surrounding property – no damaging excavation by abutters
- **Right to subjacent support** –protects property owners from actions by abutting property owners that would cause land surface to shift, collapse or erode

Manufactured vs. Modular Homes

- Manufactured homes considered personal property until affixed to foundation
- Modular homes considered real property and are built according to state codes

Townhouse Ownership

- 2-3 story dwelling units constructed with party walls
- Owners own the unit, a share of common elements, and the land
- Owners must share cost to maintain party wall

NC Condominium Act

- Condominium created upon execution and recording of declaration

  o Declaration includes covenants, conditions, plat map, plan of the property, bylaws

- Must also provide disclosures via public offering statements
- Buyers have a 7-day rescission period on first-time sales
- Resale sellers must give buyer a resale certificate detailing dues, assessments and fees

Adverse Possession & Easements by Prescription

Prescription periods: fee estates

- with color of title, 7 years
- with no color of title, 20 years

Prescription periods: easements

- 20 years

Requirements for adverse possession: "HI OCEAN"
- Hostile
- Intentional
- Open
- Continuous
- Exclusive
- Adverse
- Notorious

Additional conditions:
- Owner may or may not be aware – does not matter
- Adverse possessor must file ;suit to quiet title' to gain title

Forms of Legal Description Used in NC

- Metes and bounds
- By reference to recorded plat
- By reference to recorded deed

Mechanic's liens

Filing deadlines:
- Must file within 120 days after last service rendered
- Must take action to enforce within 180 days after last service rendered

Other characteristics;
- Lien agent must be appointed for liens exceeding $30,000
- Mechanics liens' date of recordation can jump back to first day labor or materials were provided

NC Housing Finance Agency

NC Housing Finance Agency

- Public agency created by legislature in 1973

- Mission: provide affordable housing opportunities

  - Offers low-cost mortgages and downpayment assistance
  - Protects borrower against loss of home in event of job loss
  - Issues Mortgage Credit Certificate to reduce homeowner's tax liability
  - Administers HUD rent assistance contracts

- Targeted to moderate- and low-income individuals who haven't owned a home in 3 years (first-time homebuyers)

The Sale of Mortgaged Property and USDA Loans

Sale of mortgaged property

- Conventional sale extinguishes liens for clear, marketable title conveyance
- Mortgages stay in place for assumptions and subject-to sales
- Parties should obtain lender approval as they risk loan acceleration and foreclosure

U.S. Department of Agriculture Rural Development Loans
- Rural Development loans issued by USDA for low-income rural residents 'principal residences

Title Transfer and Recording

Title theory vs. lien theory state

- NC is title theory state where lender or 3rd party trustee has legal title until debt is repaid

Recording

- Must be recorded to be enforceable against third party claims:

  - deeds
  - mortgages
  - land contracts

o   assignments
  o   options
  o   leases exceeding 3 years (NC Conner Act)
  o   easements
  o   restrictive covenant documents

NC Marketable Title Act

- Purpose is to limit the time period for making claims that cloud title
- If chain of title has been without a claim against it for the previous 30 years, the title is marketable
- Claims before this period can be nullified

Interstate Land Sales

- "Interstate Land Sales Full Disclosure Act" regulates property sales across state lines
- Requires developers with 25+ lot projects to register with HUD
- All buyers must be given a property report
- Buyers are allowed a 7-day right of rescission after signing sales contract

Agreements for Preemptive Rights

Right of First Refusal
- seller grants third party right to buy if ever seller sells

Right of First Opportunity
- seller grants third party a purchase right just prior to putting property on market

Short Sales

- A short sale is where a property for sale has more debt than its market value
- Lienholders have primary rights to convey or not convey
  o   Lienholders have to grant some degree of debt forgiveness
- Licensees must disclose short sale as material fact and that major delays in closing are possible
- Brokers should employ NC Standard form 2A14-T

Ad Valorem Taxation & Homestead

Ad valorem taxation

- Machinery Act -- can charge taxes based on assessed value of the property; tax rate is set by jurisdiction's budget
- Listed, taxable property is assessed every 8 years or more often
- A lien may be filed

Principal exemptions from real property taxation

- Nonprofit and religious organizations
- Charitable and educational organizations
- Property classified as agricultural, horticultural, forest
- Certain elderly & handicapped owner-occupants

92

Property tax homestead exclusion

- Must be a North Carolina resident
- Must be an owner-occupant
- Protection against general liens less than or equal to $35,000, and $60,000 for qualified individuals aged 65 or older

Ad valorem taxing cycle

- Tax lien attaches January 1st
- August 1 deadline: levy the tax rate
- September 1 deadline: taxes levied are due and payable
- Taxes late when paid after January 5th of the following year

Home ownership taxation

- Homeowners allowed to deduct real estate taxes and mortgage interest
- Deduction must be taken in the year paid

Vacation home taxation

- Vacation homes can be tax deduction as income property provided personal use is limited to two weeks per year or 10% or less of the period the property was rented
  - if used more than that, deductions will be disallowed

NC Land Use Planning and Control

Enabling Acts

- North Carolina Enabling Acts delegated power to local jurisdictions to enact public land use restrictions – zoning, building codes, ordinances, highway access restrictions

Land use verification

- Licensees have duty to know or verify material facts and problems relating to land use
- Licensees must avoid misrepresenting
  - zoning
  - flood zone exposure
  - deed covenants
  - major changes in transportation systems and patterns

Subdivisions

- Agent may not sell lots prior to approval of subdivision
- Subdivision developer must disclose whether streets are public or private
- Agents must disclose whether subdivision streets are public or private as a material fact

NC Environmental Issues

- Lead: if built prior to 1978, must disclose lead by completing Lead-Based Paint Hazard addendum to purchase contract
- Lead-Based Paint Poisoning Act
- Leaking Petroleum Underground Storage Tank Cleanup Act

- Coastal Area Management Act -- limits development in estuary areas
- Dredge and Fill Act -- permit to dredge
- Sediment Pollution Control Act -- requirement to control erosion
- Other issues:
  - Meth labs; mold; PCB's; contaminated soil; exterior insulation finishing systems (EIFS)
  - Licensee's risk management strategy: encourage principal to seek professional assistance such as an environmental engineer

Closings

Excise tax

- Excise tax is payable by sellers at closing as a real estate conveyance tax
- Excise tax rate is $1 for every $500 or fraction thereof of the purchase price – round up fractional dollars to the next highest dollar
- Excise tax stamps, or revenue stamps attached to the deed evidence the tax payment

Prorations

- NC uses the 360-day year/30-day month method of prorations, unless otherwise stated
  - Seller pays or is paid through the day of closing (ie, seller 'owns day of closing) unless otherwise stated
- For NC closing cost prorations, seller owns day of closing

Closing statement accuracy and delivery

- Broker is responsible for accuracy of those items on the closing statement for which s/he has actual knowledge
- Primary source for verification of settlement statement accuracy is the sale contract (OPC)
- Broker is responsible for delivery of the closing statement at closing or within 5 days following closing

Government Regulation of Residential Construction

North Carolina Uniform Residential Building Code

- NC Uniform Residential Building Code sets forth minimum building and materials standards
- These standards are enforced by inspectors

HUD minimum standards

- HUD has minimum building standards for properties to become collateral for FHA, VA loans

Contractor licensing

- Residential construction general contractors must be licensed if they construct improvements costing over $30,000

NCREC guidelines for representing living area

- Agents are not required to disclose property's square footage
- If they represent the living area size, agents are expected to be reasonably accurate according to the guidelines

- To qualify as living area, the space must be:

  o have a minimum height of 7' (6'4" under ducts and beams)
  o under fixtured heat (e.g., not portable heaters)
  o finished (construction completed)
  o directly accessible from other living area

- Not necessary to distinguish above-grade from below-grade

Section IV: National Practice Tests

Test 1: Rights; Interests and Estates; Ownership

1.1   Which of the following would be defined as real estate as opposed to real property?

   a. Wells, driveways, and signs on a parcel of land.
   b. Mobile homes temporarily parked on a parcel of land.
   c. Timber that has been cut and is lying on a parcel of land.
   d. Business equipment an owner or tenant has placed on a parcel of land.

1.2   Which of the following would be considered a property improvement?

   a. An alteration to land to make it more useful.
   b. An increase in the value of a property.
   c. A chicken coop permanently attached to land.
   d. A parcel of land that has passed a percolation test.

1.3   Which of the following best describes the physical boundaries of land?

   a. The surface of the earth and infinite space above the surface.
   b. The center of the earth and infinite space above the earth.
   c. The surface of the earth and all water and minerals on or below the surface to the center of the earth.
   d. The surface of the earth and the air rights above the surface to the point defined by local zoning.

1.4   The "bundle of rights" refers to a set of rights

   a. enjoyed by the owner of a property.
   b. that is synonymous with the Bill of Rights.
   c. guaranteed to citizens by the Statute of Rights.
   d. specified in a deed or land contract.

1.5   Which of the following best describes the legal concept of personal property?

   a. Any item which is acquired in a fee simple sale transaction.
   b. Any item of property that is not definable as real property.
   c. Any movable property owned by an individual, partnership, or corporation.
   d. Any item that is not a natural item affixed to the earth.

1.6   The right to encumber a property means that the owner can

   a. sell the property to an encumbered party.
   b. pledge the property as collateral for debt.
   c. lease the property.
   d. assign the bundle of rights to another.

1.7   A property owner leases 60 acres of agricultural land for a renewable period of 5 years. In the context of real estate rights, this lease represents a(n)

   a. transfer of a portion of the bundle of rights.
   b. encroachment on the bundle of rights.
   c. conveyance of the complete bundle of rights.
   d. encumbrance of the tenant's rights.

1.8   A homeowner is very upset over a drone that a neighbor flies over his house. He takes his case to court to end this possible violation of rights. Does he have a case, and on what basis?

a. No. The neighbor is not physically on his property.
b. No. The drone is in the air, so he cannot exercise any surface rights.
c. Yes. The owner has the right to stop encroachments.
d. Yes. The drones infringe on his air rights.

1.9   Littoral rights apply to which of the following?

a. Boatable ponds entirely contained within the boundaries of an owner's property.
b. Streams and rivers.
c. Navigable lakes, seas, and oceans.
d. Navigable streams and rivers.

1.10   A retired couple has just bought a retirement home with a pier on a large lake. In this case the retirees' water rights extend to

a. the high water mark of the body of water at the shoreline.
b. the low water mark of the body of water at the shoreline.
c. the center of the lake.
d. the end of the pier.

1.11   A waterfront homeowner has just died. What will become of the water rights the owner enjoyed while living in the home?

a. They revert to the state when the property is sold.
b. They are extinguished.
c. They are a personal right belonging to an individual owner, not attaching to the real property.
d. They transfer with the property when the property is sold.

1.12   Riparian rights concern which of the following bodies of water?

a. Lakes.
b. Seas and oceans.
c. Streams and rivers.
d. Navigable lakes.

1.13   Which of the following best describes a "fixture?"

a. Any item of personal property positioned within the boundaries of a parcel of real estate.
b. An item of personal property that has been converted to real property.
c. An item of real property temporarily placed on land for the purpose of conducting a business.
d. An item of personal property that has been left in one location for a period of six months.

1.14   An item may be considered personal property as opposed to real property provided that

a. the owner intended to remove it after a period of time.
b. it can be removed without altering the appearance of the structure.
c. it is unnecessary to the physical integrity of the structure.
d. the owner installed it at some time after acquiring the real property.

1.15   Two people own a house, each having an undivided equal interest. Which of the following best describes what each party owns?

a. Fifty percent of the physical house and the land it rests on.
b   One hundred percent of the home and the land.
c. Fifty percent of the estate consisting of the indivisible whole of the real property.
d. Each owns one hundred percent of the estate represented by the real property and fifty percent of the physical house and the land it rests on.

1.16 A real property interest that includes the right to possess is considered

    a. an estate in land.
    b. a leasehold estate.
    c. a fee simple estate.
    d. the bundle of rights.

1.17 The right to control land usage by zoning and eminent domain is an example of

    a. a public interest.
    b. a police interest.
    c. an encumbrance.
    d. an estate in law.

1.18 If the duration of an owner's rights in an estate is not determinable, the owner has

    a. a tenancy at sufferance.
    b. a leased fee simple estate.
    c. a freehold estate.
    d. a leasehold estate.

1.19 The distinguishing feature of a leasehold estate is

    a. ownership of an interest by a tenant.
    b. temporary ownership of the full bundle of rights in a property.
    c. unlimited ownership of one right in the bundle of rights in a property.
    d. that the estate is limited by a lease term.

1.20 A landowner conveys a parcel of property with the provision that the land cannot be developed for retail purposes. The new owner immediately begins to develop a retail shopping outlet, the grantor finds out and takes the property back. What kind of estate did this landowner convey?

    a. Fee simple absolute.
    b. Life estate with reversion.
    c. Life estate with condition subsequent.
    d. Fee simple defeasible.

1.21 Ned grants his sister Alice an estate for as long as she lives. Her descendants, however, cannot inherit the estate. What kind of estate is it?

    a. An estate pur autre vie.
    b. An estate for years.
    c. An ordinary life estate.
    d. A legal life estate.

1.22 Homestead estates are examples of

    a. a conventional life estate.
    b. a legal life estate.
    c. an estate created by an owner's agreement.
    d. a fee simple absolute.

1.23 Louis owned a boat and a house before marrying Barbara. While she was single, Barbara owned a new car. The two got married and bought a second home. As a wedding present, Barbara's father bought Louis a motorcycle. Under the law of community property, what property can Louis sell without his wife's consent or signature?

a. The boat and house.
b. The boat, house, and motorcycle.
c. The second home and the motorcycle.
d. The boat and motorcycle.

1.24 Katelyn rents an apartment for one year. What rights has she acquired under the leasehold?

a. The right to exclude everyone from the premises.
b. The right to encumber the fee interest.
c. The right to sell the premises.
d. The right to possess and use the premises.

1.25 An estate from period-to-period will continue as long as

a. the tenant makes, and landlord accepts, regular rent payments.
b. the term specified in the lease.
c. the period is less than a year.
d. the landlord has not sold the property.

1.26 An estate at will

a. cannot be terminated.
b. is terminated only if so stated in the lessee's last will and testament.
c. terminates on the death of lessor or lessee.
d. terminates on the date specified in the lease agreement.

1.27 A tenant continues to occupy an apartment after lease expiration without the consent of the landlord. This type of estate is called

a. an estate at sufferance.
b. a holdover estate.
c. a canceled leasehold.
d. a hostile leasehold.

1.28 A tenant without a lease has been sending the landlord monthly rent checks, and the landlord continues to accept the payments. What kind of leasehold estate exists?

a. Estate for years.
b. Estate from period to period.
c. Estate at will.
d. Estate at sufferance.

1.29 A fee or life estate is held by an individual. This form of estate is referred to as a(an)

a. tenancy in severalty.
b. tenancy by the entireties.
c. absolute fee simple.
d. legal fee simple.

1.30 Six people have identical rights in a property and enjoy an indivisible interest. However any of the owners may sell or transfer his/her interest without consent of the others. This form of ownership is a

a. joint tenancy.
b. homestead ownership.

c. tenancy in common.

d. estate in severalty.

1.31 The "four unities" required to create a joint tenancy include which of the following conditions?

a. Parties must acquire respective interests at the same time.

b. Parties must be residents of the same state at the time of acquiring the interest.

c. Parties must be family members.

d. Parties must have joint financial responsibility.

1.32 Unlike tenants in common, joint tenants

a. own distinct portions of the physical property.

b. cannot will their interest to a party outside the tenancy.

c. may own unequal shares of the property.

d. cannot encumber their interest to outside parties.

1.33 Which of the following life estates is created by operation of law rather than by the owner?

a. Conventional life estate.

b. Ordinary life estate.

c. Legal life estate.

d. Community property life estate.

1.34 Which of the following is true of a homestead?

a. A homestead interest cannot be conveyed by one spouse.

b. A homestead interest cannot be passed to the children of the head of household.

c. A homestead interest is a form of conventional life estate.

d. A homestead is a primary or secondary residence occupied by a family.

1.35 A tenant in common can

a. sell or transfer his interest without the consent of the other tenants in common.

b. use his or her interest in the estate to encumber the entire estate.

c. sell, encumber or transfer his or her interest only to the other tenants in common.

d. sell, encumber or transfer his or her interest only with the consent of all the other tenants in common.

1.36 Which of the following would be considered community property?

a. Property acquired before marriage

b. A motorcycle bought after the marriage with separate property funds

c. Income derived from community property

d. A mother's heirloom wedding ring gifted to the wife after her wedding

1.37 When real property is held in a land trust, who controls the property?

a. The trustor

b. The trustee

c. The beneficiary

d. The mortgagee

1.38 In a community property state, John marries Patricia. Prior to the marriage John owned an SUV. During the marriage, John bought a Buick, John and Patricia bought a second property with money earned from Patricia's job, and each individual received a motorcycle from Patricia's uncle as a gift. What property is community property in this marriage?

a. The SUV, the Buick, and the second property.

b. The SUV, the Buick, the second property, and the motorcycles.

    c. The Buick and the second property.

    d. The Buick, the second property, and the motorcycles.

1.39   Which of the following is true of a cooperative?

    a. A cooperative may hold an owner liable for the unpaid operating expenses of other tenants.

    b. The owners have a fee simple interest in the airspace of their respective apartments.

    c. Owners may sublease their apartments even if they sell their stock in the cooperative.

    d. The proprietary lease is guaranteed to have a fixed rate of rent over the life of the lease term.

1.40   Which of the following is true of a tenancy in common?

    a. The co-owners must be related.

    b. The owners enjoy an indivisible interest.

    c. The tenants must acquire their interests at the same time.

    d. The tenants must pay equal amounts for their interest in the estate.

1.41   Carissa and Robert acquire a condominium as tenants in common. In this circumstance, Carissa can

    a. sell her interest to a third party without the consent of Robert.

    b. use her interest in the estate to mortgage the entire estate.

    c. sell her interest only to Robert.

    d. sell encumber or transfer her interest only with the consent of Robert.

1.42   When a tenant in common dies, what happens to the tenant's interest in the estate?

    a. It is divided equally among the surviving tenants in common.

    b. The surviving tenants must buy the interest from the deceased tenant's heirs or sell their interests to the heirs.

    c. It becomes a joint tenancy.

    d. It passes by probate to the deceased tenant's heirs.

1.43   Which of the following is true of a joint tenancy?

    a. The tenants can determine the size of the share owned by each tenant.

    b. The size of the tenant's shares is determined by the amount of equity each has invested in the property.

    c. The tenants have an equal and indivisible ownership interest.

    d. There can be no more than two co-owners, and each has a fifty percent interest.

1.44   In contrast to a tenancy in common, in a joint tenancy

    a. there is a single title to the property.

    b. there are as many titles to the property as there are co-owners.

    c. title is held by a trustee.

    d. co-owners who are married hold separate titles.

1.45   If a joint tenant sells his or her interest to an outside party,

    a. the new owner becomes a tenant in common with the other owners, who continue to hold a joint tenancy with each other and a tenancy in common with the new owner.

    b. the joint tenancy continues with the new owner as the third joint tenant.

    c. the joint tenancy terminates and all owners become tenants in common.

    d. the joint tenancy terminates and the owners must create a new joint tenancy to include the new owner.

1.46   When a joint tenant dies, what happens to the tenant's interest in the estate?

    a. It passes to the decedent's heirs, who become joint tenants.

    b. It passes as a tenancy in common to the decedent's heirs.

c. The joint tenancy terminates and becomes a tenancy in common with the decedent's heirs and the surviving tenants as co-owners.

d. It passes to the surviving joint tenants.

1.47 Under what conditions can two individuals own a property as tenants by the entireties?

a. If they so elect at the time of acquiring title.

b. If they are blood relatives.

c. If they are married.

d. If they incorporate.

1.48 When an estate is held in a trust, which party holds legal title?

a. The beneficiary.

b. The trustor.

c. The trustee.

d. The grantor.

1.49 Tanya buys a 4-bedroom condominium. As the new owner, she has the right to

a. sell or mortgage the unit without impediment from individual owners of neighboring units.

b. sell the interest in the physical unit separately from the interest in the common elements.

c. prevent non-owners from using the unit owner's portion of the common elements.

d. exclusively possess and use those portions of the common areas structurally or functionally necessary for the operation of the unit.

1.50 A condominium owner's share of maintenance and operations expenses are based on

a. the unit's pro rata share of floor space.

b. the unit's pro rata share of the property value as defined in the declaration.

c. the number of shares the owner purchased in the condominium association.

d. the assessed value of the condominium unit.

1.51 By contrast to a condominium, the owner of a cooperative owns

a. shares in a corporation or association and a proprietary lease in a physical unit.

b. a fee simple interest in a physical unit plus a tenancy in common in common elements.

c. a tenancy in common in a physical unit and the common areas.

d. a ground lease in the physical unit's pro rata share of land and a proprietary lease in the unit.

1.52 In a cooperative, real property is owned only by

a. the individual unit owners.

b. the individual unit owners and the cooperative association.

c. the cooperative developer.

d. the corporate entity of the cooperative association.

1.53 In a time-share freehold, owners acquire

a. undivided interests in the property as tenants in common.

b. a renewable periodic tenancy from for a portion of a year.

c. a pro rata share of a leased fee.

d. a tenancy in severalty for a portion of a year.

Test 2: Encumbrances; Liens; Title Transfer and Recording; Leases

2.1   Which of the following describes an encumbrance?

a. A third party's right encroach upon a property without the permission of the property owner.
b. A third party's right to claim the sale proceeds of a property that has been mortgaged as collateral for a loan.
c. A third party's interest in a real property that limits the interests of the freehold property owner.
d. Another's right to acquire a freehold interest in a property against the property owner's wishes.

2.2   Which of the following is true of easements in general?

a. They involve the property that contains the easement and a non-owning party.
b. They apply to a whole property, not to any specific portion of the property.
c. They only involve the legal owner of the property.
d. They may require a specific use, but cannot prohibit one.

2.3   Mr. King wants to offer 100 acres of his property for sale. Since the property is landlocked, he will have to put in a driveway to the road that will run across his remaining property. What kind of easement will he have to grant?

a. An easement in gross.
b. A commercial easement.
c. A personal easement.
d. An easement appurtenant.

2.4   If property Alpha has a court-ordered easement across property Beta in order for Alpha to have access to a public road, the easement is a(n)

a. easement by prescription.
b. personal easement.
c. easement by necessity.
d. easement in gross.

2.5   An encroachment is

a. an easement that has not been recorded on the title of the burdened property.
b. an unauthorized physical intrusion of one property into another.
c. a right granted by a property owner to the owner of an adjoining property to build a structure that protrudes across the property boundary.
d. a structure that does not comply with a zoning ordinance.

2.6   A court might grant an easement by prescription if

a. a town needs to dig a trench across an owner's property to install a sewer line to a neighboring property, and the owner refuses permission.
b. a property owner sells the front half of a lot and wants to continue using the driveway to access the rear of the lot.
c. a trespasser has been using an owner's property for a certain period with the owner's knowledge but without permission.
d. a property owner wants to prevent the owner of an adjoining property from building a an improvement that blocks her view.

2.7   The purpose of a deed restriction is to enable an owner to specify

      a. the form of ownership in which a property may be held.
      b. how long a property must be owned before it can be legally transferred.
      c. what groups of people are legally excluded from future ownership of a property.
      d. how a property may be used and what improvements may be built on it.

2.8   Melinda purchases a house and finances it. The lender in turn places a lien on Melinda's title. The lien in this mortgage transaction is

      a. evidence of debt incurred by a property owner.
      b. a promissory note granted by a property owner as security for a debt.
      c. the creditor's claim against the property as collateral security for the loan.
      d. the document required to clear clouded title.

2.9   In a lien-theory state, what kind of interest does a mortgage lender have in the liened property?

      a. A possessory interest.
      b. A tenancy-by-mortgagee interest.
      c. A legal interest in a pro rata share of the property.
      d. An equitable interest.

2.10 How is a lien terminated?

      a. Payment of the debt that is the subject of the lien and recording of the satisfaction.
      b. Transfer of the property that has the lien.
      c. Recording of another lien that is superior.
      d. Death of the lienor or lienee.

2.11 A judge rules in favor of the creditor in a court proceeding and places a judgment lien against all the debtor's assets, including his real property. This is an example of a(n)

      a. voluntary junior lien.
      b. involuntary superior lien.
      c. involuntary specific lien.
      d. involuntary general lien.

2.12 A real estate tax lien, a federal income tax lien, a judgment lien, and a mortgage lien are recorded against a property. Which lien will be paid first when the property is sold?

      a. Real estate tax lien.
      b. Federal income tax lien.
      c. Judgment lien.
      d. Mortgage lien.

2.13 A lien holder can change the lien priority of a junior lien by agreeing to

      a. change the date of recording.
      b. lower the amount of the claim.
      c. cancel the lien.
      d. subordinate the lien.

2.14 Which of the following accurately describes the act of foreclosure?

      a. A court-ordered acceleration of loan payments.
      b. The final step in a bankruptcy filing.
      c. A proceeding to enforce a lien by forcing the sale or transfer of a secured property.
      d. A proceeding to take equitable title to a property that was liened as security for a mortgage loan.

2.15   A property is secured by a mortgage that does not contain a "power of sale" clause. To foreclose, the lien holder will have to

a. file a deficiency suit.
b. file a foreclosure suit.
c. file a suit to quiet title.
d. obtain a quit claim deed.

2.16   A homeowner defaults on his mortgage loan. In the subsequent foreclosure action, the lender takes title to the liened property directly instead of initiating a court-ordered public sale. This is an example of

a. strict foreclosure.
b. judicial foreclosure.
c. non-judicial foreclosure.
d. deed in lieu of foreclosure.

2.17   A property owner gives Deanna permission to cross his property as a shortcut to her kindergarten school bus. One day the property owner dies. What right was Deanna granted originally, and will it survive the owner's death?

a. A personal easement in gross, which continues after the owner's death.
b. An easement by prescription, which continues after the owner's death.
c. A license, which continues after the owner's death.
d. A license, which terminates upon the owner's death.

2.18   On two adjacent properties, there is an easement that allows property A to use the driveway that belongs to property B. Here, property A is said to be which of the following in relation to property B?

a. Subservient estate.
b. Servient tenement.
c. Senior tenant.
d. Dominant tenement.

2.19   A property owner who is selling her land wants to control how it is used in the future. She might accomplish her aim by means of

a. an injunction.
b. a deed restriction.
c. an easement.
d. a land trust.

2.20   What distinguishes a lien from other types of encumbrance?

a. It involves a monetary claim against the value of a property.
b. It lowers the value of a property.
c. It is created voluntarily by the property owner.
d. It attaches to the property rather than to the owner of the property.

2.21   Which of the following defines actual notice?

a. It is notice published in a newspaper.
b. It is knowledge one could have or should have obtained.
c. It is notice explicitly stated in a legal document.
d. It is knowledge received or imparted through direct experience.

2.22   Which of the following defines constructive notice?

    a. It is notice published in a newspaper.
    b. It is knowledge one could have or should have obtained.
    c. It is notice explicitly stated in a legal document.
    d. It is knowledge received or imparted through direct experience.

2.23   Ownership of real estate can be transferred voluntarily or involuntarily. The three ways title can be transferred voluntarily are by

    a. grant, deed, and will.
    b. escheat, deed, and covenant.
    c. title certificate, will, and deed.
    d. sale contract, deed, and warrant of seizin.

2.24   What is the function of recording a deed?

    a. It makes the deed valid.
    b. It causes title to pass.
    c. It gives constructive notice of ownership.
    d. It removes all prior recorded encumbrances.

2.25   The only clause that is actually required in a deed is the

    a. habendum clause.
    b. granting clause.
    c. reserving clause.
    d. tenendum clause.

2.26   The type of deed that offers the grantee the fullest protection against claims to the title is the

    a. general warranty deed.
    b. special warranty deed.
    c. quitclaim deed.
    d. bargain and defend deed.

2.27   What is one of the purposes of a lawsuit to "quiet title"?

    a. To force the grantor to defend the title against a third party claim.
    b. To terminate a co-ownership estate when one co-owner is unwilling.
    c. To keep the owner's name out of the title records.
    d. To have an encumbrance removed if the lienholder cannot prove its validity.

2.28   Which of the following best describes the documentary stamp tax?

    a. A transfer tax based on the price of the property being conveyed.
    b. A tax a title company must pay in order to examine title records in the recorder's office.
    c. A tax collected by attorneys and paid to the state when transfer documents are prepared.
    d. A tax on stamps used to certify the authenticity of a conveyance.

2.29   The court proceeding that generally settles a decedent's estate is called

    a. testate.
    b. probate.
    c. escheat.
    d. distribution.

2.30   If an owner of real property dies intestate and has no legal heirs, what will happen to the property?

   a. It will escheat to the state or county.
   b. It will transfer to the decedent's executor.
   c. It will be divided equally among adjoining property owners.
   d. It will become a public easement.

2.31   A municipality wants to build a sewage treatment facility which will require the acquisition of several parcels of privately owned land. What legal power enables the municipality to buy the necessary properties, even against the owners' wishes?

   a. Estoppel.
   b. Escheat.
   c. Alienation.
   d. Eminent domain.

2.32   An adverse possessor must be able to successfully demonstrate that he or she has been

   a. openly possessing and claiming the property without the owner's consent.
   b. occupying the property without an occupancy permit.
   c. using the property intermittently and without permission over a period of years.
   d. building a permanent structure on the property.

2.33   A buyer has signed a contract to purchase a property, but is uncertain of the condition of the title. Which of the following parties is legally responsible for knowing the condition of the title?

   a. The County Recorder.
   b. The seller's agent.
   c. The buyer.
   d. The mortgage lender.

2.34   A break in the chain of title to a property results in

   a. a clouded title.
   b. a title plant.
   c. a lien of indeterminate ownership.
   d. a duplicate title.

2.35   Wayne and Leota obtain an insurance policy that protects them from liabilities and losses resulting from title defects. The kind of policy they bought is a

   a. a homeowner's insurance policy.
   b. standard owner's title insurance policy.
   c. lender's title insurance policy.
   d. private mortgage insurance policy.

2.36   An owner transfers title to a property to a buyer in exchange for a motorcycle. This is an example of

   a. voluntary alienation.
   b. involuntary liquidation.
   c. hypothecation.
   d. 1031 exchange.

2.37   A person wishes to convey any and all interests in a property to another without assurance of the property's marketability. This party would most likely use which of the following types of deed?

   a. A sheriff's deed.
   b. A special warranty deed.
   c. A partition deed.
   d. A quitclaim deed.

2.38 Jennifer owns a one-half interest in a condominium as a tenant in common with her business partner. If Jennifer has several heirs and dies without a will, the property will

a. pass to the heirs by the laws of descent and distribution.
b. escheat to the state.
c. pass to the surviving spouse based on homestead law.
d. pass to the surviving heirs according to the provisions of the will.

2.39 A drifter secretly lives in an abandoned shack on a large ranch property. After twenty years, the person makes a claim of ownership to the shack and the land immediately surrounding it that he had cleared. This claim will likely be

a. upheld through adverse possession.
b. upheld because of the length of possession.
c. declined through the doctrine of prior appropriation.
d. declined because possession was secretive.

2.40 To be marketable, title must be

a. insured.
b. free of undisclosed defects and encumbrances.
c. abstracted by an attorney.
d. guaranteed by a title certificate.

2.41 Which of the following types of leasehold estate lacks a specific term?

a. Estate for years.
b. Estate from period-to-period.
c. Estate at will.
d. Estate by the entireties.

2.42 A landlord generally has the right to enter the leased premises

a. at any time without notice.
b. for specified reasonable purposes.
c. provided the tenant gives prior permission.
d. only thirty days prior to lease expiration.

2.43 When a tenant rents an apartment, he or she is usually responsible for

a. compliance with the rules and regulations of the building.
b. payment for any alterations to the leased space.
c. recording the lease in title records.
d. occupying the premises throughout the lease term.

2.44 Under landlord-tenant laws, landlords must treat tenants fairly and honestly. In a residential leasehold, this requirement would include

a. insuring the tenant against loss of personal property.
b. providing required building support and services.
c. guaranteeing that a fair rent is being charged.
d. insuring the property for the value of the leasehold.

2.45 While a one-year lease is in effect, the tenant dies of a sudden illness. In this situation,

a. the lease automatically terminates.
b. the tenant's estate has the option of canceling the contract.
c. the landlord can record a lien against the leased fee interest.
d. the tenant's estate is still obligated under the lease.

2.46 Three students rent a house together, and all three sign a one-year lease. Six months later, two students move out. Which of the following is true of the remaining rent obligation?

a. The remaining tenant is responsible for the full rent obligation.
b. The remaining tenant is responsible for one third of the rent obligation.
c. The lease is cancelled due to abandonment. Therefore, the rent obligation is extinguished.
d. The departing tenants have no further rent obligation.

2.47 A tenant transfers a portion of the leasehold interest to another party. The instrument that accomplishes this transfer is a(n)

a. deed.
b. novation.
c. sublease.
d. reconveyance

2.48 Vijay enters into a lease for his new store. The provisions of the lease require Vijay to pay the operating expenses of the premises such as janitorial and repair expenses. This is an example of a

a. gross lease.
b. percentage lease.
c. land lease.
d. net lease.

2.49 A tenant obtains a full-service lease where the landlord agrees to pay all operating expenses in exchange for an additional $5.00 rent per square foot. Another term for this lease is a(n)

a. gross lease.
b. proprietary lease.
c. exchange lease.
d. full service net lease.

2.50 Which of the following circumstances is the most likely scenario for a ground lease?

a. A developer wants to acquire a necessary parcel that separates two parcels she already owns.
b. An owner-developer wants to retain ownership of the land portion of the improved real property.
c. A fast food company wants to place a restaurant in an existing building without buying either land or improvement.
d. A farmer wants to sell his property to a mining company.

2.51 A tenancy at will can usually be terminated by

a. either party giving proper notice.
b. either party without notice.
c. a sublease, with the lessor's approval.
d. an assignment by the lessor.

2.52 Under the Uniform Residential Landlord and Tenant Act, if a lease does not state a clear expiration date, the lease is regarded as

a. invalid.
b. a tenancy from period-to-period.
c. a tenancy at will.
d. a tenancy for years.

2.53   The Uniform Residential Landlord and Tenant Act generally does not apply to

a. a hotel.
b. a single-family residence.
c. a unit in an apartment building that has fewer than ten units.
d. a duplex in which the owner occupies one of the units.

2.54   In executing a condominium lease, a tenant has acquired

a. a temporary transfer of legal title.
b. a limited freehold interest in the air space of her unit.
c. a temporary possessory interest.
d. a title conveyance in exchange for rent.

2.55   When a tenant acquires a leasehold estate through a lease, what does the property owner acquire?

a. A freehold estate for years.
b. A reduced leasehold estate.
c. A defeasible estate.
d. A leased fee estate.

2.56   When an owner leases her property, she temporarily relinquishes the right to

a. transfer the property.
b. encumber the property.
c. occupy the property.
d. maintain the property.

2.57   Which of the following happens when a leased property is sold?

a. The buyer acquires title subject to the lease, which remains in effect.
b. The lease is cancelled.
c. The lease expires within thirty days unless renewed.
d. A new lease is automatically executed.

2.58   If a lease does not state a specific ending date, when does it terminate?

a. Immediately, since it is an invalid lease.
b. After one year.
c. When either party gives proper notice.
d. Whenever the property is sold.

2.59   In accordance with the statute of frauds,

a. leases in excess of one year must be recorded to be enforceable.
b. oral leases are not enforceable.
c. a five-year lease must be in writing to be enforceable.
d. an unwritten lease is fraudulent.

2.60   Which of the following is true of a sublease?

a. The subtenant takes over sole responsibility for performance of the original lease contract.
b. The original tenant retains primary responsibility for performance of the original lease contract.
c. It does not convey any of the leasehold interest.
d. It conveys the entire leasehold interest.

3.1   Which of the following is true regarding master planning and zoning?

    a. The aggregate of zoning ordinances is the master plan.
    b. A master plan eliminates the need for zoning ordinances.
    c. Master planning is a county-level function; zoning is limited to the city level.
    d. Zoning ordinances are a primary means of keeping land use in harmony with the master plan.

3.2   The basic intent of zoning ordinances is to

    a. establish the basis for public ownership of land for the common good.
    b. establish subdivision rules and regulations.
    c. specify usage for every parcel within the zoning authority's jurisdiction.
    d. restrict development in unincorporated areas.

3.3   Why do zoning authorities create different types of zones?

    a. To ensure that a variety of building structures are available in the community.
    b. To separate land uses so that they do not interfere with each other.
    c. To preserve high density land uses.
    d. To discourage industrial and commercial users from relocating.

3.4   The key consideration in granting a zoning exception known as a special exception is which of the following?

    a. Hardship
    b. Change of zones
    c. The public interest
    d. The use was legal prior to the new zone creation

3.5   The intensity of land usage generally refers to what?

    a. The number of residential building lots per acre.
    b. The number of people per square mile.
    c. The number of building permits issued per year within a zoning jurisdiction.
    d. The area of a commercial or industrial facility in relation to the size of the site.

3.6   How does Planned Unit Development zoning vary from ordinary zoning?

    a. It applies only to office parks.
    b. It incorporates a number of different zones within a single property boundary.
    c. It requires that multiple tracts of land be developed according to a single design.
    d. It requires developers to obtain a separate building permit for every structure.

3.7   Which of the following situations is most likely to represent an illegal nonconforming use?

    a. A homeowner in a residential zone converts her residence to a private school.
    b. A homeowner builds a toolshed in a neighborhood where there are no toolsheds.
    c. A storeowner remodels a storefront in accordance with regulations, and then the zoning is changed to residential.
    d. A new zoning ordinance outlaws two-story additions after a homeowner completes an addition.

3.8   What is the difference between a variance and a nonconforming use?

    a. A variance, once granted, is unconditional and permanent.
    b. A variance is granted by the zoning board if the owner has a justifiable reason.
    c. A nonconforming use is allowed if the owner requests it in advance of building.

d. A nonconforming use violates current zoning, but a variance does not.

3.9 A document certifying that a structure complies with building codes and is ready for use is referred to as a(n)

a. inspection report.
b. satisfaction bond.
c. certificate of occupancy.
d. user permit.

3.10 Which of the following is true of an eminent domain proceeding?

a. It cancels the property owner's mortgage loan balance.
b. It leaves the property owner with equitable title in place of legal title.
c. It conveys legal title to the acquiring entity.
d. It clouds the chain of title by canceling the original grant.

3.11 Among other provisions, the Superfund Act (CERCLA) and Superfund Amendment and Reauthorization Act of 1986 provided that

a. large development projects undergo an environmental impact survey immediately after completion of construction.
b. industrial users of real estate comply with air quality standards.
c. the EPA would give financial help to homeowners to remedy any hazardous situation resulting from radon, asbestos, or lead-based paint.
d. parties responsible for improper disposal of hazardous waste could be charged for the cleanup costs.

3.12 Public land use planning strives to balance which of the following potentially conflicting interests?

a. Individual property rights and the public's interest.
b. Public policy makers and community business leaders.
c. Tenant occupancy specifications and construction contractors.
d. Individual property owners and municipal planning agencies.

3.13 Zoning, building codes, and environmental restrictions are forms of local land use control known as

a. master planning.
b. preemption.
c. police power.
d. concurrency.

3.14 If a municipality exerts its power of eminent domain against a certain property owner, what happens?

a. The owner must pay higher property taxes or give up the property.
b. The owner must cede an easement without receiving any compensation.
c. The municipality annexes the property.
d. The owner must sell the property in exchange for market-value compensation.

3.15 To be valid, a local zoning ordinance must

a. reasonably promote community health, safety and welfare.
b. comply with federal zoning laws.
c. apply only to unique properties.
d. published periodically in the local newspaper.

3.16 Why do communities require building permits?

  a. To promote development.
  b. To establish the basis for an inspection.
  c. To promote certificates of occupancy.
  d. To ensure that improvements comply with codes.

3.17 What is the purpose of residential zoning?

  a. To increase home values in a neighborhood.
  b. To regulate the density of dwellings in the residential zone.
  c. To prevent families from residing in commercial and industrial sites.
  d. To maximize intensity of usage.

3.18 A non-profit organization wants to erect an urgent care facility in a residential zone. Given other favorable circumstances, the local authorities may grant permission by allowing

  a. a special exception.
  b. an illegal nonconforming use.
  c. an easement.
  d. a license.

3.19 A property that conformed with zoning ordinances when it was developed but does not conform to new ordinances is said to be

  a. an illegal special exception.
  b. a variance.
  c. a legal nonconforming use.
  d. unmarketable.

3.20 The approval process for development of multiple properties in an area includes submission of

  a. a covenant of restriction.
  b. a plat of subdivision.
  c. a court order.
  d. a developer's pro forma.

3.21 A legal description of a property is one which

  a. accurately identifies the boundaries of the property as distinct from all other properties.
  b. accurately describes the location and dimensions the lot and improvements on the property.
  c. is accepted by a licensed surveyor as suitable for inclusion in a survey of the property.
  d. is written by an attorney licensed to practice real estate law in the state in which the property is located.

3.22 The essential elements of the metes and bounds system are

  a. parallels, base lines, and meridians.
  b. boundaries, distances, and a base line.
  c. reference points, angles, and distances.
  d. lot numbers, sections, and ranges.

3.23 In the Rectangular Survey System, a range is the area in between

  a. any row of sections in a township.
  b. two consecutive meridians.
  c. a principal meridian and a base line.
  d. a parallel and a meridian.

3.24   In the Rectangular Survey System, a tier is defined by

a. six consecutive sections of a township.
b. two consecutive meridians.
c. two consecutive parallels.
d. a parallel and a meridian.

3.25   In the Rectangular Survey System, what are the dimensions of a township?

a. One mile square.
b. Six miles by six miles, or 6 miles square.
c. Thirty-six miles square.
d. The north and south boundaries are one mile apart; the east and west boundaries are indeterminate.

3.26   What portion of a section is ten acres?

a. 1/8.
b. 1/16.
c. 1/32.
d. 1/64.

3.27   The lot and block system of legally describing property is used for

a. farm properties.
b. any property in an unincorporated area.
c. properties where metes and bounds is not acceptable.
d. properties in a subdivision.

3.28   A certain legal description contains the phrase, "...northwesterly along Erie Road to the POB...". What kind of description is this?

a. Plat survey.
b. Government grid.
c. Metes and bounds.
d. Rectangular survey.

3.29   How many sections are there in a township?

a. One.
b. Six.
c. Twelve.
d. Thirty-six.

3.30   In the Rectangular Survey System, a section contains how many acres?

a. 640.
b. 320.
c. 160.
d. 40.

3.31   The valuable consideration necessary to make a contract valid must be

a. money.
b. something tangible.
c. something of value traded in exchange for something of value.
d. something of equal value with whatever is received in exchange.

3.32 A real estate sales contract, to be enforceable, must

   a. contain a legal description of the property.
   b. be written on a form approved by the state bar association.
   c. be acknowledged by three witnesses.
   d. be recorded within three days to be enforceable.

3.33 How much time does a seller have to accept a buyer's offer?

   a. Forty-eight hours from the time of the offeror's signing of the offer.
   b. Twenty-four hours from the time of the offer's delivery to the seller.
   c. Within 24 hours following the stated expiration.
   d. A reasonable time, or until the expiration date on the offer.

3.34 A buyer submits an offer to a seller and then dies in a car accident. Before learning of the buyer's death, the seller accepts the offer. Which of the following is true?

   a. The seller can force the buyer's estate to go through with the purchase.
   b. The buyer's death terminated the offer.
   c. The seller must make a new offer with the same terms to the buyer's heirs.
   d. The buyer's heirs have the option of enforcing the contract.

3.35 Which of the following contracts can be assigned to another party?

   a. An exclusive listing agreement.
   b. A personal services agreement.
   c. A contract for the sale of undeveloped land.
   d. An employment contract between a broker and a salesperson.

3.36 An implied agency relationship may be deemed to exist if

   a. the parties do not disavow an express contract that has expired.
   b. the parties act is if there is a contract.
   c. an offering party does not receive written notice that the offer has been rejected.
   d. the parties promise to perform their part of the agreement if the other party performs.

3.37 Which of the following is an executory contract?

   a. An expired lease.
   b. A sale contract before closing.
   c. A recorded sale contract.
   d. An option to buy after it is exercised.

3.38 A bilateral contract is one in which

   a. both parties promise to do something in exchange for the other party's performance.
   b. both parties receive equal consideration.
   c. two parties agree to perform a service together.
   d. both parties promise to do something if the other party performs first.

3.39 A homeseller signs a listing agreement with a broker then subsequently revokes the listing. Which of the following is true?

   a. The seller continues to have contractual obligations to the broker.
   b. The contract remains in full force until the expiration date.
   c. The broker may have a claim for marketing expenses expended during the listing term.
   d. The seller cannot sign a listing agreement with another broker.

3.40 A breach of contract is

    a. a termination of the contract by the mutual consent of the parties.
    b. financial damage suffered by a party because another party has nullified a contract provision.
    c. a lawsuit to force a party to discharge the contract.
    d. the failure of a party to perform according to the terms of the contract.

3.41 What is rescission?

    a. The act of withdrawing an offer before it has been accepted.
    b. The act of declaring that a contract is no longer in effect for a given party.
    c. The act of declaring a contract unenforceable.
    d. The act of modifying the terms of an offer.

3.42 To be valid, a valid contract must

    a. reflect a mutual understanding or agreement.
    b. use precise wording in a document.
    c. not be executable.
    d. be created only by an attorney.

3.43 Two parties enter into a contract. The agreement fulfills all the requirements for a valid contract, with no disqualifying circumstances. Given this situation, it is still possible that the contract may be

    a. void.
    b. illegal.
    c. unenforceable.
    d. voidable.

3.44 The guardian for a mentally incompetent party enters into an oral contract with another party to buy a trade fixture on behalf of the incompetent party. This contract

    a. does not meet validity requirements.
    b. is possibly valid and enforceable.
    c. must be in writing to be valid.
    d. is valid but unenforceable.

3.45 A prospective homebuyer submits a signed offer with the condition that the seller pay for the inspection at closing. The seller disagrees, crosses out the provision, then signs and returns the document to the buyer. At this point, assuming all other contract validity items are in order, the original offer is now

    a. an accepted offer, therefore a valid contract.
    b. an executable option.
    c. a counteroffer.
    d. an invalid offer.

3.46 A construction contractor executes a contract with a buyer. In the agreement, the contractor promises to complete construction by November 20. This promise can be construed as

    a. an option.
    b. mutual consent.
    c. a meeting of the minds.
    d. valuable consideration.

3.47 A seller contracts to sell a property that she does not own. The sale contract for this transaction

    a. is executable.
    b. must be in writing.
    c. is void.

d. is illegal yet potentially enforceable.

3.48 The statute of limitations requires that parties to a contract who have been damaged or who question the contract's provisions

    a. must act within a statutory period.
    b. must select a specific, limited course of action for recouping their losses.
    c. must arbitrate prior to taking court action.
    d. must wait a statutory period before they may take legal action.

3.49 The purpose of the statute of frauds is to

    a. invalidate certain oral contracts.
    b. require certain conveyance-related contracts to be in writing.
    c. nullify oral leases and listing agreements.
    d. eliminate fraud in real estate contracts.

3.50 A seller immediately accepts a buyer's offer but waits ten days before returning the accepted document to the buyer. Meanwhile, the offer has expired. Which of the following is true?

    a. The buyer is bound to the contract since it was accepted immediately.
    b. The buyer has no obligations to the seller whatsoever.
    c. The buyer may not rescind the expired offer.
    d. The seller may sue for specific performance.

4.1   The agency relationship is defined by

    a. the Realtor Code of Ethics.
    b. the laws of agency, or in some states, by statute.
    c. the law of real estate contracts.
    d. the agreement between a principal and an agent.

4.2   Which of the following is true of the connection between compensation and the agency relationship?

    a. An agreement to give and receive compensation creates an agency relationship.
    b. If an agency relationship exists, the principal must provide valuable consideration to the agent.
    c. The relationship is independent of any compensation arrangement.
    d. If an agency relationship exists, the agent is entitled to compensation.

4.3   One of the parties to an agency relationship defaults, and the agreement terminates. Which of the following is true?

    a. All obligations are extinguished.
    b. Both parties must continue to perform all other obligations of the agreement.
    c. The defaulting party may have a financial consequence.
    d. The damaged party has no claim against the defaulting party.

4.4   Among the fiduciary duties imposed on a real estate agent is the requirement to

    a. refuse offers the agent knows will be unacceptable to the principal.
    b. present all offers to the principal regardless of their amount.
    c. advise the principal against accepting an offer that is below full price.
    d. advise a prospect that the principal will not accept the prospect's offer in order to elicit a better offer.

4.5   One of the agent's fiduciary duties that continues even after a listing agreement expires is

    a. obedience.
    b. diligence.
    c. confidentiality.
    d. disclosure.

4.6   The standard of care and competence that a principal can expect from an agent is generally that which is

    a. specified in the agency agreement.
    b. necessary to earn the promised compensation.
    c. necessary to procure a customer.
    d. comparable to that of other practitioners in the area.

4.7   Agent Michael is showing his new listing to a buyer who informs him that he has just inherited five million dollars. Michael is now bound by fiduciary duty to

    a. keep the information in confidence.
    b. disclose the information to the buyer's agent.
    c. disclose the information to the seller.
    d. verify the buyer's statements before disclosing them to the client.

4.8 Agent Gerry has executed an exclusive buyer broker agreement with the Andersons. The agent subsequently places an offer with Melinda, the exclusive selling agent for the Lincolns, to buy their lakefront property. The offer contains provisions for the Lincolns to pay the brokerage commission, which the Lincolns agree to. Given this set of circumstances, Gerry owes the full set of fiduciary duties to

a. the Andersons.
b. the Lincolns.
c. Gerry's broker.
d. Melinda's broker.

4.9 A subagent is the agent of

a. the seller.
b. the buyer.
c. a broker who has an agency relationship with a client.
d. the client's and the customer's agents.

4.10 Which of the following is a dual agency situation?

a. Two agents share the exclusive right to represent the same client on all transactions.
b. One agent represents both sides in a transaction.
c. A selling agent from one brokerage works with a listing agent from another brokerage to complete a transaction.
d. One agent represents two sellers at the same time.

4.11 The duties of a transaction broker or facilitator include

a. preserving the confidentiality of information received from either party.
b. helping the two parties achieve their respective objectives.
c. disclosing material facts that affect the value of the property to both parties.
d. choosing to obey the instructions of one party and informing the other party of the decision.

4.12 In which of the following contact situations would a seller's agent be expected to disclose his agency relationships?

a. The agent is showing the client's property to a prospective buyer.
b. The agent tells an acquaintance at a party about the client's property.
c. The agent answers questions about the client's property for a telephone caller responding to a newspaper ad.
d. The agent is showing a potential buyer houses in a certain price range in the multiple listing book.

4.13 The essential foundation of the agency relationship consists of

a. mutual respect, compensation, and confidentiality.
b. diligence, results, and compensation.
c. service, marketing, and respect.
d. good faith, trust and confidence.

4.14 Audrey wants to take a vacation. To do so, she authorizes an agent to conduct the operations of one of her business enterprises. The kind of agency she has established is

a. limited.
b. general.
c. universal.
d. special.

4.15 A property seller empowers an agent to market and sell a property on his behalf. The kind of agency represented is

a. general.
b. special.
c. universal.
d. no agency.

4.16 Implied agency arises when

a. an agent accepts an oral listing.
b. a principal accepts an oral listing.
c. a party creates an agency relationship outside of an express agreement.
d. a principal agrees to all terms of a written listing agreement, whether express or implied.

4.17 An agency relationship may be involuntarily terminated for which of the following reasons?

a. Condemnation of the property.
b. Mutual consent.
c. Full performance.
d. Renewal of the agent's license.

4.18 A principal discloses that she would sell a property for $500,000. During the listing period, the house is listed and marketed for $530,000. No offers come in, and the listing expires. Three weeks later, the agent confides to a customer that the seller would have sold for less than the listed price. Which of the following is true?

a. The agent has violated the duty of confidentiality.
b. The agent has fulfilled all fiduciary duties, since the listing has expired.
c. The agent is violating the duties owed this customer.
d. The agent has created a dual agency situation with the customer.

4.19 A principal instructs an agent to market a property only to families on the west side of the university campus. The agent refuses to comply. In this case,

a. the agent has violated fiduciary duty.
b. the agent has not violated fiduciary duty.
c. the agent is liable for breaching the listing terms.
d. the agent should obey the instruction to salvage the listing.

4.20 An owner's agent is showing a buyer a residential property for sale. The buyer notices water stains on the foundation walls and floor, and informs the agent. The appropriate course of action for the agent is to

a. immediately contract to paint the ceiling.
b. immediately contract to repair the roof.
c. suggest the buyer make a lower-price offer.
d. inform the seller.

4.21 The meaning and salient characteristics of the agency relationship should be disclosed to the client

a. prior to completing a listing agreement.
b. prior to or upon completion of an offer.
c. upon the initial contact with the person.
d. prior to showing properties.

4.22   When must a listing agent disclose his or her agency relationship to prospective tenants or buyers?

a. Immediately prior to the initial contact.
b. Upon initial contact.
c. Whenever substantive communication is made beyond casual conversation.
d. Immediately following any offer executed by the customer.

4.23   A buyer agent or tenant representative should disclose his or her agency relationship to the owner's agent

a. immediately prior to the initial contact.
b. upon initial contact.
c. immediately prior to substantive contact.
d. immediately following any offer executed by the landlord.

4.24   An agent is operating as a disclosed dual agent on a transaction. In this case, the agent

a. may not represent one party's interests to the detriment of the other.
b. must operate without a listing agreement.
c. must be obedient and loyal to both parties.
d. must require that the principals refrain from disclosing any material facts to him.

4.25   An agent informs a buyer that a provision in a contract is very commonplace. After explaining the clause, the agent assures the buyer that the clause does not mean anything significant. If something goes wrong with the transaction, the agent could be liable for

a. violating duties owed a customer.
b. misinterpreting the clause.
c. intentional misrepresentation.
d. practicing law without a license.

4.26   When a broker enters into a listing agreement, the broker has agreed to accept which of the following?

a. Fiduciary and contractual obligations with the client.
b. Fiduciary relationships with client and customer.
c. Contractual obligations with cooperating brokers.
d. Fiduciary obligations with the customer.

4.27   The degree of authority granted by a residential brokerage listing agreement generally allows the agent to

a. create contractual obligations for the client.
b. negotiate the selling price between client and customer.
c. hire inspectors, and other individuals to prepare the property for marketing.
d. market, sell and show the property.

4.28   A salesperson, without an oral or written listing agreement, brings potential buyers to the seller. The seller says, "You can bring me buyers if you want, but I'm not paying you a commission." The salesperson then continues to direct buyers to the property. Which of the following is true about this situation?

a. There is no agency relationship, and therefore the seller will owe no commission if one of the salesperson's buyers buys the property.
b. An implied agency may have been created, with obligations to perform for both seller and agent.
c. The seller and agent have an illegal, undisclosed agency relationship.
d. The agent has an open exclusive agency listing with no commission agreement, and therefore owes no fiduciary duties to the seller.

4.29   An agent enters into a listing agreement with a homeseller, but then becomes too busy to
        professionally fulfill the terms of the agreement. To solve the dilemma, the agent assigns the
        agreement to another licensee in the office. Which of the following is true about this situation?

        a. The agent cannot assign the listing agreement.
        b. The new listing agent acquires the full set of fiduciary duties owed to the client.
        c. The new broker has to split any commission that results with the assigning broker.
        d. The original broker has to disclose the assignment to the seller.

4.30   From an agent's point of view, the most desirable form of listing agreement is a(n)

        a. exclusive agency.
        b. exclusive right to sell.
        c. open listing.
        d. net listing.

4.31   What is a multiple listing?

        a. A listing shared by a listing agent and a selling agent.
        b. A listing that a listing agent delegates to a subagent.
        c. A listing that is entered in a multiple listing service to enable cooperation with member brokers.
        d. A listing that authorizes a listing agent to market more than one property for a seller.

4.32   Which of the following conditions is necessary for a customer to qualify as "ready, willing, and
        able" in the context of a commissionable transaction?

        a. The customer's offer must be accepted.
        b. The customer must be legally competent to undertake the transaction.
        c. The customer must have a commitment from a lender.
        d. The customer must have no business relationship with the agent.

4.33   Although a listing broker may delegate listing tasks to an employed licensee, the broker may not
        delegate the authority to

        a. obtain and distribute compensation.
        b. provide cooperating brokers with information about the property.
        c. advertise the property.
        d. inspect the property for hazardous substances.

4.34   Agent Peter has an open listing with Frank. Paul is Peter's broker. Agent Perry's customer buys
        Frank's house. Patrick has a commission agreement with Frank. Who is most likely to be
        compensated in this scenario?

        a. Peter, since he has a written listing agreement.
        b. Paul, since he is Peter's broker
        c. Perry, since he found the customer.
        d. Patrick, since he has a commission agreement.

4.35   If an agent has an exclusive listing to sell a property, and the property is then taken by eminent
        domain, what is the status of the listing?

        a. The seller's obligations under the listing are assigned to the agency that takes the property.
        b. It becomes a voidable contract.
        c. The commission clause of the agreement is canceled.
        d. It may be terminated against the agent's will.

4.36 A broker obtains an exclusive listing to sell a house, but after two months, he abandons the listing because the seller is too demanding and hot-tempered. What can the seller do in this situation?

a. Have the licensee's license revoked for negligence.
b. Sue the broker for money damages.
c. Sign a listing agreement with another broker and force the first broker to pay the commission.
d. Force the broker to perform the contract without compensation.

4.37 An owner agrees to pay a broker for procuring a tenant unless it is the owner who finds the tenant. This is an example of a(n)

a. exclusive right-to sell agreement.
b. exclusive agency agreement.
c. open listing.
d. net listing.

4.38 A landlord promises to compensate a broker for procuring a tenant, provided the broker is the procuring cause. This is an example of a(n)

a. exclusive right-to rent agreement.
b. exclusive agency agreement.
c. open rental listing.
d. net lease listing.

4.39 A property owner agrees to pay a broker an open-ended commission as the difference between the sale price and a net amount, provided the owner receives a minimum amount of proceeds from the sale at closing. This is an example of a(n)

a. exclusive right-to sell agreement.
b. exclusive agency agreement.
c. open listing.
d. net listing.

4.40 In the context of agency law, the legal difference between an owner representation agreement and a buyer representation agreement is

a. the client.
b. the commission amount.
c. fiduciary duties.
d. regulatory approvals.

4.41 A multiple listing authorization gives a broker what authority?

a. To list the owner's property in a multiple listing service.
b. To sell several properties for the owner at once.
c. To represent both seller and buyer, if necessary, in selling the property.
d. To delegate the listing responsibilities to other agents.

5.1   Which of the following business entities is generally prohibited from brokering real estate?

    a. Sole proprietorship.
    b. Partnership.
    c. Corporation for profit.
    d. Non-profit corporation.

5.2   A joint venture may generally broker real estate if the co-venturers

    a. form a business trust.
    b. form a co-operative association.
    c. are properly licensed.
    d. are limited partners.

5.3   A licensed salesperson may work only for

    a. a client who has signed a listing agreement with a licensed broker.
    b. a single employing broker who has an active broker's license.
    c. a client who has signed an authorization agreement with a licensed salesperson.
    d. an employer who has an active or inactive broker's license.

5.4   Which of the following activities is a licensed salesperson allowed to engage in?

    a. Accept a listing that is in an associate's name.
    b. Accept a commission directly from the MLS.
    c. Offer a property for lease on behalf of the employing broker.
    d. Sign a contract with a management company on behalf of a client.

5.5   If a salesperson has worked on a completed transaction that involved a listing agent, a selling agent, and several subagents for each of these, from whom will the salesperson receive any compensation that is due?

    a. The listing agent.
    b. The selling agent.
    c. The seller.
    d. The employing broker.

5.6   A property has sold for $380,000. The listing agreement calls for a commission of 6.5%. The listing broker and selling broker agree to share the commission equally. What will the listing agent receive if the agent is scheduled to get a 40% share?

    a. $4,445.
    b. $3,556.
    c. $2,667.
    d. $4,940.

5.7   A real estate salesperson finds a buyer to a For Sale By Owner property. The home sells for $245,000, and the seller agrees to pay a commission of 3%. The salesperson is on a 65% commission schedule with her broker, who pays her 65% minus office expenses of $500. How much will the salesperson receive from this transaction?

    a. $4,778.
    b. $4,452.
    c. $4,278.
    d. $3,175.

5.8   A salesperson makes a listing presentation to a homeseller and obtains a signed listing agreement. The first thing the salesperson must now do is

        a. make a final pricing determination for the property.
        b. negotiate the commission with the client.
        c. complete the signing of the listing.
        d. explain the agency relationship to the client.

5.9   Juan shows a customer a property that is listed by another brokerage firm.   He obtains an offer that is $5,000 less than the listing price. How should Juan deal with this offer?

        a. Advise the buyer that the offer will be rejected.
        b. Present the offer to the seller at the earliest possible moment.
        c. Ask the listing broker to lower the listing price.
        d. Counter the offer.

5.10   A broker receives an earnest money deposit from a buyer and signs the check over to the listing agent as a partial commission advance. What is wrong with this procedure?

        a. Nothing, provided the deposit clears the bank and doesn't bounce.
        b. The broker and the agent are guilty of price fixing.
        c. The broker has illegally converted security funds for business use.
        d. The agent may not be able to return the advance if the transaction falls through.

5.11   Under what circumstance may a property listed for sale with a brokerage be advertised without identifying the broker?

        a. When the salesperson is an out-of-state licensee.
        b. When the ad is restricted to the brokerage's website.
        c. When the advertisement is a silent ad.
        d. Never.

5.12   Competing brokers in a county seat agree on a standard commission rate for principals within the county. This is a possible violation of

        a. fair trade and anti-trust laws.
        b. the Statute of Frauds.
        c. contract law.
        d. the Uniform Commercial Code.

5.13   What is co-brokerage?

        a. An owner agent and a buyer agent combine efforts to complete a sale.
        b. Outside brokers assist a listing agent in procuring a buyer.
        c. An owner or buyer lists with several brokers to complete a transaction.
        d. Agents from a single agency cooperate to generate listings for the broker.

5.14   Which of the following may associate his or her name or title with the term "Realtor®"?

        a. Any active or inactive broker in the country.
        b. Any duly licensed, active agent or broker.
        c. Any member in good standing in a properly chartered real estate trade organization.
        d. Only members of the National Association of Realtors®.

5.15   Real estate sales agents are legally authorized to

        a. represent their employing broker in procuring clients and customers.
        b. act directly on a client's behalf to discharge the broker's listing responsibilities.
        c. negotiate and execute contracts for sale on behalf of the client.
        d. take on the listing responsibilities for other listings in MLS.

5.16 How does the position of an independent contractor licensee (IC) differ from that of an employee licensee?

a. The IC is responsible for his or her own taxes; the broker does not withhold.
b. The IC must obtain his or her own training; it is not provided by the broker.
c. The employee is not entitled to company benefits.
d. The IC must abide by all office meeting schedules.

5.17 A salesperson's commission rate and structure is established by

a. state regulation.
b. competitive conditions.
c. agreement with other brokers in the market.
d. negotiations with the client.

5.18 In obtaining offers from a buyer, an agent must be careful to

a. pursue only those offers which are at or near the listing price.
b. balance the owner's price expectations with the buyer's opinion of value.
c. avoid disclosing what price the owner will accept.
d. avoid completing offers that are beneath market value.

5.19 Commingling is the practice of

a. blending escrow funds on a number of properties in one escrow account.
b. mixing socially with prospects at open houses or other marketing functions.
c. allocating commission funds from a transaction for use in the agency's business.
d. mixing escrow funds with the broker's operating funds.

5.20 Three leading agencies charge identical commission rates for brokering office properties in Phoenix. Based on this information alone, which of the following is true?

a. There is insufficient evidence of anything other than a normal business practice.
b. The brokers have engaged in legal collusion.
c. The brokers have allocated the Phoenix market.
d. The brokers have illegally fixed prices.

5.21 A real estate sale contract is an executory contract until

a. the completed sale transaction is recorded.
b. the buyer and seller have agreed to all provisions and have signed the contract.
c. all the obligations and promises are performed and the transaction is closed.
d. the loan has been approved, the title insurance has been obtained, and the closing date is set.

5.22 In assisting a buyer or seller to complete an offer to purchase, what should an agent do to reduce the risk of committing an unauthorized practice of law?

a. Use a standard contract promulgated by a state agency or a real estate board.
b. Observe ethical standards promulgated by real estate trade organizations.
c. Offer legal advice only on points of the contract that the agent is absolutely certain about.
d. Write contract terms that are fair to both buyer and seller.

5.23 To be enforceable, a contract for the conveyance of real estate must

a. be acknowledged by witnesses.
b. be written.
c. be recorded.
d. have an expiration date.

5.24 A buyer makes an offer to purchase a house, and the seller accepts the offer. However, before the salesperson can inform the buyer of the seller's decision, the buyer delivers a written notice that she is opting out and cancelling the agreement.   At this point, which of the following is true?

a. The contract has been legitimately cancelled and is null and void.
b. The seller must give the buyer an opportunity to make a new offer.
c. The buer must perform under the terms of the contract
d. The seller must notify the buyer in writing that the buyer is in default.

5.25 Which of the following is an essential element of a valid contract for the sale of real estate?

a. A valid blank form that the contract is written on.
b. A habitable property.
c. An offer and acceptance.
d. A marketable title.

5.26 What kind of interest does the buyer acquire once a real estate sale contract is signed by the principal parties?

a. Legal title.
b. Lienholder interest.
c. Reversionary interest.
d. Equitable title.

5.27 A contingency in a sale contract is

a. a promise by buyer or seller to perform a specific action.
b. a condition that, if unmet, renders the contract unenforceable.
c. one of several alternative actions that buyer or seller may take to satisfy contract requirements.
d. an optional, unilateral action that either party may take at the request of the other party.

5.28 A clause in a sale contract stipulates that the seller must provide evidence that the property is free of active termite infestation. On the day of closing, the buyer learns that inspection service did not provide the required written documentation. The buyer then proceeds to declare that the sale is off. Which of the following is true of this situation?

a. The seller can sue for specific performance.
b. The buyer will be in default, and liable for damages, if he does not complete the transaction.
c. The buyer may be able to have the contract canceled.
d. The contract is automatically void.

5.29 A buyer signs an earnest money agreement and gives it to the broker who showed her the property she is buying. After leaving the broker's office, she reconsiders and decides she prefers a different property. How long does she have to take back her offer?

a. Until the seller communicates acceptance of the offer.
b. Until the earnest money deposit check is cashed.
c. She can take it back at any time, but must forfeit the earnest money.
d. She cannot take it back until after the expiration date of the offer.

5.30 On Wednesday, Fred offers to sell his property to Jack for $275,000, with the offer to remain open until 5 p.m. the next day. On Thursday morning, Sally offers Fred $280,000 for the property and Fred accepts. At 1 p.m. on Thursday afternoon, Jack accepts. Which of the following is true of this situation?

a. The acceptance by Sally creates a contract and terminates Fred's offer to Jack.
b. Fred has entered into contracts with both Jack and Sally to sell the same property.
c. Fred's acceptance of Sally's offer is invalidated by Jack's acceptance, because Fred's offer to Jack was made prior to Sally's offer to Fred.
d. No contract has been created because it is impossible to have two valid sale contracts for the same property.

5.31 Among the items that normally must be disclosed in a sale contract or its addenda is/are the

a. buyer's financial capability.
b. buyer's source of funds for the down payment.
c. seller's acceptable price range.
d. agency relationships and property condition.

5.32 To create an enforceable option-to-buy contract, there must be an exchange of

a. a promise to sell and a promise to buy.
b. valuable consideration and a right to buy.
c. valuable consideration and a promise to buy.
d. a down payment and a post-dated contract for sale.

5.33 Mary Carboy buys a house from Jim Schmidt and at the same time obtains an option to purchase the adjoining vacant lot for $10,000 within one year. A few months later, Carboy informs Schmidt that she is ready to exercise her option, but finds that Schmidt has received an offer of $12,000 from another party. Schmidt states that he will accept the offer unless Carboy is willing to match the $12,000 offer. Which of the following is true of this situation?

a. Schmidt must sell to Carboy for $10,000.
b. Carboy must pay $12,000 or lose the property.
c. Schmidt may sell to Carboy or the other party, but the price cannot exceed $10,000.
d. If the other party delivers payment before Carboy does, the option is canceled.

5.34 Which of the following is true regarding the assignability of an option?

a. It is assignable only if the contract specifically allows assignment.
b. It is never assignable.
c. It is assignable only if the option is exercised.
d. It is always assignable unless the contract prohibits assignment.

5.35 Which of the following is true of a contract for deed transaction?

a. At the end of the contract period, the vendee receives equitable title, provided all required periodic payments have been made.
b. The vendee has no right to possess or occupy the property during the contract period.
c. At the end of the contract period, the vendor conveys legal title, provided the vendee has fulfilled all obligations.
d. The vendor may cancel the contract at any time before the final payment has been received.

5.36   Several buyers are competing for the last available home in a desirable new subdivision. One buyer calls the owner-developer directly on the phone and offers $20,000 over and above the listed price. The developer accepts the offer. At this point,

a. the parties have a valid, enforceable sale contract on the home.
b. the parties have completed a verbal, executory contract.
c. the parties may not cancel their contract.
d. the developer could not entertain other offers on the property.

5.37   An owner completes a sales contract on her property with a buyer. Before closing, the seller runs into financial trouble and assigns the contract to her principal creditor. The buyer cries foul, fearing the property will be lost. Which of the following is true?

a. The buyer can sue the assignee to disallow the illegal assignment.
b. The buyer can take legal action against the assignor.
c. The assignor has completed a legal action.
d. The sale contract is nullified.

5.38. A due-on-sale clause in a sale contract puts parties on notice that

a. the full price of the property is due the seller at closing.
b. any loans surviving closing become immediately payable.
c. all of the seller's debts must be retired before or upon closing.
d. any conveyance may trigger an acceleration of any loans secured by the property.

5.39   A tenant has an option-to-purchase agreement with the landlord that expires on June 30. On July 1, the tenant frantically calls the landlord to exercise the option, offering the apology that she was busy with a death in the family. Which of the following is true?

a. Since options contain grace periods, the landlord must sell.
b. The tenant loses the right to buy, but can claim the money paid for the option from the landlord.
c. The landlord does not have to sell, but must renew the option.
d. The option is expired, and the tenant has no rightful claim to money paid for the option.

5.40   Two parties enter into a contract for deed agreement. In this form of agreement,

a. title is conveyed to the buyer, but the seller retains possession for a stipulated time period.
b. the buyer contracts to pay all cash at closing in exchange for the deed.
c. the seller retains legal title while the buyer makes partial payments until the contract is fully executed.
d. the buyer immediately acquires legal title and takes possession.

6.1   If the price of an item is increasing, one can usually assume that

a. demand for the item is decreasing in relation to supply of the item.
b. demand for the item is increasing in relation to supply of the item.
c. supply of the item is increasing.
d. demand for the item and supply of the item are increasing.

6.2   When the market for an item has achieved market equilibrium, which of the following statements is true?

a. New suppliers will enter the market and drive the price down.
b. Demand will slowly taper off, driving the price down.
c. Unmet demand for the item is directed toward demand for some other item.
d. Supply and demand are equal, and price and value are equal.

6.3   As an economic product, real estate is distinguished by

a. its homogeneity.
b. its variety.
c. the uniqueness of every parcel.
d. its ability to appreciate in value.

6.4   The city of Stevensville has declared a moratorium on new construction. If demand is increasing, what will be the likely effect on real estate prices in the area?

a. Prices level off.
b. Prices continue to follow the trend that preceded the moratorium.
c. Prices fall.
d. Prices rise.

6.5   If Okapi, Inc., a company that markets its sports clothing worldwide, moves into Stevensville and hires 100 employees, it is reasonable to expect that the town will experience

a. an immediate rise in the demand for industrial real estate, but no other changes in the real estate market.
b. an increase in demand for all types of real estate.
c. a housing boom, but no other changes in the real estate market.
d. an immediate increase in the prices for industrial and office real estate, but no impact on the residential market.

6.6   What is "absorption?"

a. The amount of new space that is added to available space over a period of time.
b. The number of houses that are built over a period of time.
c. The amount of space that is occupied at any given time.
d. The number of available units that become occupied over a period of time.

6.7   When vacancies are declining in a real estate market, it is common for the market to experience

a. rising prices.
b. falling prices.
c. falling construction activity.
d. falling absorption.

6.8   The price for any product is a function of four fundamental determinants of value. These are

a. durability, feasibility, mobility, and location.
b. desire, utility, scarcity, and purchasing power.
c. popularity, recognizability, promotion, and rebate.
d. fungibility, costs, convenience, and uniqueness.

6.9   A town is rapidly growing, but all the buildable vacant lots in the most desirable area have already been occupied. In this case, it is likely that the price of existing homes in that area

a. will stabilize, since the population must stabilize.
b. will increase.
c. will decline, since no further building can take place.
d. will not show any predictable movement.

6.10   If there is a significant undersupply of homes in a market, construction will tend to increase. This is an example of

a. supply outstripping demand.
b. demand outstripping value.
c. consumer optimism.
d. the market tending toward equilibrium.

6.11   If commercial real estate rental prices are falling in a market, it is likely that

a. demand has outstripped supply of space.
b. the market is in equilibrium.
c. the market is over-supplied.
d. employment is increasing.

6.12   A construction boom in a market is an indication that prices

a. have been increasing.
b. have been declining.
c. have been in equilibrium.
d. have exceeded supply.

6.13   Why is real estate traditionally considered a relatively illiquid economic product?

a. Its physical form is fixed.
b. Real estate is defined as land, not water.
c. It is often difficult to convert to cash.
d. It cannot be moved.

6.14   What does "base employment" refer to in the context of real estate demand?

a. The lowest category of employment in terms of wages and desirability
b. The number of persons employed in base industries in an area
c. The number of persons employed on military bases in an area
d. The labor pool available for employment in all industries in an area

6.15   What is "vacancy" in real estate market economics?

a. A property that has no owner-occupant
b. The total number of properties of a certain type that are on the market at a given time
c. The absence of certain types of users in a given market area
d. The total existing space of a certain type that is unoccupied at a given time

6.16 A moratorium on new construction is an example of

    a. local government influencing the real estate market, regardless of demand.
    b. the natural result of demand exceeding supply in a local market.
    c. government promotion of the free market concept in the local real estate market.
    d. a government policy that aims to restrain a trend of rising prices in the local real estate market.

6.17 Of the following potential influences on a local real estate market, which one would be considered local, rather than regional, national, or global?

    a. Changes in money supply
    b. Federal Reserve interest rates
    c. In- and out-migrations of major employers
    d. Trade imbalances with foreign trading partners

6.18 There is a lot of new construction going on in the town of Florence. Which of the following would most likely be the immediate effect on the real estate market?

    a. Demand increases and prices rise.
    b. Vacancy rises and prices fall.
    c. Absorption and vacancy decrease.
    d. Supply decreases relative to demand.

6.19 What kind of real estate users are most concerned with neighborhood quality, access to services, property amenities, and quality of life in their demand for real estate?

    a. Retail
    b. Office
    c. Industrial
    d. Residential

6.20 One distinguishing feature of real estate as an economic product is

    a. its easy convertibility to cash.
    b. its quick response to changes in supply-demand balance.
    c. its susceptibility to swings in the local economy.
    d. the easy substitutability of one item for another.

6.21 Bill Parsons paid $150,000 for a house to operate as a rental property, figuring that he could rent it out at a rate of $900 a month. In paying a price based on the property's ability to generate a desired future income, Parsons was motivated by the economic principle known as

    a. substitution.
    b. anticipation.
    c. supply and demand.
    d. utility.

6.22 Which of the following situations illustrates the principle of contribution?

    a. A homebuyer makes a down payment of 20% instead of the 10% the lender requires.
    b. A homeowner adds a third bathroom to a house and thereby increases the appraised value by $10,000.
    c. The appraised value of a house goes up by $20,000 over a two-year period because of the prices recently paid for other houses in the neighborhood.
    d. Because of a decline in mortgage interest rates, a homeowner in a certain market is able to list her house at a higher price.

6.23 When a property owner combines two adjacent properties to create a single property with a higher value than the sum of the values of the two separate properties, the applicable principle of value is called

    a. assemblage.
    b. accretion.
    c. progression.
    d. subdivision.

6.24 What is the difference between market value and market price, if any?

    a. There is no difference.
    b. Market value is a broker's estimate; market price is a precise number derived by a licensed appraiser.
    c. Market value is an average price derived from comparable sales; market price is a price based on the cost of creating the property.
    d. Market value is an estimate; market price is the price at which a property sold.

6.25 The first step in the appraisal process, regardless of the appraisal method, is to

    a. identify the highest and best use of the property to be appraised.
    b. collect and analyze property data.
    c. estimate the value of the land as if it were vacant.
    d. define the appraisal problem and the purpose of the appraisal.

6.26 In the final step of an appraisal, the appraiser reconciles the value estimates derived by the various appraisal approaches by

    a. disregarding the high and low extreme results.
    b. averaging the results of all three approaches.
    c. weighing the applicability of the approaches and considering the quality of data supporting each approach.
    d. choosing the result that is closest to the average for properties in the immediate neighborhood.

6.27 Which of the following statements properly describes the central concept of the sales comparison approach?

    a. Find the median price of recently sold comparable properties and add or subtract dollar amounts in the subject property to account for competitive differences.
    b. Make dollar adjustments to the sale prices of comparable properties to account for competitive differences with the subject.
    c. Find at least three comparable properties that are currently for sale and make dollar adjustments to the listing prices to account for competitive differences with the subject.
    d. Apply an appreciation factor to the price at which the subject property most recently sold and make dollar adjustments to account for competitive differences with comparable properties currently for sale.

6.28 One of the strengths of the sales comparison approach is that it

    a. takes into account the subject property's investment value.
    b. reveals the profit margin of the builder or developer of the subject property.
    c. discovers the underlying value of the subject property apart from the influence of competing properties.
    d. takes into account the competitive value of specific amenities of the subject property.

6.29   In making dollar adjustments in the sales comparison approach, the appraiser

    a. adds value to a comparable that is inferior to the subject property.
    b. adds value to the subject property if it is inferior to a comparable.
    c. subtracts value from a comparable that is inferior to the subject property.
    d. subtracts value from the subject property if it is inferior to a comparable.

6.30   The best comparable property for use in the sales comparison approach is the one that

    a. requires the most and largest adjustments.
    b. requires the fewest and smallest adjustments.
    c. sold most recently at the highest price.
    d. is located closest to the subject property.

6.31   A house is being appraised using the sales comparison approach. The house has three bedrooms, two bathrooms, and a patio. The appraiser selects a comparable house that has three bedrooms, 3 bathrooms, and no patio. The comparable house just sold for $200,000. A bath is valued at $7,000, and a patio at $2,000. Assuming all else is equal, what is the adjusted value of the comparable?

    a. $202,000.
    b. $207,000.
    c. $195,000.
    d. $205,000.

6.32   Which of the following statements properly describes the central methodology of the cost approach to appraisal?

    a. Apply a depreciation factor to the reported actual cost of acquiring and improving the subject property.
    b. Estimate the cost of building the improvements on the subject property.
    c. Estimate the land value and add to this the actual cost of the improvements adjusted for competitive differences with similar properties.
    d. Add the estimated land value and cost of improvements and subtract the accrued depreciation of the improvements.

6.33   One of the strengths of the cost approach is that it

    a. takes into account the amount of money required to develop a similar property.
    b. is very accurate for a property with new improvements that represent the highest and best use.
    c. results in an actual price in dollars instead of an estimated value.
    d. reveals the owner's return on money invested in the cost of development.

6.34   The principle underlying depreciation from physical deterioration is that

    a. eventually, a property loses all of its value.
    b. a property loses a portion of its value each year because of economic obsolescence.
    c. a property loses the same increment of value each year over the economic life of the property.
    d. the value lost to depreciation is incurable.

6.35   A property is being appraised by the cost approach. The appraiser estimates that the land is worth $30,000 and the replacement cost of the improvements is $95,000. Total depreciation from all causes is $10,000. What is the indicated value of the property?

    a. $135,000.
    b. $130,000.
    c. $125,000.
    d. $115,000.

134

6.36 Which of the following statements properly describes how to apply the income capitalization approach to appraisal?

    a. Apply a rate of return to the price paid for an income property.
    b. Divide the income a property generates by a rate of return.
    c. Estimate the amount of income a property must generate to return the capital amount invested in it.
    d. Estimate the rate of return a property owner receives from income generated by the property.

6.37 A strength of the income capitalization approach is that it

    a. uses a rate of return that is required for all potential purchasers in a market.
    b. yields an accurate projection of investment income.
    c. uses a method that is also used by investors to determine how much they should pay for an investment property.
    d. can be used with any type of property in any market.

6.38 A property is being appraised using the income capitalization approach. Annually, it has an estimated gross income of $60,000, vacancy and credit losses of $3,000, and operating expenses of $20,000. Using a capitalization rate of ten percent, what is the indicated value (to the nearest $1,000)?

    a. $370,000.
    b. $400,000.
    c. $570,000.
    d. $600,000.

6.39 An apartment building that sold for $450,000 had monthly gross rent receipts of $3,000. What is its monthly gross rent multiplier?

    a. 12.5
    b. .01.
    c. .08.
    d. 150.

6.40 A rental house has monthly gross income of $1,200. A suitable gross income multiplier derived from market data is 14.1. What estimated sale price (to the nearest $1,000) is indicated?

    a. $169,000.
    b. $102,000.
    c. $203,000.
    d. $173,000.

6.41 A certified appraiser is one who has received certification by

    a. a licensed real estate school.
    b. the Appraisal Institute.
    c. the state in which the appraiser operates.
    d. the Appraisal Review Board.

6.42 The act that required federally-related appraisals to be conducted by a certified appraiser is known as

    a. The Financial Institutions Reform, Recovery and Enforcement Act (FIRREA).
    b. The Uniform Standards of Professional Appraisal Practice Act (USPAPA).
    c. The Appraisal Foundation Authorization and Reform Act (AFAR).
    d. The Federal Institution for Regulation and Enforcement of Appraisal Act (FIREAA).

6.43 As a component of real estate value, the principle of substitution states that

a. if two similar properties are for sale, a buyer will purchase the cheaper of the two.
b. if one of two adjacent homes is more valuable, the price of the other home will tend to rise.
c. if too many properties are built in a market, the prices will tend to go down.
d. people will readily move to another home if it is of equal value.

6.44 Highest and best use of a property is that use which

a. is physically and financially feasible, legal, and the most productive.
b. is legal, feasible, and deemed the most appropriate by zoning authorities.
c. entails the largest building that zoning ordinances will allow developers to erect.
d. conforms to other properties in the area.

6.45 Lynne just bought a house. She paid $187,500, for it, even though it had been listed at $195,000. An adjoining property owner, Ken, had tried to buy the property for $185,000, but had been refused. He now offers Lynne $190,000 for the house. Lynne is interested, so she hires an appraiser. The appraiser returns an estimate of value of $200,000. Which of these numbers can be called the market value?

a. $187,500.
b. $190,000.
c. $195,000.
d. $200,000.

6.46 A notable weakness of the sales comparison approach to value is that

a. there may be no recent sale price data in the market.
b. the approach is not based on the principle of substitution.
c. the approach is only accurate with unique, special purpose properties.
d. sale prices cannot be compared, since all real estate is different.

6.47 In the market data approach, an appraiser

a. chooses nearby comparables, adjusts the subject for differences, and estimates the value.
b. gathers relevant price data, applies the data to the subject, and estimates the value.
c. selects comparable properties, adjusts the comparables, and estimates the value.
d. identifies the price previously paid, applies an appreciation rate, and estimates the value.

6.48 In the sales comparison approach, an adjustment is warranted if

a. the buyer obtains conventional financing for the property.
b. the seller offers below-market seller financing.
c. a comparable is located in another, albeit similar neighborhood.
d. one property has a hip roof and the other has a gabled roof.

6.49 To complete the sales comparison approach, the appraiser

a. averages the comparable values.
b. weights the comparables.
c. identifies the subject's value as that of the middle value of the comparables.
d. identifies the subject's value as that of the nearest comparable.

6.50 One weakness of the cost approach for appraising market value is that

a. builders may not pay market value for materials or labor.
b. market value is not always the same as what the property cost.
c. comparables used may not have similar quality of construction.
d. new properties have inestimable costs and rates of depreciation.

6.51   The cost of constructing a functional equivalent of a subject property is known as

    a. reproduction cost.
    b. replacement cost.
    c. restitution cost.
    d. reconstruction cost.

6.52   An office building lacks fiber optic cabling to accommodate the latest communications equipment. This is an example of

    a. physical deterioration.
    b. economic obsolescence.
    c. incurable depreciation.
    d. functional obsolescence.

6.53   A home is located in a neighborhood where homeowners on the block have failed to maintain their properties. This is an example of

    a. curable external obsolescence.
    b. incurable economic obsolescence.
    c. functional obsolescence.
    d. physical deterioration.

6.54   In appraisal, loss of value in a property from any cause is referred to as

    a. deterioration.
    b. obsolescence.
    c. depreciation.
    d. deflation.

6.55   In the cost approach, after estimating the value of the land and the cost of the improvements, the appraiser

    a. estimates depreciation, subtracts depreciation from cost, and adds back the land value.
    b. subtracts deterioration from cost, estimates land depreciation, and totals the two values.
    c. estimates depreciation of land and improvements and subtracts the total from original cost.
    d. estimates obsolescence and subtracts from the cost of land and improvements.

7.1   What is a lien-theory state?

    a. A state in which a mortgagee holds legal title to a secured property.
    b. A state in which a mortgagee has equitable title to a secured property.
    c. A state that allows a real estate owner's creditors to record liens against the owner's property.
    d. A state in which a lien is considered as a conveyance.

7.2   What is the function of a note in a mortgage or trust deed financing arrangement?

    a. It is the lender's security instrument in the collateral property.
    b. It is evidence of ownership of the mortgage or trust deed.
    c. It contains the borrower's promise to maintain the value of the property given as collateral for a loan.
    d. It is evidence of the borrower's debt to the lender.

7.3   When homebuyer Henry pledges his newly purchased home as collateral for a mortgage loan, the evidence of the pledge is the

    a. trust deed or mortgage.
    b. promissory note.
    c. loan commitment.
    d. loan receipt.

7.4   The borrower in a mortgage loan transaction is known as the

    a. mortgagee.
    b. mortgagor.
    c. lienor.
    d. trustee.

7.5   If a borrower obtains an interest-only loan of $200,000 at an annual interest rate of 6%, what is the monthly interest payment?

    a. $1,200.
    b. $600.
    c. $500.
    d. $1,000.

7.6   If a borrower's monthly interest payment on an interest-only loan at an annual interest rate of 6% is $500, how much was the loan amount?

    a. $72,000.
    b. $100,000.
    c. $120,000.
    d. $50,000.

7.7   A borrower of a $50,000 interest-only loan makes annual interest payments of $3750. What interest rate is the borrower paying?

    a. 7.5%.
    b. .75%.
    c. 3.75%.
    d. 8.5%.

7.8   Maria borrows $100,000 and pays two points for the loan. How much does she pay in points?

    a. $200.
    b. $2,000.
    c. $1,200.
    d. It depends on the interest rate.

7.9   Which of the following is true of an amortizing loan?

    a. The amount of annual interest paid is the same for every year of the loan term.
    b. Part of each periodic payment is applied to repayment of the loan balance in advance and part is applied to payment of interest in arrears.
    c. Except for any points that may be paid, the interest on the loan balance is usually paid in advance.
    d. The interest rate is reduced each year to maintain equal payments even though the outstanding loan balance is smaller.

7.10   For a loan that is not backed by the Federal Housing Administration or Veterans Administration, and for which the borrower is making a down payment of less than 20%, the lender is likely to require the borrower to obtain

    a. a subrogation agreement.
    b. private mortgage insurance.
    c. a letter of credit.
    d. a co-signer on the note.

7.11   What is a loan-to-value ratio?

    a. The percentage of a lender's portfolio that is composed of mortgage loans.
    b. The ratio of borrowed principal plus total interest to the appraised value of the collateral property.
    c. The ratio of a lender's return on a mortgage loan to the value of the collateral property.
    d. The fraction of the appraised value of the property offered as collateral which the lender is willing to lend.

7.12   The difference between what a borrower has to pay to purchase a property and the amount a lender will lend on the property is the

    a. mortgage insurance coverage amount.
    b. lender's profit margin.
    c. buyer's down payment.
    d. origination fee.

7.13   The Equal Credit Opportunity Act prohibits a lender from

    a. refusing a loan because the borrower does not match the lender's target market.
    b. including income from self-employment in the borrower's qualifying income.
    c. requiring both spouses to sign the loan application form.
    d. refusing a loan because a borrower has a defective credit report.

7.14   A loan applicant has an annual gross income of $72,000. How much will a lender allow the applicant to pay for monthly housing expense to qualify for a loan if the lender uses an income ratio of 28%?

    a. $2,160.
    b. $1,680.
    c. $1,068.
    d. $840.

7.15 AMC Bank discovers, in considering buyer Bob's application for a mortgage loan, that Bob has borrowed the down payment from an uncle and has to repay that loan. Bob should expect that AMC Bank will

a. refuse the application.
b. adjust the applicant's debt ratio calculation and lower the loan amount.
c. increase the loan amount to enable the borrower to pay off the loan to the relative.
d. require the borrower to make payments to an escrow account for repayment of the relative's loan.

7.16 The Federal Reserve's Regulation Z applies to which loans?

a. All loans.
b. All loans secured by real estate.
c. All loans secured by a residence.
d. All loans over $25,000.

7.17 If a particular loan falls under Regulation Z's right of rescission provision,

a. the lender has the right to change the terms of the loan within a certain period.
b. the lender has the right to accelerate repayment of the loan because of a change in the borrower's credit status.
c. the borrower has the right to pay off the loan ahead of schedule with no penalty.
d. the borrower has a limited right to cancel the transaction within a certain period.

7.18 Under the Equal Credit Opportunity Act, a lender, or a real estate agent who assists a seller in qualifying a potential buyer, may not

a. tell a rejected loan applicant the reasons for the rejection.
b. ask the buyer/borrower about his/her religion or national origin.
c. ask the buyer/borrower to explain unconventional sources of income.
d. use a credit report that has not been provided to the borrower.

7.19 A conventional mortgage loan is one that is

a. backed by the Federal National Mortgage Association.
b. insured under Section 203(b) of the Federal Housing Administration loan program.
c. guaranteed by the Government National Mortgage Association.
d. not FHA-insured or VA-guaranteed.

7.20 The assumability of an FHA-insured loan is

a. unrestricted.
b. limited by when the loan was originated.
c. limited to owner-occupied properties.
d. prohibited on all existing loans under current regulations.

7.21 A VA certificate of eligibility determines

a. how long an individual served in the military.
b. the maximum loan amount an approved lender can give to veterans.
c. how much of a loan the VA will guarantee.
d. whether a lender is approved to issue VA-guaranteed loans.

7.22 A borrower obtains a 30-year, fully amortizing mortgage loan of $50,000 at 8%. What is the principal balance at the end of the loan term?

a. $2,000.
b. $50,000.
c. $220.
d. Zero.

7.23   Which of the following describes a purchase money mortgage financing arrangement?

a. A bank gives a buyer a senior mortgage loan that fully covers the cost of purchasing the property.
b. The buyer gives the seller a mortgage and note as part of the purchase price of the property.
c. A land trust holds title to the property while the buyer makes periodic installment payments to the seller.
d. The seller uses the purchase money obtained from the buyer's mortgage loan to repay the seller's outstanding loan balance.

7.24   A homeowner borrows money from a lender and gives the lender a mortgage on the property as collateral for the loan. The homeowner retains title to the property. This is an example of

a. intermediation.
b. forfeiture.
c. hypothecation.
d. subordination.

7.25   Which of the following correctly describes the flow of money and documents in a mortgage loan transaction?

a. The borrower gives the lender a note and a mortgage in exchange for loan funds.
b. The lender gives the borrower a mortgage and receives a note in exchange for loan funds.
c. The borrower receives a note in exchange for a mortgage from the lender.
d. The lender gives the borrower a note, loan funds and a mortgage.

7.26   In a deed of trust transaction, which of the following occurs?

a. The beneficiary conveys title to a trustee in exchange for loan funds.
b. The trustee conveys title to a beneficiary in exchange for loan funds.
c. The trustor conveys title to a trustee in exchange for loan funds from the beneficiary.
d. The trustee conveys title to a trustor in exchange for loan funds from the beneficiary.

7.27   A lender lends money to a homeowner and takes legal title to the property as collateral during the payoff period. They are in a

a. title-theory state.
b. lien-theory state.
c. state allowing land trusts.
d. state where hypothecation is illegal.

7.28   A lender who charges a rate of interest in excess of legal limits is guilty of

a. redlining.
b. usury.
c. profit-taking.
d. nothing; there are no legal limits to interest rates.

7.29   A lender is charging 2 points on a $60,000 loan. The borrower must therefore pay the lender an advance amount of

a. $120.
b. $300.
c. $1,200.
d. $3,000.

7.30 The difference between a balloon loan and an amortized loan is

   a. an amortized loan is paid off over the loan period.
   b. a balloon loan always has a shorter loan term.
   c. an amortized loan requires interest-payments.
   d. a balloon loan must be retired in five years.

7.31 A distinctive feature of a promissory note is that

   a. it is not assignable.
   b. it must be accompanied by a mortgage.
   c. it is a negotiable instrument.
   d. it may not be prepaid.

7.32 When the terms of the mortgage loan are satisfied, the mortgagee

   a. may retain any overage in the escrow account.
   b. may inspect the property before returning legal title.
   c. may be entitled to charge the borrower a small fee to close the loan.
   d. may be required to execute a release of mortgage document.

7.33 In addition to income, credit, and employment data, a mortgage lender requires additional
      documentation, usually including

   a. an appraisal report.
   b. a criminal record report.
   c. a subordination agreement.
   d. a default recourse waiver.

7.34 The three overriding considerations of a lender's mortgage loan decision are

   a. points, interest rate, and loan term.
   b. the location of the mortgaged property, the borrower's cash, and the amount of the borrower's
       equity.
   c. the ability to re-pay, the value of the collateral, and the profitability of the loan.
   d. the amount of the loan, the borrower's income, and the down payment.

7.35 The reason lenders consider the loan-to-value ratio important in underwriting is that

   a. they don't want to lend borrowers any more money than necessary.
   b. they want to ensure there is more than enough collateral to cover the loan amount.
   c. borrowers can only afford to borrow a portion of the entire purchase price.
   d. the higher the loan-to-value ratio, the more profitable the loan.

7.36 The Equal Credit Opportunity Act (ECOA) requires lenders to

   a. extend equal credit to all prospective borrowers.
   b. consider the income of a spouse in evaluating a family's creditworthiness.
   c. discount the income of a person involved in child-rearing or child-bearing.
   d. specialize lending activity by geographical area for improved customer service.

7.37 Lenders use an income ratio in qualifying to

   a. insure a borrower has the earning power to make the loan payments.
   b. compare a borrower's earnings to the borrower's short-term debt.
   c. identify the highest possible interest rate that the borrower can afford.
   d. quantify the borrower's assets to the fullest extent.

7.38 The debt ratio formula used to qualify borrowers is

a. total debt divided by debt payments.
b. gross income divided by assets.
c. gross income divided by debts.
d. debt payments divided by gross income.

7.39 At the closing of a mortgage loan

a. the borrower pays off the note and receives clear title.
b. the lender issues a firm loan commitment.
c. the parties complete all loan origination documents and the loan is funded.
d. the borrower's loan application is complete and the file closed.

7.40 Which laws or regulations require mortgage lenders to disclose financing costs and annual percentage rate to a borrower before funding a loan?

a. The Equal Credit Opportunity Act.
b. Truth-in-Lending laws and Regulation Z.
c. The Real Estate Settlement and Procedures Act.
d. Federal Fair Housing Laws.

7.41 Which laws or regulations prevent mortgage lenders from discriminating in extending credit to potential borrowers?

a. The Equal Credit Opportunity Act.
b. Truth-in-Lending laws.
c. The Real Estate Settlement and Procedures Act.
d. Federal Fair Housing Laws.

7.42 Which laws or regulations require mortgage lenders to provide an estimate of closing costs to a borrower and forbid them to pay kickbacks for referrals?

a. The Equal Credit Opportunity Act.
b. Truth-in-Lending laws.
c. the Real Estate Settlement and Procedures Act.
d. Federal Fair Housing Laws.

7.43 Which of the following are methods used by the Federal Reserve System to regulate the money supply?

a. Selling securities, printing money, and controlling lending underwriting requirements.
b. Buying securities, changing the discount rate, and controlling banking reserves.
c. Printing money, changing interest rates, and selling T-bills.
d. Controlling the prime rate, trading securities, and purchasing loans.

7.44 How does the secondary mortgage market aid borrowers seeking a mortgage loan?

a. It cycles funds back to primary lenders so they can make more loans.
b. It issues second mortgages and sells them in the home equity market.
c. It lends funds to banks so they can make more loans.
d. It pays off defaulted loans made by primary mortgage lenders.

7.45 The major organizations operating in the secondary mortgage market are

a. Fannie Mae, Freddie Mac, and Ginnie Mae.
b. Fannie Mae, GMAC, and MGIC.
c. Freddie Mac, FHA, and VA.
d. Fannie Mae, Freddie Mac, and the Federal Reserve.

7.46   What is the role of Fannie Mae in the secondary mortgage market?

   a. It guarantees FHA-backed and VA-backed loans.
   b. It insures FHA-backed and VA-backed loans.
   c. It purchases FHA-backed and VA-backed loans.
   d. It originates FHA-backed and VA-backed loans.

7.47   What is the role of the Federal Housing Authority in the mortgage lending market?

   a. It guarantees loans made by approved lenders.
   b. It insures loans made by approved lenders.
   c. It purchases loans made by approved lenders.
   d. It originates loans made by approved lenders.

7.48   What is the role of the Veteran's Administration in the mortgage lending market?

   a. It guarantees loans made by approved lenders.
   b. It insures loans made by approved lenders.
   c. It purchases loans made by approved lenders.
   d. It originates loans made by approved lenders.

7.49   In a graduated payment mortgage loan,

   a. loan funds are disbursed to the borrower on a graduated basis.
   b. the interest rate periodically increases in graduated phases.
   c. the loan payments gradually increase.
   d. the loan payments gradually increase and the loan term gradually decreases.

7.50   In a buydown,

   a. the lender lowers the interest rate on a loan in exchange for a prepayment of principal.
   b. the borrower pays additional interest at the onset in order to obtain a lower interest rate.
   c. the lender requires the borrower to buy down the price of the property by increasing the down payment.
   d. the borrower pays the lender additional funds to buy down the term of the loan.

8.1   When an investor has to pay a lender more to finance the investment than the investment property generates in income, the investor suffers from

   a. negative amortization.
   b. negative leverage.
   c. a reverse mortgage.
   d. a debt investment.

8.2   Cost recovery is allowed as a federal tax deduction on

   a. principal residences that do not have a home office.
   b. income properties.
   c. land.
   d. commercial properties owned by the federal government.

8.3   A homeowner paid $200,000 for a house three years ago. The house sells today for $239,000. How much has the property appreciated?

   a. 8.4 %.
   b. 6.5 %.
   c. 19.5 %.
   d. 16.3 %.

8.4   The primary tax benefit in owning a non-income property such as a residence is

   a. depreciation of improvements.
   b. appreciation of land.
   c. a deduction for costs of operating the property.
   d. a deduction for mortgage interest.

8.5   A house sold for $250,000. The seller paid a brokerage commission of six percent, legal fees of $600, and had other closing costs of $1,500. What are net proceeds from the sale?

   a. $235,000.
   b. $234,000.
   c. $233,500.
   d. $232,900.

8.6   A homeowner bought a house five years ago for $150,000. Since then, the homeowner has spent $3,000 to pave the driveway and has added a central heating/airconditioning system at a cost of $4,000. What is the homeowner's adjusted basis if the house is sold today?

   a. $156,000.
   b. $157,000.
   c. $144,000.
   d. $145,000.

8.7   A homeowner sold her house and realized a net proceeds amount of $210,000. Her adjusted basis in the home was $176,000. She immediately bought another house for $200,000. What was her capital gain?

   a. $10,000.
   b. $24,000.
   c. $34,000.
   d. None.

8.8   After five years of owner-occupancy, Simon Wilson sells his principal residence for a gain of $150,000, and the next month buys another principal residence that costs more than the adjusted sale price of the old home. Which of the following is true of the treatment of the tax on gain?

a. There is no taxable gain.
b. It must be paid in the year of the sale.
c. The homeowner may choose to pay it or defer it.
d. Tax is due on the difference between the cost of the new home and adjusted basis of the old one.

8.9   Ralph Roberts buys a small office building as an investment and participates actively in the management and operation of the building. This is an example of

a. syndication.
b. equity investment.
c. direct investment.
d. illiquidity.

8.10 Elmo Gilmore owns a small retail property that he inherited from his father. There are no mortgages or interest expenses connected with the property. Elmo takes an annual cost recovery expense of $5,000. The property has a monthly gross income of $1,500 and monthly operating expenses of $500. Elmo's taxable income from this property will be taxed at a rate of 30%. What is the tax liability for the year?

a. $2,100.
b. $3,600.
c. $3,900.
d. $7,000.

8.11 All investors desire their investments to increase in value. However,

a. the degree of return is inversely related to the degree of risk.
b. the more the investor stands to gain, the greater the risk that the investor may lose.
c. investments requiring intense management have lesser returns.
d. the more liquid an investment is, the greater the chances are that the investment will not appreciate.

8.12 Two of the financial rewards that investments offer are

a. income and tax benefits.
b. negative leverage and appreciation.
c. appreciation and taxation.
d. positive leverage and prestige.

8.13 Because a real estate investment can take a long time to sell, real estate investments are considered to be

a. management intensive.
b. insensitive to marketing.
c. vulnerable to seller's markets.
d. relatively illiquid.

8.14 Compared to a stock portfolio, a real estate investment would be considered

a. a riskier investment.
b. a more management-intensive investment.
c. a shorter-term investment.
d. a more leveraged investment.

8.15 Six investors purchase a shopping center. One investor manages the tenants and another handles the marketing and leasing. Two investors manage accounting and finance, and the remaining two run the management office. This is a possible example of

a. a general partnership.
b. a limited partnership.
c. a real estate investment trust.
d. an investment conduit.

8.16 The formula for determining taxable income produced by an income property is

a. gross income minus expenses plus land and building depreciation.
b. gross income minus expenses minus land and building depreciation.
c. gross income minus building depreciation plus land depreciation.
d. gross income minus expenses minus building depreciation.

8.17 In deriving taxable income on an investment property, it is generally legal to

a. deduct principal and interest payments from income.
b. deduct principal payments from income.
c. deduct interest payments from income.
d. deduct principal and interest payments from income and capital gain.

8.18 Jake does not use any part of his principal residence as a home office. Which of the following is true of the tax treatment of this property?

a. The owner may deduct the property's interest and principal from ordinary income.
b. The owner may depreciate the property and deduct depreciation expenses from ordinary income.
c. The owner can deduct any capital gain when the property is sold.
d. The owner may be able to avoid capital gain tax when the property is sold.

8.19 An investment property seller pays $14,000 in closing costs. These costs

a. may be deducted from personal income.
b. may be deducted from the property's income.
c. may be deducted from the sale price for gains tax purposes.
d. may be deducted from the adjusted basis for gains tax purposes.

8.20 The formula for calculating capital gain tax is the taxpayer's tax bracket multiplied by

a. the sum of the beginning basis plus gain.
b. the difference between amount realized and adjusted basis.
c. the sum of net sale proceeds and capital gain.
d. the difference between net sale proceeds and capital gain.

8.21 Which of the following entities can legally levy annual real property taxes?

a. The Internal Revenue Service.
b. A utility company.
c. A tax district.
d. A court of law.

8.22 Certain classes of property owner and types of property are exempted or immune from real property taxation in many areas. The protected categories usually include

a. recreational properties.
b. properties owned by a government agency.
c. properties that comply with the Americans with Disabilities Act.
d. properties occupied by single-parent families.

147

8.23 What is the purpose of an equalization factor in ad valorem taxation?

   a. It modifies a local tax rate to bring it into conformity with statutory tax rates.
   b. It changes the assessed value of an individual property to make it reflect the assessed values of other properties in the same neighborhood.
   c. It adjusts assessments in a locality to make them more consistent with an average level for the state or other higher level jurisdiction.
   d. It adjusts the amount of the homestead exemption in a certain area to make it proportionally equivalent to the average homestead exemption in other areas.

8.24 A school district's tax rate is 10 mills. The school district's required revenue from real estate taxes is $20,000,000. What is the tax base of the area?

   a. $20,000,000.
   b. $200,000,000.
   c. $2,000,000,000.
   d. $200,000,000,000.

8.25 A homeowner receives a tax bill that includes an amount for the library district, taxed at $1.00 per $1,000, and the fire protection district, taxed at $2.00 per $1,000. How much does the taxpayer have to pay for these two items if the property's taxable value is $147,000?

   a. $1,567.
   b. $157.
   c. $1,410.
   d. $441.

8.26 A town is replacing a sidewalk that serves five homes. The length of the sidewalk is 200 feet. Mary's property has 38 feet of front footage. If the cost of the project to be paid by a special assessment is $30,000, what will Mary's assessment be?

   a. $6,000.
   b. $5,700.
   c. $789.
   d. $1,579.

8.27 What is a tax deed?

   a. A conveyance instrument for a property that is sold to enforce a tax lien.
   b. A document recorded in title records showing that property taxes have been paid.
   c. A notice to a homeowner that a tax lien has been entered against the property.
   d. A document that gives a municipal authority the power to collect an individual tax bill.

8.28 If a property owner has the right to redeem his or her property after a tax sale, the owner has

   a. a legal right of rescission.
   b. an equitable right to acquire title.
   c. a right of homestead exclusion.
   d. a statutory right of redemption.

8.29 The formula for deriving a municipal jurisdiction's ad valorem tax base is

   a. the jurisdiction's annual budget times the tax rate.
   b. the total of all assessed values of properties minus exemptions.
   c. the total amount of ad valorem taxes required by the budget.
   d. the municipality's budget multiplied times the millage rate.

8.30 A homeowner's total tax bill is derived by

a. dividing the tax requirement by the tax base.
b. multiplying each district's tax rate times the market value of the property.
c. multiplying each district's tax rate times the taxable value of the property.
d. averaging the tax rate for each tax district, and multiplying the average tax rate times the assessed value.

8.31 The fair housing law that first protected people against discrimination in housing based on race was the

a. Civil Rights Act of 1866.
b. Civil Rights Act of 1968.
c. Executive Order 11063 of 1962.
d. Title VIII amendment to the Fair Housing Act.

8.32 The classes protected against discrimination by the Fair Housing Act of 1968 are

a. race only.
b. religion and gender only.
c. race, color, religion, and national origin.
d. age and gender only.

8.33 An agent is committing an act of discriminatory advertising by doing which of the following?

a. Telling prospective buyers about the positive and negative aspects of a certain neighborhood.
b. Telling a prospective seller that now would be a good time to put a property on the market.
c. Advertising a property as available to individuals of a particular race.
d. Telling a prospective buyer that the agent is too busy to show the buyer properties personally on a given day.

8.34 Which of the following is an example of blockbusting?

a. An agent shows a minority home buyer properties located in a neighborhood where there are no other minority home owners.
b. An agent persuades a minority home buyer to avoid looking in a neighborhood where there are no minority home owners.
c. An agent persuades a family to put their house on the market because ethnic minority families are beginning to move into the neighborhood.
d. An agent persuades a minority home buyer to buy a property located in an area where most of the home owners belong to minority groups.

8.35 The practice of redlining is specifically prohibited by

a. The Home Mortgage Disclosure Act.
b. The Real Estate Settlement Procedures Act.
c. The Civil Rights Act of 1866.
d. The Americans with Disabilities Act.

8.36 Title VIII of the Civil Rights Act of 1968 applies to the sale of

a. all single-family residences.
b. all privately owned single-family residences.
c. privately owned single-family residences listed with a broker.
d. privately owned single-family residences for sale by owner.

8.37 A broker signs a listing agreement to sell a home for $200,000. An immigrant couple are interested in the house and ask the agent the price. The agent states the price as $210,000. According to the fair housing laws, such an action is

    a. illegal, because the agent changed the terms of the sale to discourage this particular couple.
    b. illegal, because the agent violated the listing agreement.
    c. legal, because the quoted price increase did not exceed 10% of the listing price.
    d. legal, because the increased price does not necessarily exclude the couple.

8.38 Which of the following actions is allowed under federal fair housing laws?

    a. A broker, following the instructions of the seller, advertises the property as for sale to Christian families only.
    b. A home seller, acting without a broker, places a "for sale-- mature, single men only" sign in front of the house.
    c. The owner of four rental houses advertises one of the properties for rent to married couples, no children, no pets.
    d. The owner of a duplex who resides in one of the units refuses to rent the other unit to a non-Christian.

8.39 Cecily Longstreet believes a real estate agent has kept her from seeing a certain property for rent because she is a woman. What actions should she take if she wants legal satisfaction for her complaint?

    a. File charges of illegal discrimination with the police department that has jurisdiction over the local area.
    b. File a complaint with HUD and/or file suit against the offending parties in a state or federal court within the prescribed time period.
    c. Wait two years and then file a civil suit in federal court.
    d. Sue HUD for damages under the Civil rights Act of 1866.

8.40 George Scott hires Shannon Lang to sell his house, with the condition that he will not be the first one in the neighborhood to sell to members of a certain ethnic group. What should Shannon do about this condition?

    a. Inform Scott that the condition is illegal and that she cannot comply with it.
    b. Note the condition on the listing agreement and have Scott initial it.
    c. Pretend that she did not hear the condition and proceed to market the property to all groups.
    d. Tell Scott that she will try to discourage members of that group from looking at the property, but that she cannot control cooperating brokers.

8.41 Under federal fair housing laws, the owner of a ten-unit apartment building may legally

    a. advertise that the property is not available to anyone requiring wheelchair access.
    b. refuse to rent to aliens.
    c. require families without children to pay the same security deposit that families with children must pay.
    d. require tenants to move out when they become 62 years old.

8.42 Sam Gough wants to rent out his home, but wants to exclude families with children because of his belief that they cause damage. Under what conditions would federal fair housing laws allow Gough to rent on these terms?

    a. The owner has a consistent no-children policy in all his rental properties.
    b. The owner can prove that costs to repair damage caused by previous tenants with children exceeded the tenants' security deposit.
    c. It is a single-family house that is part of a federally-designated planned unit development.
    d. It is a single-family house, and the owner owns only one other rental home in addition to his own residence.

8.43 Which of the following laws or rulings extended discrimination to include gender, handicapped status, and family status?

   a. Executive Order 11063.
   b. the Civil Rights Act of 1968.
   c. the Fair Housing Amendments Act of 1988.
   d. Jones v Mayer.

8.44 The Wallaces, a minority family, would like to buy a home in a certain price range. Agent Ambrose shows the family all available properties in a neighborhood of families with similar backgrounds. Ambrose does not mention a number of homes in the family's price range in other neighborhoods. This agent could be liable for

   a. blockbusting.
   b. providing unequal services.
   c. steering.
   d. nothing; his services were legal and acceptable.

8.45 An agent does not like a particular minority buyer, and is very short with the person, refusing to engage in lengthy conversation or show him any properties. A second minority party visits the office the next day. The agent is very forthcoming, and shows the person five prospective properties. This agent could be liable for

   a. providing unequal services.
   b. steering.
   c. misrepresentation.
   d. nothing; both parties were minorities, and therefore no discrimination occurred.

8.46 Following the client's recommendation, an agent conceals the availability of a property from an employed but pregnant and unmarried minority woman. This agent could be liable for

   a. discriminatory misrepresentation by omission.
   b. steering.
   c. violating fiduciary duty.
   d. nothing: an agent may show or not show any property at his or her discretion.

9.1   The conditions of an escrow agreement cannot be met and the related transaction cannot be completed. In such a case, the escrow agent

    a. levies a fine against the defaulting party.
    b. assigns his or her fiduciary responsibilities to the seller's broker.
    c. returns funds to the buyer.
    d. cancels the sale contract and destroys the transaction documents.

9.2   To avoid violating the Real Estate Settlement Procedures Act, parties who are providing services to the buyer or seller in a transaction must

    a. be paid before the closing date for any service they provide.
    b. inform the closing agent of the cost of their services at least one week before the closing date.
    c. receive payment only from the funds held in escrow, not directly from buyer or seller.
    d. disclose in writing any business relationships they have with other parties involved in the transaction.

9.3   A certain item is to be prorated between a buyer and seller. If no outside party is concerned, which of the following statements is true?

    a. The item must be prorated and recorded as a debit to one party and a credit to the other party for the same amount.
    b. The item must be prorated and recorded as a debit to one party; the remainder is recorded as a credit to the other party.
    c. The party who is owed money receives a credit for the entire item and a debit for the prorated amount.
    d. The party who owes money receives a debit for the portion owed and a credit for the portion that is not owed.

9.4   An item is said to be paid in arrears if it is normally paid

    a. on a monthly or yearly basis.
    b. at some time after the expense is incurred.
    c. only after it is billed.
    d. whenever it is incurred.

9.5   A seller received a rental payment of $900 in advance. At closing, the seller has earned only $320 of this rent. What should appear on the closing statement?

    a. A debit to the seller and credit to the buyer for $320.
    b. A debit to the seller for $580 and a credit to the buyer for $320.
    c. A debit to the seller for $320 and a credit to the buyer for $900.
    d. A debit to the seller and credit to the buyer for $580.

9.6   A buyer will receive a water bill for an estimated $100 at the end of the month. At closing, the seller has used an estimated $43 in water. What should appear on the closing statement?

    a. A debit to the seller and credit to the buyer for $57.
    b. A debit to the seller and credit to the buyer for $43.
    c. A debit to the buyer and credit to the seller for $57.
    d. A debit to the buyer and credit to the seller for $43.

9.7 A sale transaction closes on April 1, the ninety-first day of the tax year. The day of closing belongs to the seller. Real estate taxes for the year, not yet billed, are expected to be $2,190. According to the 365-day method, what is the seller's share of the tax bill?

   a. $1,644.00.
   b. $546.00.
   c. $959.30
   d. $1,364.66.

9.8 A sale transaction closes on July 4. The day of closing belongs to the seller. On January 1, the seller paid a hazard insurance premium of $375 for the calendar year. According to the 12-month/30-day method, what is the seller's share of the insurance premium?

   a. $183.33.
   b. $187.50.
   c. $189.05.
   d. $191.67.

9.9 Waldo is buying Marianne's house. The closing date (day belongs to seller) of the sale transaction is September 1 (day 244 of the year). Current Year real estate taxes are $1,100 (will be billed to buyer next year). Use the 365-day method for prorating. What is Marianne's share of the real estate taxes?

   a. $364.66.
   b. $367.67.
   c. $732.33.
   d. $735.34.

9.10 Christie is buying John's house. The closing date (day belongs to seller) of the sale transaction is September 1 (day 244 of the year). Existing hazard insurance of $350 has been paid by John through December 31. Use the 365-day method for prorating. What is Christie's share of the existing hazard insurance already paid in full?

   a. $116.03.
   b. $117.99.
   c. $232.01.
   d. $233.97.

9.11 Julie is buying Florence's house. The closing date (day belongs to seller) of the sale transaction is September 1 (day 244 of the year). The buyer's loan amount is $78,750 (90%; 30 years @ 8%). The monthly payment on this loan is $577.84, with $525 going to interest in the first month. At closing, Julie must pre-pay interest for the period of Sept. 2-Sept. 30. Use the 365-day method for prorating. What is Julie's prepaid interest amount?

   a. $507.50.
   b. $525.00.
   c. $543.10.
   d. $558.58.

9.12 Melissa is buying Raymond's house. Melissa's loan amount is $88,750. She has agreed to pay 2 points at closing. How much will Melissa pay for points?

   a. $157.50.
   b. $177.50.
   c. $1,775.00.
   d. $887.50.

9.13 Tina is buying Terrell's house for $187,500. The broker's commission, to be paid by the seller, is 6%. How much will Terrell pay the broker?

    a. $31,250.
    b. $2,625.00.
    c. $4,725.
    d. $11,250.

9.14 A sale contract stipulates that a buyer is to pay the seller's transfer tax expenses. This practice is not customary in the area. In this case,

    a. the buyer and seller must amend the contract before closing.
    b. the contract is voidable, since the seller must pay the expense.
    c. the buyer may pay or not pay the expense, at his or her option.
    d. the buyer must pay the expense.

9.15 What a buyer has to pay at closing is equal to

    a. the excess of the buyer's debits over the buyer's credits.
    b. the excess of the buyer's credits over the buyer's debits.
    c. the excess of the seller's debits over the seller's credits.
    d. the excess of the seller's credits over the seller's debits.

9.16 The standard E & O policy covers damages resulting from

    a. failure to disclose an environmental condition.
    b. antitrust violations.
    c. mishandling of earnest money deposits.
    d. negligence, error or omission in carrying out professional services.

9.17 Which of the following is a common risk relating to the agency relationship?

    a. Failing to inform and disclose properly.
    b. Failing to take a personal interest in a transaction.
    c. Acting as an exclusive agent without an oral agency agreement.
    d. Forgetting to record the listing agreement.

9.18 Even after giving buyer and seller the required information about property condition disclosures, the licensee may still be subject to legal action for

    a. failing to detect customer misrepresentations.
    b. failing to disclose known adverse facts.
    c. relying on publicly available market information.
    d. advising the purchaser to exercise due diligence.

9.19 A licensee performing a comparative market analysis must be careful to

    a. use the term "market value" whenever possible in the report.
    b. show a low suggested selling price to avoid a complaint of misrepresenting the value.
    c. include the results of a certified appraisal in the analysis.
    d. avoid creating a false impression that the licensee is a certified appraiser.

9.20 One of the major risk areas in fulfilling a listing agreement is

    a. finding a buyer who turns out to be unqualified.
    b. exceeding the authority of the agreement.
    c. showing the property without the presence of the owner.
    d. cooperating with other licensees.

9.21 To reduce the risk of committing an error or omission in the contracting process, it is a good idea to

a. use a checklist of all items, contingencies, dates and responsibilities that must be met.
b. delegate some of your responsibilities to the licensee who represents the other party in the contract.
c. call the buyer and seller daily to check on progress.
d. cut the list of necessary tasks down to a few essentials and concentrate on tracking those.

9.22 Regarding contracts and forms,

a. once written and signed they cannot be changed except by a lawyer.
b. real estate licensees may alter forms but not contracts.
c. whoever originates them can make changes without the risk of unauthorized practice of law.
d. the principals may make changes as long as they sign or initial each change.

9.23 Fair housing laws are easily violated. An effective way for agents to minimize the risk of doing so is to

a. deal only with consumers who do not belong to a protected class.
b. obtain education in the content and intent of the laws.
c. make sure there is always a witness present at all meetings with consumers.
d. stay away from transactions involving public housing.

9.24 A licensee risks violating antitrust law by

a. being present at a conversation where the setting of commission rates is discussed.
b. being present at a discussion of antitrust laws.
c. charging a commission rate that happens to be the same as that charged by another firm.
d. cooperating with another firm to do market research.

9.25 How is an intentional misrepresentation penalized?

a. License discipline, fines, and possible incarceration.
b. License discipline and fines, but no incarceration.
c. License discipline only.
d. Fines only.

9.26 Of the following actions, the only one which avoids any risk of committing unintentional misrepresentation is

a. measuring and reporting property dimensions.
b. describing properties and amenities.
c. stating that a client should seek legal counsel.
d. making statements about the presence or absence of hazardous substances.

9.27 To reduce risks inherent in reporting transaction progress to a client, the licensee should

a. make reports orally only, never in writing.
b. leave progress reporting to the inspectors and other experts.
c. advise the client that it is company policy to make no progress reports until the contingency period is over.
d. avoid speculative statements in all reports

9.28 How does sharing the qualifying function with a lender protect a licensee?

a. It guarantees that a buyer will have a loan.
b. It reduces the chance of presenting an offer from an unqualified buyer.
c. It relieves the licensee of his or her due diligence responsibilities.
d. It allows the licensee to avoid asking embarrassing questions.

9.29 The area of agent activity where there is the greatest risk of failing to maintain client confidentiality is

   a. trust fund handling.
   b. office management.
   c. the agency relationship.
   d. the closing process.

9.30 The area of agent activity where there is the greatest risk of creating a false impression that the licensee is a certified appraiser is

   a. performing a comparative market analysis.
   b. writing property advertisements.
   c. presenting written offers.
   d. researching ownership documents

9.31 One of the major risk areas in advertising a listed property is that an advertisement will

   a. describe the property in excessively glowing terms.
   b. fail to appear at the same time in all available media.
   c. omit any mention of the owner's main selling points.
   d. make a substantial misrepresentation.

9.32 Property managers have a _____ relationship with the property owner.

   a. non-binding
   b. partnership
   c. fiduciary
   d. subagency

9.33 One of the property manager's fundamental responsibilities is

   a. obtaining construction loans for the principal.
   b. financial reporting to the principal.
   c. finding a buyer for the property.
   d. maintaining good standing in a managers' professional association.

9.34 Effective gross income is defined as

   a. the total of scheduled rents.
   b. the total of all rents and revenues generated by a property.
   c. potential gross income minus debt service and reserves.
   d. revenue from all sources minus losses from uncollected rents, vacancies, and evictions.

9.35 The efficiency of marketing activities can be measured in terms of

   a. cost per tenant prospect generated per lease.
   b. number of ads produced per marketing dollar.
   c. dollars expended per square foot of vacant space.
   d. percentage of reserves expended on marketing.

9.36 If a property's vacancy rate is significantly lower than market rates, it may be a sign that the manager needs to

   a. lower rental rates.
   b. raise rental rates.
   c. find better tenants.
   d. improve management quality.

9.37 What are the three kinds of maintenance a manager has to carry out for a managed property?

a. Constructive, deconstructive, and reconstructive
b. Routine, preventive, and corrective
c. Scheduled, planned, and improvised
d. Emergency, elective, and optional

9.38 The Americans with Disabilities Act requires property managers to

a. ensure that disabled employees have the same level of access to facilities that all employees have.
b. hire the disabled whenever possible.
c. remove all existing barriers to the free movement of disabled persons within the property, regardless of the cost.
d. remodel the ground floor of the property in accordance with ADA standards if it was built before 1978.

9.39 Commercial fire and hazard insurance policies usually require coverage to equal at least 80 percent of the property's

a. replacement value.
b. reproduction value.
c. original cost.
d. depreciated basis.

9.40 Trust funds to be handled by a property manager are likely to include all of the following except

a. rents collected from tenants.
b. cash for the management firm's operating expenses.
c. security deposits.
d. capital contributions from the property owner.

9.41 What kind of agency is commonly created by a management agreement?

a. Universal
b. Specific
c. General
d. Vicarious

9.42 Which of the following describes a gross lease?

a. The tenant pays a base rent plus some or all of the operating expenses.
b. The tenant pays a fixed rent, and the landlord pays all operating expenses.
c. The tenant pays a base rent plus an amount based on income generated in the leased space.
d. The tenant pays a rent that increases at specified times over the lease term.

9.43 If an apartment contains a refrigerator that is not included in the lease,

a. the lessee is required to buy it from the landlord.
b. the landlord is required to remove it.
c. the lease is invalidated because of an incomplete property description.
d. the property manager does not have to maintain it.

9.44 A basic responsibility of a landlord is to

a. provide leased space at market rental rates.
b. deliver a habitable property.
c. keep the rental space freshly painted.
d. refrain from entering the leased space at any time during the lease term.

9.45   How does a constructive eviction occur?

   a. A landlord obtains a court order to force the tenant to vacate the leased premises.
   b. A court officer forcibly removes the tenant from the premises.
   c. A tenant declares a landlord in default and vacates the leased premises.
   d. A landlord declares a tenant in default and takes possession of the leased premises.

9.46   Among the essential elements of a management plan is consideration of

   a. the competitive market for the property.
   b. the property manager's career goals.
   c. the property owner's net worth.
   d. the management firm's income goals.

10.1   A licensee sells 5/6 of an acre for $28,000, and receives a 6% commission. If she splits with her broker 50-50, what did she receive per square foot?

    a. $.023 / SF
    b. $.046 / SF
    c. $.037/ SF
    d. $.002 / SF

10.2   Lots in the South Hyde subdivision are selling for approximately $.50 / SF. The Grandersons want to build a 2,500 SF home on a 1.5 acre corner lot. The custom builder can build the home for $135 / SF. What will the completed property cost the Grandersons?

    a. $359,170
    b. $370,170
    c. $32,670
    d. $374,070

10.3   Ivan owned a 1/4 acre lot. He wanted to construct a 120' x 80' tennis court on the lot. What approximate percentage of the lot will be left over, if any, when he has completed the construction?

    a. 12%
    b. 88%
    c. 3%
    d. 15%

10.4   A developer wants to develop a 16-acre subdivision. He figures that the streets and common area will take up about 30% of this overall area. If the minimum lot size is to be 12,000 SF, how many lots can the developer have on this property?

    a. 42
    b. 487
    c. 40
    d. 57

10.5   A homeowner wants to insulate the new recreation room in her basement. She has been told that 3" of insulation would do the job. The walls are all 9' high and respectively measure 13', 13', 18', and 18' in length. How many rolls will she need if each roll measures 3" x 2' x 50'?

    a. 6
    b. 56
    c. 5
    d. 9

10.6   Maria plans to mulch the flower area around her house. The house measures 40' x 30', and she figures she'll mulch an area 8' in width to form a big rectangle all around the perimeter. What is the square footage of the resulting mulched area?

    a. 64 SF
    b. 2,576 SF
    c. 1,824 SF
    d. 1,376 SF

10.7. Calculate how many acres are in the Southeastern ¼ of the Western ½ of the Eastern ½ of Section 9.

a. 20 acres
b. 40 acres
c. 60 acres
d. 5 acres

10.8. Homeowner Savannah owns the Southeastern ¼ of the Southwestern ¼ of the Northwestern ¼ of Section 4. How many acres is that property?

a. 4 acres
b. 40 acres
c. 10 acres
d. 8 acres

10.9 Yard of Pizza has a percentage lease on its 1,800 SF space in Lincoln Shops. The terms are $1.40 / SF / month rent plus 1.75% of the store's gross income. If monthly sales averaged $41,500 last year, how much annual rent did Yard of Pizza pay last year?

a. $38,955
b. $43,420
c. $30,240
d. $21,525

10.10 A home appreciated 2 2/3% one year, then 5 1/5% the next year, then 7 1/4% the third year. What was the average appreciation over the 3-year period expressed as a decimal?

a. 5.04%
b. 15.24%
c. 7.56%
d. 4.8%

10.11 A homeowner paid $185,000 for a house three years ago. The house sells today for $239,000. How much has the property appreciated?

a. 23 %
b. 77 %
c. 29 %
d. 123 %

10.12 Seller Frank receives an offer of $290,000 on a property he listed at $308,000. How much is the offer as a percent of the listing price?

a. 87%
b. 91%
c. 94%
d. 106%

10.13 A property is being appraised using the income capitalization approach. Annually, it has potential gross income of $30,000, vacancy and credit losses of $1,500, and operating expenses of $10,000. Using a capitalization rate of 9%, what is the indicated value (to the nearest $1,000)?

a. $206,000
b. $167,000
c. $222,000
d. $180,000

10.14 If gross income on a property is $75,000, net income is $30,000 and the cap rate is 8%, the value of the property using the income capitalization method is

a. $625,000
b. $375,000
c. $3,750,000
d. $937,500

10.15 The roof of a property cost $16,000. The economic life of the roof is 20 years. Assuming the straight-line method of depreciation, what is the depreciated value of the roof after 3 years?

a. $16,000
b. $13,600
c. $18,400
d. $12,000

10.16 Lee had to report his home office depreciation for the tax year. He has a 2,500 SF home and a 500 SF office area. Lee paid $280,000 for his home, and he figures the land portion carries about 25% of that value. If Lee depreciates on a 39-year basis, how much can he write off for his home office depreciation per year?

a. $1,077
b. $1,436
c. $5,384
d. $2,108

10.17 A property is being appraised by the cost approach. The appraiser estimates that the land is worth $40,000 and the replacement cost of the improvements is $175,000. Total depreciation from all causes is $27,000. What is the indicated value of the property?

a. $148,000
b. $228,000
c. $162,000
d. $188,000

10.18 An apartment owner paid $500,000 for her complex 5 years ago. An appraiser at that time valued the land @ $100,000, but land has appreciated 25% over this period. The investor has used a 40-year straight-line depreciation method to depreciate the property. What is its current value using the cost approach?

a. $437,500
b. $462,500
c. $475,000
d. $546,875

10.19 An apartment building that recently sold for $400,000 had monthly gross rent receipts of $3,200. What is its monthly gross rent multiplier?

a. 80
b. .01
c. 110
d. 125

10.20 A rental home has monthly gross income of $1,100. A suitable gross income multiplier derived from market data is 14.7. What estimated sale price (to the nearest $1,000) is indicated?

a. $99,000
b. $162,000
c. $194,000
d. $173,000

161

10.21 Amy obtains a 75% LTV loan on her new $200,000 home with an annual interest rate of 6%. What is the first month's interest payment?

a. $900
b. $250
c. $1,000
d. $750

10.22 Emily has an interest-only home equity loan at an annual interest rate of 5.3%. If her monthly payment is $790, how much is the loan's principal balance (to the nearest $1,000)?

a. $222,000
b. $179,000
c. $95,000
d. $146,000

10.23 The loan officer at Sixth Fourth Bank tells Amanda she can afford a monthly payment of $1,000 on her new home loan. Assuming this is an interest-only loan, and the principal balance is $249,000, what interest rate is Amanda getting?

a. 4.82%
b. 5.03%
c. 6.25%
d. 3.69%

10.24 The Keegans obtain a fixed-rate amortized 30-year loan for $280,000 @ 6.25% interest. If the monthly payments are $1,724, how much interest do the Keegans pay in the second month of the loan?

a. $1,748.33
b. $1,456.95
c. $1,458.33
d. $1724.00

10.25 A lender offers the Greys two alternative loan packages for their $60,000 home equity application. One option is an interest-only loan for 5 years @ 6.5% interest with no points, and the second, a 6.25% interest-only loan for 5 years with 1 point to be paid at closing. Which loan will cost the Greys less total interest, and by how much?

a. The first option, by $150.
b. The second option, by 150.
c. The second option, by $750.
d. Both options charge the same amount of interest.

10.26 Jose recently obtained a 90% loan on his $410,000 home, and he had to pay $6,150 for points. How many points did he pay?

a. 1.4 points
b. 1.67 points
c. 2.48 points
d. 1.5 points

10.27 Mack is buying Roy's house for $500,000. Mack's loan amount is $325,000. He has agreed to pay 1.5 points at closing. How much will Mack pay for points?

a. $450
b. $4,500
c. $4,875
d. $7,500

10.28 A lender determines that a homebuyer can afford to borrow $130,000 on a mortgage loan. The lender requires an 80% loan-to-value ratio. How much can the borrower pay for a property and still qualify for this loan amount?

a. $138,000
b. $104,000
c. $162,500
d. $170,000

10.29 Home buyer Janet pays $1,600 / month for the interest-only loan on her new house. The loan's interest rate is 6.75%. If she obtained a 75% loan, what was the purchase price?

a. $313,333
b. $31,604
c. $379,259
d. $256,000

10.30 Loan applicant Taylor has an annual gross income of $76,000. How much will a lender allow Taylor to pay for monthly housing expense to qualify for a loan if the lender uses an income ratio of 30%?

a. $2,160
b. $1,900
c. $1,215
d. $4,433

10.31 An investor paid $80,000 for a lot and $600,000 to have an apartment building constructed on it. He has depreciated the property for the past 10 years on a 39-year straight-line schedule. If he sells the property this year and realizes $780,000, what is his capital gain?

a. $253,846
b. $274,000
c. $100,000
d. $179,000

10.32. A homeowner bought a house five years ago for $250,000. Since then, the homeowner has spent $2,000 to build a screened porch and has added a central air-conditioning system at a cost of $5,000. What is the homeowner's adjusted basis if the house is sold today?

a. $256,000
b. $257,000
c. $244,000
d. $245,000

10.33 A homeowner sold her house and had net proceeds of $265,000. Her adjusted basis in the home was $231,000. She immediately bought another house for $301,000. What was her capital gain?

a. $265,000
b. $36,000
c. $34,000
d. None

163

10.34 Debra bought a home for $120,000, paying $24,000 down and taking a mortgage loan of $96,000. The following year she had a new roof put on, at a cost of $5,000. What is Debra's adjusted basis in the house if she now sells the house for $150,000?

a. $29,000
b. $96,000
c. $101,000
d. $125,000

10.35 A certain investor wants an 11% return on investment from any real estate investment. A property priced at $360,000 has gross income of $60,000 and expenses of $22,000. Approximately how much too high or too low is the price of this property for the investor to obtain her desired return exactly?

a. $1,000 overpriced.
b. $8,000 underpriced.
c. $15,000 overpriced.
d. $16,000 underpriced.

10.36 An office building investor sees a listing of an office building which is priced at $2 million. He loves the property, but he knows he needs to make a return of at least 8% to satisfy his partners. If the building is 25,000 SF, rents for $10/SF per year, has 5% vacancy, and annual expenses of $70,000, should he buy it? What is his return?

a. No, since he will yield 2.00%.
b. Yes, since he will yield 8.375%.
c. Yes, since he will yield 8%.
d. Yes, since he will yield 9.125%.

10.37 Chad owns a small retail property that he inherited from his father. There are no mortgages or interest expenses connected with the property. Chad takes an annual cost recovery expense of $7,000. The property has a monthly gross income of $1,650 and monthly operating expenses of $600. Chad's taxable income from this property will be taxed at a rate of 30%. What is the tax liability for the year?

a. $1,680
b. $5,940
c. $2,100
d. $7,000

10.38 A property has a net income of $150,000, interest payments of $105,000, principal payments of $30,000, and annual cost recovery of $7,000. The property's tax rate is 28%. What is the property's annual tax on income?

a. $14,550
b. $40,040
c. $10,640
d. $2,240

10.39 An investor bought 4 oversized lots in order to subdivide. He paid $70,000 for the lots. After subdividing, the investor was able to sell each lot for $23,000. Excluding commissions and closing costs, what per cent profit did the investor realize?

a. 0%
b. 45%
c. 23.9%
d. 31.4%

10.40 A school district's tax rate is 10 mills. The school district's required revenue from taxes is $10,000,000. What is the tax base of the area?

a. $10,000,000
b. $100,000,000
c. $1,000,000,000
d. $100,000,000,000

10.41 A homeowner's residence has an assessed valuation of $140,000, and a market value of $170,000. The homestead exemption is $25,000. Tax rates for the property are 7 mills for schools; 3 mills for the city; 2 mills for the county; and 1 mill for the local community college. What is the homeowner's tax bill?

a. $1,495
b. $1,820
c. $1,150
d. $2,210

10.42 The village of Goodsprings has an annual budget requirement of $8,000,000 to be funded by property taxes. Assessed valuations are $400,000,000, and exemptions total $25,000,000. What must the tax rate be to finance the budget?

a. 2.00%
b. 2.13%
c. 1.32%
d. 21.33%

10.43 A property has sold for $127,000. The listing agreement calls for a commission of 7%. The listing broker and selling broker agree to share the commission equally. What will the listing agent receive if the agent is scheduled to get a 40% share from his broker?

a. $4,445
b. $3,556
c. $2,667
d. $1,778

10.44 Kevin, who works for selling broker Paul, sells a house listed by listing broker Adams. The house sells for $325,000. The co-brokerage split between Paul and Adams is 50-50. Kevin is on a 65% commission schedule with Paul. If the total commission rate is 6.5%, what is Kevin's commission?

a. $6,866
b. $5,282
c. $10,563
d. $13,731

10.45. A sale transaction closes on April 1, the ninety-first day of the tax year. The day of closing belongs to the seller. Real estate taxes for the year, not yet billed, are expected to be $3,150. According to the 365-day method, what should appear on the closing statement?

a. A debit to the buyer and credit to the seller for $2,364.62
b. A debit to the buyer and credit to the seller for $785.34
c. A credit to the buyer and debit to the seller for $785.34
d. A credit to the buyer and debit to the seller for $2,364.62

10.46 Alexis is buying Jack's house. The closing date (day belongs to seller) of the sale transaction is September 1 (day 244 of the year). Her loan has a monthly payment of $577.84, with $525 going to interest in the first month. At closing, Alexis must pre-pay interest for the period of Sept. 2-Sept. 30. Use the 365-day method for prorating. What is her prepaid interest amount?

a. $507.50
b. $525.00
c. $543.10
d. $558.58

10.47 A sale transaction on rental property closes on December 16. The landlord received the December rent of $1,380 on December 1. Assuming the closing day is the buyer's, and that the 365-day method is used for prorating, which of the following entries would appear on the settlement statement?

a. Debit seller $667.74.
b. Credit seller $1,380.00.
c. Debit buyer $712.26.
d. Credit buyer $712.26.

10.48 A home sells for $322,600 in Primm County. Here, transfer taxes are set at $1.00 per $500 of the sale price. Title insurance runs $450, and the attorney costs $550. The agent's commission is 7%, and the mortgage balance is $210,000. Annual real estate taxes are estimated to be $4,000, half of which will have to be charged to the seller. If the seller pays all of these expenses, what will she net at closing?

a. $86,873
b. $88,371
c. $81,372
d. $86,372

10.49 A farmer wants to net at least $5,000/acre on the sale of his 300-acre property. If he allows for 10% commissions and closing costs, and to allow for negotiating room, he wants to get 95% of the listing price as the selling price, what should his listing price be per acre?

a. $5,750
b. $5,882
c. $4,250
d. $5,848

10.50. The Wildes have purchased a $740,000 home. The land is worth 25%, and they insure the improvements @ 75% of their replacement value. If the Wildes suffer damage estimated at $500,000, and they have an 80% co-insurance clause, what will their recovery be from the policy?

a. Zero
b. $531,915
c. $500,000
d. $468,750

10.51 The Uptons carry a $140,000 property insurance policy which covers 75% of the replacement cost of their insurable property, valued at $190,000. They have an 80% co-insurance requirement in the policy. If the family incurs a $150,000 loss, what if any amount will the Uptons recover?

a. $159,999
b. $140,625
c. $140,000
d. $187,500

Section V: North Carolina State-Level Practice Tests

Test 11: Licensing and Regulation

11.1 Any provisional broker who fails to complete the postlicensing education requirement within the prescribed period of time

    a. will have his or her license cancelled.
    b. will have his or her license converted to inactive status.
    c. must apply for a time extension to complete the requirement.
    d. will be permanently barred from broker licensure in North Carolina.

11.2 Harold, a broker, filed his request for license activation from inactive status exactly two weeks ago. To date he has not heard from the NCREC regarding his filing. What is the status of Harold's license?

    a. It is inactive until he receives acknowledgment.
    b. It remains inactive for a 45-day period following the filing, regardless of acknowledgment.
    c. It remains active during a 45-day probationary period, after which the license becomes inactive if the NCREC does not acknowledge the filing.
    d. It is active immediately upon filing unless the NCREC fails to acknowledge within 30 days from the date on the activation form.

11.3 Provisional brokers are required to

    a. complete a 30-hour postlicensing education requirement within 3 years of the first license renewal.
    b. complete 2 annual postlicense classes of 45 hours apiece within 2 years of the first license renewal.
    c. complete a 90-hour postlicensing education requirement within 3 years of initial licensure.
    d. complete a 90-hour postlicensing requirement and a 24-hour broker transition course.

11.4 The North Carolina Real Estate Commission consists of

    a. seven members nominated by the Governor and appointed by the General Assembly.
    b. nine members, all appointed by the Governor.
    c. nine members, seven appointed by the Governor and two appointed by the General Assembly.
    d. seven members appointed by the Governor.

11.5 Broker-in-charge Allison failed to complete her continuing education requirement for the current license period. What are the consequences for this?

    a. Her license is cancelled.
    b. She will be on inactive status and lose her BIC status at the end of the license period.
    c. Her BIC status is suspended pending completion of the requirement within 30 days following the end of the license period.
    d. Her BIC status is terminated and her license is revoked.

11.6 Which of the following is the most accurate definition of real estate broker?

    a. A person who buys and sells real estate for others, regardless of compensation.
    b. A person who buys, sells and manages real estate for a broker-in-charge for compensation.
    c. A person who buys or sells real estate on behalf of others for compensation.
    d. A person who buys, sells, or manages real estate on behalf of others

11.7 James is unhappy as a broker-in-charge with Johnson Realty. James decides to quit and go to work immediately for a competitor, Benson Realty. What must James do to qualify as a broker-in-charge for Benson?

a. He must re-satisfy all the educational requirements, since his BIC status with Johnson was terminated.
b. He must notify the Commission of the change.
c. He must now demonstrate 2 year's prior full-time experience to qualify.
d. He must re-take the 12-hour BIC course.

11.8 To initially activate or reactivate a provisional broker's license, the provisional broker and the broker-in-charge must certify that the provisional broker

a. has completed the prelicensing requirement.
b. has completed the continuing education requirement and has sold at least five properties in the last two years.
c. has completed the CE requirement and any postlicensing if required.
d. has not previously been a broker-in-charge.

11.9 To qualify to be a broker-in-charge, a licensee must

a. have a broker's license, two years' full-time experience or its equivalent within the 5 prior years and satisfy an educational requirement.
b. satisfy an experience requirement and complete the 90-hour postlicensing education requirement.
c. have five years of full-time experience or its equivalent.
d. complete the 24-hour broker transition course within 120 days after obtaining the designation.

11.10 In which of the following circumstances is a person or business required to have a real estate license?

a. A property manager leases and sells his own apartment buildings.
b. An attorney handles a purchase for a client.
c. A professional negotiator assists clients in obtaining the best price for their properties.
d. A guardian acts under court order.

11.11 If a general partnership applies for a real estate license,

a. all participants in the partnership may practice real estate.
b. The qualifying broker must be a general partner of the partnership.
c. the limited partners may not practice real estate under any circumstances.
d. all general partners must be licensed as active brokers.

11.12 Christine has an active broker license on February 14th, 2016. Christine just earned her broker's license. When would her license lapse assuming she does not complete her continuing education requirement?

a. June 30, 2016.
b. February 14, 2017.
c. June 30, 2017.
d. February 14, 2018.

11.13 Licensees may be disciplined or lose even their licenses if they are guilty of misrepresentation, provided that

a. a party incurs sufficient financial damage.
b. a material fact was either misstated or omitted.
c. a material fact was misstated and not omitted altogether.
d. it is proven that the misstatement was in fact made.

11.14 The partnership of Blake & Anderson decides to incorporate. Bill Blake, the partnership's qualifying broker becomes the CEO of the new firm. In this case, what happens to the partnership's real estate license with respect to the new corporation?

a. The active license transfers to the corporation, provided the qualifying broker remains the same person.
b. The partnership license becomes inactive.
c. The partnership license is terminated and the corporation must apply for a new license.
d. The license transfers to the corporation as an inactive license.

11.15 It is required that the North Carolina Real Estate Commission consist of

a. five licensed brokers and at least two non-licensees.
b. at least three individuals who are exempt from licensure.
c. at least four individuals who are not involved in real estate.
d. at least three licensed brokers and at least two individuals who are not involved in real estate.

11.16 Dorothy has an exclusive listing to sell lots in a new subdivision. A prospective buyer has only one reservation about placing an offer: if she drills a well, will it yield water? Dorothy knows that three of the eight lots already sold have failed to show water on the first drilling. However, she fails to disclose this. Is Dorothy guilty of anything here?

a. No, since the buyer is not her client.
b. No, since there is never a guarantee that a well will find water.
c. Yes, she is guilty of negligent omission.
d. Yes, she is guilty of willful omission.

11.17 Wally had his licensed revoked six months ago. He would like to continue to practice real estate. What must Wally do?

a. Wait until the statutory 12-month period has expired, then re-apply.
b. Follow the procedure for a licensee whose license has been expired for more than 6 months.
c. Appeal the revocation in civil court.
d. Wally cannot restore his license to active status.

11.18 Any licensee who violates the provisions of the real estate license law

a. is subject to license suspension, revocation, censure or reprimand by the Real Estate Commission.
b. will automatically have his or her license suspended.
c. must face an investigation followed by due process in superior court.
d. is in most cases guilty of a felony.

11.19 To satisfy the continuing education requirement, a non-resident licensee

a. must take the 4-hour general update course offered in North Carolina.
b. need only take the 4-hour general update course or its equivalent in the state where the licensee is practicing.
c. may take the 4-hour general update course and an elective, or complete two approved 4-hour electives.
d. need only comply with the requirements where the licensee resides.

11.20 Tony is the qualifying broker for the Alpha Corporation. He has recently resigned. What happens to the company's real estate license?

a. It terminates.
b. It must be surrendered.
c. It reverts to inactive status.
d. It remains active for a period not to exceed 45 days during which time a new broker can be installed.

11.21 Kelly must renew her provisional broker's license; however, she has not completed her continuing education requirement. What happens to Kelly's license?

a. It is assigned an inactive status.
b. It must be surrendered until the requirement is satisfied.
c. It remains active during a 45-day probationary period, after which the license becomes inactive.
d. It is suspended on a dormant status.

11.22 Licensees with inactive licenses may

a. not engage in any real estate activity requiring a license.
b. engage in activities limited to referrals
c. engage in any real estate activity for others, provided no compensation is involved.
d. act as brokers-in-charge.

11.23 In North Carolina, broker's and provisional broker's licenses expire

a. on June 30th following issuance of the license.
b. every two years from the date of initial issuance.
c. on every anniversary of the issuance date.
d. on December 31st of every other year.

11.24 North Carolina real estate commissioners serve terms of

a. one year.
b. two years.
c. three years.
d. four years.

11.25 The education requirement for a new broker-in-charge is that the BIC must

a. complete a 12-hour broker-in-charge course within three years prior to or within 120 days following designation as a broker-in-charge.
b. complete a 12-hour broker-in-charge course and the 24-hour broker transition course within 90 days following designation as a broker-in-charge.
c. complete the 90-hour postlicensing course and 8 hours of BIC-specific continuing education.
d. complete a 30-hour BIC postlicensing course within one year of designation as a broker-in-charge.

11.26 In North Carolina, you are exempt from real estate licensure if you

a. negotiate leases.
b. auction real estate.
c. purchase multiple properties from a broker.
d. sell real estate on behalf of a broker.

11.27 The Real Estate Commission has historically viewed a material fact that must be disclosed as one which if it

a. relates to features of the property; facts about the property; or facts relating to the ability of the principal to complete the transaction.
b. either affects the property's value or the value of the immediate neighborhood.
c. can be demonstrably proven to be true.
d. leads or fails to lead to a completed transaction.

11.28 A newly licensed provisional broker may engage in real estate practice

    a. immediately.
    b. 30 days following the initial issuance of the license.
    c. upon conversion of the inactive license to active status.
    d. as soon as the broker-in-charge has mailed or faxed a completed supervision notification form.

11.29 Darren, who is an active salesperson who lives in a neighboring state, would like to obtain a North Carolina real estate provisional broker's license. According to license law, Darren

    a. must first move to North Carolina and become a resident.
    b. must pass the North Carolina portion of the real estate licensing exam.
    c. must complete the North Carolina prelicense course and pass both the national and North Carolina portions of the licensing exam.
    d. automatically qualifies for licensure provided his state has a reciprocal arrangement.

11.30 In addition to suspending and revoking licensees, the NCREC is also empowered to

    a. obtain injunctions against non-licensees who may be violating license law.
    b. pursue criminal charges against individuals for fraud.
    c. sue licensees for license law infractions which are felonies.
    d. regulate unfair compensation structures within brokerage companies.

11.31 To satisfy North Carolina's continuing education requirement, brokers must

    a. complete 8 hours of approved instruction every two years following initial licensure.
    b. complete 8 hours of core courses every year following initial licensure.
    c. complete 4 hours of approved instruction in the initial year of licensure, and 8 hours before each subsequent renewal.
    d. complete 8 hours of approved instruction every year following the first renewal.

11.32 Which of the following must be done in order to remove the provisional status of the broker's license?

    a. Complete the prelicense requirement for brokers.
    b. Complete the 90-hour postlicensing requirement within the prescribed period of time.
    c. Complete the 90-hour postlicensing requirement and prove 2 years' full-time experience.
    d. all of the above.

11.33 To satisfy the continuing education requirement, a broker-in-charge must

    a. take the 4-hour general update course and another 4-hour elective.
    b. take the BIC 8-hour continuing education course.
    c. take a specially-designated 4-hour continuing education course for BIC's, along with a 4-hour elective CE course within each license period.
    d. complete the 4-hour BIC continuing education course in addition to the 8-hour CE course requirement.

11.34 Ken tells a buyer that a lot has sufficient area for a large house, an outbuilding, and swimming pool area. The buyer purchases the property and later discovers that she cannot build everything she wanted on the property due to easements, restrictions, and setback requirements. Here, Ken would be guilty of

    a. negligent misrepresentation.
    b. negligent omission.
    c. intentional misrepresentation.
    d. intentional omission.

11.35 A licensee's license is inactive. In order to renew the inactive license, the licensee must

    a. submit the annual renewal fee to NCREC.
    b. submit a renewal application and complete the required continuing education.
    c. convert the inactive license to active status.
    d. re-take the license examination, re-apply, and complete the continuing education requirement.

11.36 In North Carolina, licensees may be disciplined by the Real Estate Commission for failing to deliver copies of the closing statements to buyers and sellers

    a. upon the consummation of the transaction or within 5 days of closing.
    b. within seven days following the closing.
    c. within ten days following the closing.
    d. upon their written request.

11.37 The North Carolina Real Estate Commission is empowered to regulate which of the following?

    a. The requirements for obtaining a license.
    b. Compensation of brokers.
    c. Financial arrangements made between brokers and provisional brokers.
    d. All of the above.

11.38 Terrell Adams has successfully completed all the post-licensing requirements for his broker's license. Upon initial licensure, the broker will be assigned

    a. an active license.
    b. an inactive license.
    c. an inactive license pending receipt of the broker-in-charge designation.
    d. a temporary license.

11.39 Which of the following represents a violation of North Carolina license laws?

    a. failure to deliver a copy of a purchase agreement to a seller within 5 days
    b. Using a fictitious name, albeit registered, in an advertisement.
    c. Failure to disclose a property characteristic regardless of its materiality.
    d. Paying a referral fee to a licensee who is unaffiliated with the firm.

11.40 Thomas, a provisional broker, had his active license suspended last month for a 6-month period. How can Thomas restore his license from suspended to active status?

    a. He need not restore the license to continue practicing real estate.
    b. He must wait 5 months, at which time it automatically restores to active status.
    c. He must wait 5 months, then apply to convert his license from inactive to active status.
    d. He must wait 5 months, then demonstrate he is supervised by a broker-in-charge and has completed the continuing education requirement.

11.41 A provisional broker completes her 1st 30-hour postlicensing requirement, but by the end of the second year, she fails to complete the 2nd 30-hour increment. What happens to her license?

    a. It becomes inactive.
    b. It is cancelled.
    c. It is revoked.
    d. Nothing.

11.42 A licensee informs a buyer that a residence has 4,000 square feet of living area, as indicated by an expired listing. Since the former listing agent was very reputable, the provisional broker is confident that the representation is accurate and fair. In this case, the licensee

    a. may be guilty of willful omission.
    b. may be guilty of willful misrepresentation.
    c. may be guilty of negligent omission.
    d. has not made any misrepresentation or omission because the source of the measurement is reliable.

12.1   In a residential property disclosure, if the homeseller elects to make no representation regarding the condition of a given property item, then

   a. the homeseller is absolved of the duty to disclose a defect of that item.
   b. the homeseller is assumed to be concealing a defect.
   c. the homeseller is nonetheless required to disclose a defect if it exists.
   d. none of the above.

12.2   A real estate broker and a condominium property owners' association agree that the broker will handle leasing in the condominium complex. At what point may the broker begin representing the owners' association?

   a. Immediately; condominium property owners may give oral authorization for brokers to represent them.
   b. When the broker has obtained a written agreement.
   c. Immediately, provided the broker limits activities to management as opposed to leasing.
   d. As soon as the listing agreement is recorded.

12.3   In order for a provisional broker to advertise, the provisional broker must

   a. identify herself in the ad and correctly state the name of the owner.
   b. Have their broker's and the principal's consent and identify the name of the broker or firm in the ad.
   c. have the broker review and approve the ad copy.
   d. obtain the principal's consent to advertise without mentioning the broker's or firm's name in the ad.

12.4   A broker represents a sophisticated international investor who is often difficult to reach. To accommodate the client, the broker provides for an automatic renewal of the listing agreement when it expires, unless the investor specifically cancels it. The arrangement ensures that interruptions and delays will not get in the way of a potential sales transaction. The investor likes the idea. Is this arrangement acceptable for a North Carolina broker?

   a. No, the agreement must terminate at a specific time without prior notice to the seller.
   b. No, the listing agreement as a revolving service contract may only expire upon the broker's written consent.
   c. Yes, the agreement is perfectly acceptable.
   d. It is acceptable provided the agreement is in writing.

12.5   Which of the following is a required provision that must be included in an agency agreement?

   a. A property condition disclosure.
   b. The maximum dollar amount of the commission or compensation to be paid.
   c. Compliance with the North Carolina Fair Housing Act.
   d. A liquidated damages clause with a specified dollar amount.

12.6   A broker is employed by a property owner association to handle all the business affairs of the association, including handling of funds. Which of the following is true?

   a. All trust monies must be maintained in the association's trust account exclusively.
   b. The broker must deposit association funds in his agency's trust account.
   c. The association's funds may be commingled with third party escrow funds.
   d. The funds need not be placed in a trust account.

12.7 A buyer representative recommends a mortgage lender to his client following the execution of a sale contract. The lender pays the licensee a referral fee, unbeknownst to the buyer. In this case, the licensee

   a. has not violated state regulation, since the referral is from a licensed mortgage lender.
   b. has violated state regulations by obtaining a secret profit from the buyer.
   c. must inform the buyer of the commission within three days of receipt from the lender.
   d. is required to share the commission with the buyer.

12.8 A residential provisional broker receives a $5,000 deposit from a prospective buyer in connection with an offer. In this case, the provisional broker

   a. must give the deposit to their broker immediately.
   b. must deposit the funds immediately.
   c. must deliver the funds to the Commission immediately upon acceptance of the offer.
   d. must deposit the funds within three banking days of the date of the offer.

12.9 Becky, a cooperating provisional broker, places a standard company "for sale" sign on a remote piece of land that listing agent Allen had just listed. Has Becky done anything wrong?

   a. No, since she is a cooperating selling agent working as Allen's subagent.
   b. No, provided the company sign indicates the name of Becky's company.
   c. Yes, since the law does not allow signage by provisional brokers.
   d. Yes, if neither the principal nor the listing agent has granted her permission.

12.10 A large brokerage office employs over 50 provisional brokers and brokers. In this case, this office

   a. may employ one broker-in-charge for every 10 provisional brokers.
   b. may employ an assistant broker-in-charge with prior written approval by NCREC.
   c. may only employ one broker-in-charge regardless of the number of provisional brokers employed.
   d. none of the above.

12.11 Sarah, a prospective buyer, enjoys working with buyer broker Ethan, but she is reluctant to sign a representation agreement. Ethan continues to show Sarah properties, and at one point, she wants to make an offer but still refuses to sign an agreement. Which of the following represents Ethan's situation at this point?

   a. He will be owed a commission because of an implied agency.
   b. He must cease representing Sarah and become a subagent of the seller if allowed
   c. He must become a dual agent and obtain the seller's permission.
   d. He automatically becomes the seller's subagent.

12.12 The Emersons make an offer on a property through ABC Realty, and the sellers accept. During the contingency period, the Emersons fail to obtain a loan, and the deal falls through. In this case, ABC Realty

   a. is bound by the requirement to retain records of this transaction for three years.
   b. is not required to maintain records of the failed transaction, since it did not close.
   c. must retain all records of the failed transaction for at least one year.
   d. may dispose of the transaction records at the end of the calendar or fiscal year.

12.13 Provisional broker Carmine has an acceptance for her listing from a buyer. She would be well-advised to deliver this document immediately to her seller, but her absolute deadline from the date of execution is

   a. two days.
   b. three days.
   c. five days.
   d. seven days.

12.14 A home buyer, two days after closing, discovers serious leaks in the roof. The buyer had not received a property condition disclosure statement at any time prior to the closing period. In this case, the buyer

a. may annul the purchase provided he forfeits the deposit money in the sale contract.
b. may annul the sale and receive all deposit monies back.
c. may cancel the contract provided he has not taken possession.
d. may not cancel the contract.

12.15 Under the provisions of the NC Residential Rental Agreements Act, maintaining the apartment in clean, safe, and undamaged condition is the responsibility of

a. the tenant.
b. the landlord.
c. the landlord and the property manager.
d. none of the above.

12.16 Agent Patrick has a buyer who is concerned about inheritance, probate, and the laws of descent. The buyer wants to hold title in such a way as to minimize the costs and inconvenience of transferring title to his spouse should he pass away. Agent Patrick suggests a joint tenancy would achieve this objective. In this case

a. Patrick should also suggest other forms of ownership to avoid liability.
b. Patrick has correctly solved the buyer's problem.
c. Patrick should have consulted an attorney before suggesting joint tenancy.
d. Patrick has violated the prohibition of practicing law.

12.17 In compliance with the North Carolina Residential Property Disclosure Act (NCRPDA), sellers of their single family homes

a. must disclose the condition of their property to a buyer on or before the point at which they receive an offer.
b. must disclose the condition of their property to a buyer on or before the closing.
c. must disclose the condition of their property to a buyer if they are using the services of a provisional broker or broker.
d. must disclose the condition of their property to a buyer if the buyer so requests.

12.18 A broker requests and obtains written approval from his principal to receive a modest referral fee from A-1 Carpet Cleaners for periodic carpet cleaning. In this case the broker

a. may not change vendors without the consent of the principal.
b. may not receive compensation from unlicensed parties, regardless of the principal's approval.
c. must pass the referral fee through to the principal.
d. has acted properly in view of state regulations provided the payment is made to his/her employing broker.

12.19 Agent Frank makes a hard-hitting presentation and convinces a seller to list with him. However, Frank has left his agreement forms back in the office. The seller instructs Frank to begin the listing process immediately. Does Frank have a listing agreement with the seller?

a. Yes, since the seller gave the verbal go-ahead.
b. Yes, however Frank has a 24-hour deadline to get the agreement in writing.
c. Yes, but the agreement is an open listing.
d. No, not until the agreement is in writing.

12.20 A broker who places a listing in a newspaper advertisement must clearly

    a. identify the broker's name or firm.
    b. identify the broker's telephone number.
    c. identify the broker's post office box or street address.
    d. identify all of the above.

12.21 A broker may maintain an interest-bearing trust account, provided that

    a. the principals approve of the account and agree in writing on who will receive the interest.
    b. the principals understand that the broker will receive the interest.
    c. the party depositing the funds receives the benefit of the interest.
    d. the account is a bona fide trust account and not the broker's business account.

12.22 In North Carolina, licensees may only prepare offers and sales contracts if

    a. the principals expressly agree to the terms that are drafted.
    b. the licensee limits his preparations to completing an approved, preprinted form.
    c. he is in the presence of a licensed attorney.
    d. the documents are reviewed by the principal's attorneys prior to signing.

12.23 In North Carolina, the rule regarding completion of deeds and deeds of trust is that licensees

    a. may not draft these documents without express approval of the principals.
    b. may complete any preprinted form of these documents.
    c. may complete preprinted forms approved by NCREC.
    d. may not draft or fill in the blanks of printed forms for others.

12.24 Which of the following conditions is not required in a North Carolina listing agreement?

    a. It must not automatically renew.
    b. It must have a stated expiration date.
    c. It must be on pre-printed forms approved by NCREC.
    d. It must contain a non-discrimination clause.

12.25 Provisional broker Sandra decides to leave her employing brokerage firm. What must she do to comply with state regulations?

    a. Notify her broker-in-charge of her discontinuation within three business days.
    b. Notify all principals that she is no longer practicing real estate.
    c. Surrender all of her personal records to the broker-in-charge within three business days.
    d. Notify the NCREC of the termination within 10 days following her last day.

12.26 The deadline for the broker to deliver a closing statement to a buyer and seller is

    a. one day after closing.
    b. three days after closing.
    c. five days after closing.
    d. seven days after closing.

12.27 A brokerage firm has ten offices and a headquarters office where the owner-broker conducts her business. According to North Carolina law, this brokerage must have how many brokers-in charge?

    a. Ten, one for every branch office.
    b. One for the overall firm.
    c. Two: one for the headquarters office and one for the branches.
    d. Eleven; one for each office, including the headquarters office.

12.28 What is the purpose of the booklet "Working with Real Estate Agents?"

a. To explain and promote the benefits of listing properties with a particular firm.
b. To clarify and identify whether the agent will represent the buyer or seller in the transaction.
c. To highlight the potential pitfalls of buying or selling property without the expertise of a licensee.
d. To explain real estate services and how they justify the commission to be charged.

12.29 Licensees must maintain records of trust fund deposits and of the principals who deposited such funds. The standard for sufficient trust fund accounting is that the records must

a. leave a clear audit trail, including monthly bank reconciliations.
b. comply with IRS guidelines.
c. be maintained for a period of at least five years.
d. include all deposit tickets and withdrawal receipts.

12.30 George promises to give a listing to agent Vanessa, provided she gives him a 15% kickback on her commission when the transaction closes. Instead, Vanessa cuts her commission rate charge to George to cover the amount of the fee. In this instance, Vanessa

a. has acted properly, since she did not pay a kickback.
b. has violated state law by paying a kickback to an unlicensed person.
c. has illegally conspired with her principal.
d. has violated state regulations, since the commission cut is effectively a kickback.

12.31 North Carolina regulations require that brokers must have trust accounts

a. if they are engaged in active brokerage practice.
b. regardless of whether their licenses are active or inactive.
c. that do not bear interest.
d. if they handle the funds of others

12.32 Which of the following is NOT among the group of principal responsibilities of a broker-in-charge?

a. Maintaining corporate tax and accounting records and the firm's license status.
b. Retaining provisional broker licenses and maintaining transaction records.
c. Supervising provisional brokers and verifying their experience.
d. Assuring agency disclosures and maintaining trust account records.

12.33 A buyer wants a certain repair made before closing and gives the broker a check for the repair, dated for the day the job is to be finished. Meanwhile, the broker uses funds from the buyer's trust account deposit to pay the repairman. When the work is complete, the broker promptly deposits the check into the trust fund. In this case, the broker

a. has acted properly by promptly covering the approved expenditure.
b. has misapplied trust funds in violation of state regulations.
c. has co-mingled trust funds.
d. should have received written authorization from the buyer in advance.

12.34 Broker Mike is sole proprietor of his active real estate practice, which specializes in residential home sales. The broker-in-charge rule that applies here is that

a. Mike is exempt from the rule since he has no provisional brokers working for him.
b. Mike must designate himself as broker-in-charge in order to conduct business.
c. Mike must designate himself broker-in-charge as soon as he hires any provisional broker to work for him.
d. None of the above.

178

12.35 Provisional broker Alice has completed an offer to purchase on behalf of her buyer client. In addition to the customary terms, the buyer asks Alice to write in a special financing contingency. Alice carefully enters the terms into the offer as instructed, and the buyer initials the clause. In this case, Alice

a. has violated state regulations by practicing law.
b. must have an attorney review the offer prior to submission.
c. must also initialize the contingency since she wrote it.
d. has not violated any regulation.

12.36 An agent is informed by a local home developer that he will buy any parcel of real estate within one-half mile of a new shopping center. One of the agent's listings falls within this radius. Knowing this information, the agent is considering making a full price offer on his own listing, knowing he may be able to subsequently re-sell the property for a profit. In this case, the agent

a. may not purchase the property due to a conflict of interest.
b. may make the offer without disclosing his intentions, since it is a full-price offer.
c. must disclose the developer's intentions prior to making the offer.
d. none of the above.

12.37 Buyer representative Christine receives a $2,000 earnest money deposit (in the form of cash) from her buyer. According to North Carolina regulation, these funds must be deposited in the broker's trust account

a. immediately.
b. within three banking days of acceptance of the offer.
c. within five banking days of acceptance of the offer.
d. within seven banking days of acceptance of the offer.

12.38 Which two organizations have approved a standard "Offer to Purchase and Contract" sales form commonly known as OPC Standard Form 2-T?

a. HUD and the Department of Commerce
b. The North Carolina Association of Realtors and North Carolina Bar
c. The North Carolina Real Estate Commission and the National Association of Realtors
d. The North Carolina General Assembly and the American Bar Association

12.39 In the completion and fulfillment of the Offer to Purchase and Contract's terms, which of the following statements is true?

a. Closing must occur within 30 days of the sales contract being signed.
b. If the seller defaults, the buyer may sue for specific performance.
c. At least 5% of the purchase price must be immediately escrowed.
d. The Offer to Purchase and Contract can be an oral agreement.

12.40 During the time period of a transaction between contracting and closing,

a. the contract becomes void upon major damage to the property.
b. the seller is responsible for curing reasonable wear and tear.
c. the buyer may make improvements to the property at the buyer's expense.
d. the seller is responsible for the property condition.

13.1 All of the following statements by a buyer to a seller's agent would exemplify "first substantial contact" except

    a. how long the buyer has been living in his present house.
    b. what the buyer wants to pay.
    c. what type of property the buyer needs.
    d. how much the buyer will have to borrow.

13.2 A licensee of a firm cannot be a designated agent representing the buyer in a transaction if

    a. the agent has already received confidential information from the seller in the transaction.
    b. the agent has represented a seller in earlier transactions.
    c. the agent has already received approval to be a dual agent.
    d. All of the above.

13.3 What approvals are necessary, if any, to practice designated agency?

    a. Verbal consent of both parties, followed by written consent prior to closing.
    b. Prior express approval of both principals obtained upon the formation of the relationship and reduced to writing as required.
    c. Prior written approval of the buyer.
    d. No specific approvals are necessary if the firm has a written policy authorizing designated agency.

13.4 In North Carolina, when may a broker represent both parties in a real estate transaction?

    a. Never.
    b. When the broker has obtained prior written consent of both parties.
    c. Only when the broker is acting as a designated agent in a firm.
    d. Only when the principal broker has agreed to the transaction.

13.5 An agent in a firm cannot be a designated agent representing one principal's interest if

    a. the agent has already received confidential information from the other principal party.
    b. the buyer refuses to authorize dual agency.
    c. the agent is a broker-in-charge and supervises the provisional broker representing the other party in the transaction.
    d. all of the above.

13.6 Dual agency in North Carolina

    a. is illegal.
    b. may not be practiced without consent of the customer in the transaction.
    c. may not be practiced without consent of the seller.
    d. may not be practiced without written consent of both parties to the transaction.

13.7 During telephone discussions with a buyer, a seller's agent has reached the point where the buyer is interested in making an offer. To comply with the NCREC rule on agency disclosure, the agent must now provide

    a. a verbal disclosure.
    b. a verbal disclosure followed by a written disclosure mailed within three days.
    c. a verbal disclosure followed by a confirming disclosure completed within seven days.
    d. a written notification of dual agency.

13.8 A broker-in-charge may not represent a party in a dual agency transaction

    a. under any circumstances.
    b. if a provisional broker under his or her supervision represents the other party.
    c. even if both principal parties give written authorization.
    d. without the prior verbal consent of the principals.

13.9 In North Carolina, a designated agent is

    a. an agent designated to represent either the buyer or seller in a firm's dual agency situation.
    b. a subagent to the seller.
    c. a cooperating agent.
    d. an agent representing a buyer or a seller within the same firm.

13.10 At what point must a North Carolina seller's agent disclose his agency relationship to a buyer in writing?

    a. Immediately upon first contact.
    b. Upon first substantial contact.
    c. Prior to showing any properties.
    d. Prior to completing an offer.

13.11 The North Carolina Uniform Building Code

    a. standardizes construction styles for residential properties statewide.
    b. provides appraisers with a ready-reference for valuing different methods of construction.
    c. establishes municipal zoning standards.
    d. provides building standards for local building inspectors to certify properties for occupancy.

13.12 In making representations regarding the living area of a listed residence, licensees

    a. are required to state the square footage based on their measurement.
    b. are required to identify the square footage of all properties, including out-buildings.
    c. are not required to be accurate since they are not appraisers.
    d. are not required to report square footage, but are advised to be accurate if they do so.

13.13 The North Carolina excise tax on the purchase price of property conveyances is

    a. $.50 per each $100 or fractional part thereof, paid by the seller.
    b. $.50 per each $100 or fractional part thereof, paid by the buyer.
    c. $1.00 per each $500 or fractional part thereof, paid by the seller.
    d. $1.00 per each $500 or fractional part thereof, paid by the buyer.

13.14 According to the NC Fair Housing Act, a homeseller who does not employ an agent

    a. may discriminate in the selection of a buyer.
    b. may not discriminate in the sale of his property.
    c. may discriminate in selecting a buyer, but not in any advertising.
    d. none of the above.

13.15 A homeowner in a college town wants to rent a room in her principal residence to a college student. Which provision of the NC Fair Housing Act applies?

    a. The homeowner is exempt.
    b. The homeowner is exempt, provided she does not use an agent to locate the tenant.
    c. The homeowner may not discriminate in the selection of a tenant.
    d. The homeowner may only discriminate against handicapped people.

13.16 The time limit for filing a complaint to remedy an alleged violation of the NC Fair Housing Act is

a. 60 days following the alleged violation.
b. 90 days following the alleged discriminatory violation.
c. 120 days following the alleged discriminatory violation.
d. One year following the alleged discriminatory violation.

13.17 A violation of federal fair housing laws is also a violation of

a. the North Carolina Residential Agreements Act of 1988.
b. the North Carolina Equal Credit Opportunity Act of 1977.
c. the North Carolina Fair Housing Act of 1983
d. the North Carolina Equal Opportunity Act of 1995.

13.18 North Carolina is considered to be a

a. lien theory state where borrowers take legal title to the property.
b. title theory state where borrowers take legal title to the property.
c. lien theory state where lenders take legal title to the property.
d. title theory state where trustee's take legal title to the property.

13.19 A North Carolina resident qualifies for more than the standard homestead tax exclusion of $35,000 if he or she

a. is 65 years of age or totally disabled.
b. has an income of $25,000 or greater.
c. is 55 years of age or older.
d. owns subsidized housing for the poor.

13.20 Which of the following is not exempt from real property taxation in North Carolina?

a. An FDIC-insured banking institution.
b. A protected natural area.
c. A recycling center.
d. A public park.

13.21 Which of the following series of dates represents the taxing cycle for real properties in North Carolina?

a. Taxes are levied in January; due and payable in April, and delinquent on August 6.
b. Taxes are levied, due, and payable in January, and delinquent on February 6.
c. Taxes are levied in July; due and payable in September, and delinquent on January 6.
d. Taxes are levied, due and payable in March, and delinquent on September 6.

13.22 North Carolina statutes require that real property in the state be re-assessed

a. every two years.
b. every four years.
c. every six years.
d. every eight years.

13.23 The purpose of the North Carolina Coastal Area Management Act (CAMA) is to

a. protect and preserve the state's coastal and estuary regions.
b. minimize hurricane damage to shoreline properties.
c. control fishing practices in coastal areas.
d. promote sustainable agriculture in arable coastal regions.

13.24 What right of rescission does the North Carolina Condominium Act allow the initial purchaser of a condominium?

    a. 3 days' right of rescission following the execution of a contract.
    b. 7 days' right of rescission following the execution of a contract.
    c. 10 days' right of rescission following the execution of a contract.
    d. No right of rescission.

13.25 In North Carolina, how long does a construction contractor have to file a mechanic's lien after last supplying material or labor?

    a. 60 days.
    b. 90 days.
    c. 120 days.
    d. 1 year.

13.26 Under the provisions of the North Carolina Condominium Act, re-sellers of condominium units must

    a. give buyer prospects a copy of the public offering statement.
    b. give buyer prospects a statement of monthly fees and assessments.
    c. give buyer prospects a copy of the public offering statement as well as monthly fees and expenses.
    d. give other unit owners a right of first refusal.

13.27 According to the North Carolina Condominium Act, the initial purchaser of a condominium

    a. may not be related to the condominium developer.
    b. may not be a prior resident of the property.
    c. must receive a public offering statement prior to executing a contract.
    d. none of the above.

13.28 Which of the following is not used in North Carolina to legally describe a parcel of real property?

    a. Metes and bounds descriptions.
    b. References to a recorded map.
    c. Government Survey System.
    d. Legal descriptions contained in public records.

13.29 In North Carolina, the prescriptive period for adverse possession of private property without color of title is

    a. fifteen years.
    b. seventeen years.
    c. twenty years.
    d. thirty years.

13.30 In North Carolina, the use of trust deeds with a power of sale clause enables which type of foreclosure to occur?

    a. Strict foreclosure.
    b. Non-judicial foreclosure.
    c. Judicial foreclosure.
    d. All of the above.

13.31 According to the NC Tenant Deposit Security Act, deposits may be used for

    a. any purpose.
    b. any purpose, provided the tenant has in fact defaulted.
    c. expenses specifically relating to a tenancy, if justified.
    d. expenses relating to the apartment building where the tenant resides.

13.32 The rights, obligations and remedies under a rental agreement for a dwelling unit within North Carolina are governed by

    a. the NC Tenant Security Deposit Act.
    b. the Residential Rental Agreements article of the NC Landlord and Tenant statute.
    c. the NC Vacation Rental Act.
    d. none of the above.

13.33 In North Carolina, a lease of mineral rights

    a. must be in writing and recorded to be valid.
    b. is void if its term exceeds three years.
    c. is enforceable if its term is less than three years.
    d. is enforceable provided the tenant exercises the mining option.

13.34 Licensees in North Carolina who are involved in the practice of leasing or managing vacation properties are governed by the provisions of the North Carolina

    a. Tenant Security Deposit Act.
    b. Time Share Act.
    c. Environmental Protection Act
    d. Vacation Rental Act

13.35 Under the provisions of the NC Residential Rental Agreements Act, tenants are responsible for

    a. repairing common area where damage is due to ordinary wear and tear.
    b. making repairs that are needed due to ordinary wear and tear.
    c. structural and cosmetic repairs, provided they are required during the lease term.
    d. damages caused to the interior of an apartment that is above and beyond wear and tear.

13.36 If a North Carolina tenant refuses to pay rent for an apartment and continues to occupy the premises, the landlord

    a. has grounds to evict the tenant.
    b. landlord may not evict the tenant.
    c. must wait 60 days to pursue a remedy.
    d. none of the above.

13.37 According to the NC Tenant Deposit Security Act, the maximum deposit a landlord may charge is an amount equal to

    a. one week's rent for a week-to-week rental.
    b. one month's rent for a month-to-month rental.
    c. two month's rent for rentals exceeding month-to-month.
    d. one month's rent for all tenancies.

13.38 In North Carolina, land contracts and installment sales

    a. must be in writing to be valid.
    b. are enforceable.
    c. are enforceable if the payment term is less than three years.
    d. are enforceable provided the purchaser can procure financing.

13.39 The North Carolina Vacation Rental Act applies to

    a. occupants of vacation properties.
    b. landlords and brokers of vacation properties.
    c. hotel and motel owners.
    d. all of the above.

13.40 In North Carolina, if a salaried employee of a property manager performs administrative duties on behalf of the property owner, the employee

a. must be licensed as a broker.
b. must be licensed as a broker or provisional broker.
c. need not be licensed.
d. is violating North Carolina license laws.

13.41 To be valid, a North Carolina vacation rental agreement

a. must be in writing.
b. must be acknowledged by a signature or acceptance of a deposit.
c. must describe how monies are to be handled.
d. all of the above.

13.42 According to the NC Statute of Frauds, oral leases are void if they

a. are for one year or more.
b. have terms in excess of two years.
c. exceed three years.
d. are not recorded.

13.43 Bob wants to work for his brother-in-law promoting and selling a time share project the brother-in-law is developing. What must Bob do to comply with state licensing regulations to sell time shares?

a. Pass the real estate time share exam.
b. Obtain a time share developer's license.
c. Obtain a real estate license and a securities license before engaging in any sales.
d. Obtain a certificate of occupancy for the time share project.

13.44 Bob's brother-in-law, Ted, a time share developer, hires Bob to sell time share units. Bob is properly licensed, but Ted could be committing a Class 1 felony if he lets Bob begin selling before

a. designating Bob as project broker.
b. registering the time share project with the NC Real Estate Commission.
c. paying a fee to register Bob as an agent.
d. providing Bob with certified training in the time share sales regulations.

13.45 Who is responsible for providing a time share purchaser with a public offering statement?

a. The project broker.
b. The time share developer.
c. The on-site marketing administrator.
d. The registrar.

13.46 Who is responsible for keeping accurate records of trust monies, time share sales and rentals, and registration of a time share project?

a. The time share broker.
b. The time share developer.
c. The project broker.
d. The time share registrar.

13.47 In North Carolina, when an owner in a joint tenancy dies, in the absence of express provisions for descent, his estate passes to

a. the surviving joint tenant.
b. the state.
c. the heirs of the deceased.
d. none of the above.

13.48 One of the purposes of the North Carolina Marketable Title Act is to

a. promote the marketability and transferability of North Carolina real estate.
b. establish rules as to how NC properties may be conveyed.
c. protect the interests of parties wishing to cloud title.
d. invalidate claims against one's title to real estate.

13.49 Seller Brandy has an agency agreement with broker Tabitha that itemizes authorized activities in exchange for commensurate compensation. What type of agency agreement does Brandy have?

a. An open agency agreement
b. A full service agency agreement
c. A limited service agency agreement
d. A co-agency agreement

13.50 Which statement is true regarding protection agreements?

a. They are used in FSBO transactions to ensure the property "appraises out."
b. The agreements do not create an agency relationship.
c. They are typically only used in transactions where the property is listed for more than one million dollars.
d. They are required by the North Carolina Real Estate Commission when an out-of-state buyer makes an offer on a property.

13.51 What is the purpose of Agriculture Rural Development Loans?

a. To stimulate settlement and development of rural agricultural jurisdictions.
b. To help low-income agricultural homeowners with affordable financing.
c. To subsidize rural small business owners' financing needs.
d. To prevent younger people from moving to cities.

13.52 According to the North Carolina Machinery Act, how often do all counties have to reappraise property?

a. Every 4 years
b. Every 8 years
c. Every 12 years
d. Every 20 years

Section VI: North Carolina License Examination Sample Test

Sample Test: North Carolina Practice Exam

S 1. A farmer temporarily installs produce coolers in a leased farm stand in order to prevent spoilage. The coolers would be considered which of the following?

    a.   Trade fixtures that are real property.
    b.   Trade fixtures that are personal property.
    c.   Temporary real property.
    d.   Emblements.

S 2. Property can be converted from real to personal property and from personal property to real property by means of which processes, respectively?

    a.   Assemblage and plottage.
    b.   Application and dissolution.
    c.   Severance and affixing.
    d.   Planting and harvesting.

S 3. The highest form of ownership interest one can acquire in real estate is the

    a.   legal life estate.
    b.   conventional life estate.
    c.   defeasible fee simple estate.
    d.   absolute fee simple estate.

S 4. The distinguishing feature of a defeasible fee simple estate is that

    a.   it can be passed on to heirs.
    b.   it has no restrictions on use.
    c.   the estate may revert to a grantor or heirs if the prescribed use changes.
    d.   it is of unlimited duration.

S 5. Maria acquires a property from her uncle Alfonso. When Maria dies, the estate will pass to Alfonso's other niece, Serena. The type of estate that Maria has in the property is a

    a.   conventional life estate.
    b.   legal life estate.
    c.   fee simple defeasible estate.
    d.   tenancy by the entireties.

S 6. One difference between a cooperative estate and a condominium estate is that

    a.   a condominium owner owns a unit of air space whereas the co-op owner owns a proprietary lease.
    b.   a condominium sale adversely affects other unit owners.
    c.   the coop owner owns stock and a freehold real estate interest whereas the condominium owner simply a proprietary lease.
    d.   the condominium owner owns the common elements and the airspace whereas the coop owner only owns the apartment.

S 7.   Who are the essential parties involved in an estate in trust?

   a.   Owner, trustor and lawyer.
   b.   Owner, trustor and trustee.
   c.   Trustee, title company, and beneficiary.
   d.   Trustor, trustee and beneficiary.

S 8.   A condominium owner enjoys a

   a.   share in an association that owns one's apartment.
   b.   tenancy in common interest in airspace and common areas of the property.
   c.   fee simple ownership of the airspace in a unit and an undivided share of the entire property's
        common areas.
   d.   fee simple ownership of a pro rata share of the entire property.

S 9.   With various types of junior liens, the order of payment priority is generally established according to

   a.   the date of recordation.
   b.   what form of tax is in question.
   c.   the order of disbursement.
   d.   whether the lien was subordinated.

S 10.   What is a lien-theory state in contrast to a title-theory state?

   a.   A state in which liens are given priority over other encumbrances.
   b.   A state in which a mortgagor retains title to the property when a mortgage lien is created.
   c.   A state in which the holder of a mortgage lien receives title to the mortgaged property until the
        debt is satisfied.
   d.   A state in which liens must be recorded to be enforceable.

S 11.   A property owner has an easement appurtenant on her property. One day the property is sold to
        another party who is opposed to the easement. Following the closing, this particular form of
        easement

   a.   terminates.
   b.   transfers with the property.
   c.   transfers with the owner to a new property.
   d.   becomes a license on the property.

S 12.   What fundamental legal purpose is fulfilled by title records?

   a.   Keeping the county apprised of tax payments.
   b.   Preventing identity theft.
   c.   Giving constructive notice of one's rights and interests in the property.
   d.   Assembling all relevant documents in a single place.

S 13.   What is "chain of title?"

   a.   The list of all parties who have ever owned real estate.
   b.   The bundle of rights linked to the recorded title to a parcel.
   c.   A chronology of successive owners of record of a parcel of real estate.
   d.   Involuntary conveyance of title by statutory rules of descent.

S 14.   Which of the following provides the strongest evidence of marketable title?

   a.   A general warranty deed.
   b.   A title certificate.
   c.   Title insurance.
   d.   An attorney's opinion.

S 15. A store owner enters into a lease that charges rent per square foot, a common area fee, and a portion of the store owner's gross income from the property. This kind of lease is a

    a. triple charge, or triple net lease.
    b. proprietor's lease.
    c. percentage lease.
    d. retailer's gross lease.

S 16. An owner leases a property to a business in exchange for rent. The tenant is required to pay all operating expenses as well. This is an example of a

    a. proprietary lease.
    b. percentage lease.
    c. gross lease.
    d. net lease.

S 17. A lease automatically terminates under which of the following circumstances?

    a. The tenant fails to pay rent.
    b. The leased property is foreclosed.
    c. The tenant goes out of business.
    d. The landlord cancels the lease.

S 18. A county or municipal authority usually grants a certificate of occupancy for new construction only after

    a. all contractors' work has been inspected.
    b. all work has been completed for at least sixty days.
    c. the construction conforms to building codes.
    d. the tax assessor has valued the improvement.

S 19. A property owner is precluded by deed restriction from developing a thirty foot boat dock. The limitation prompts the owner to sell to another party. The new owner

    a. is free to build the dock since the next door neighbor built a similar dock two weeks later.
    b. takes title subject to the same restriction.
    c. can build the dock with special permission from the zoning board.
    d. may build, since the restriction is extinguished by the sale.

S 20. Emily sells Rycole a property containing a deed condition. The condition stipulates that the forested portion of the property must never be razed for development. Three months later, Rycole proceeds to harvest the trees and turn the area into an executive golf course. What recourse, if any, does Emily have under the deed condition?

    a. She has the right to re-possess the property because the grantee has violated the condition.
    b. The condition has ceased to apply because she allowed the violation to continue for a certain period of time.
    c. She can claim the proceeds from the harvested trees.
    d. She can force Rycole to sell the property to a new owner who agrees to comply with the condition.

S 21. What is the essential purpose of legal descriptions of real property?

    a. To create a consistent, unchanging standard for uniquely locating a property.
    b. To enable courts and attorneys to calculate property size accurately.
    c. To comply with common law for real property.
    d. To eliminate cumbersome metes and bounds descriptions.

S 22. Which of the following characterizes metes and bounds descriptions?

    a.   They use meridians and base lines.
    b.   They identify an enclosed area, beginning and ending at the same point.
    c.   They use lot and block numbers.
    d.   They incorporate elevation into the descriptions.

S 23. A buyer agrees to all terms of a seller's offer except the length of time for a contingency to procure financing. The buyer extends the financing period in the offer by one week, signs the form, and mails it back to the seller. At this point, the seller's offer

    a.   is void.
    b.   becomes an executory contract.
    c.   becomes a counteroffer.
    d.   has been accepted, since the modification was a contingency.

S 24. Real estate contracts that are not personal service contracts

    a.   may be assigned.
    b.   are not assignable.
    c.   must be in writing.
    d.   are exempt from the statute of frauds.

S 25. Which of the following contracts must be in writing to be enforceable?

    a.   A parol contract.
    b.   A six-month lease.
    c.   A two-year lease.
    d.   An executory contract.

S 26. Agent Bob, who works for Broker Bill, obtains an owner listing to lease a building. Bill's other agent, Sue, locates a tenant for Bob's listing. Broker Bill in this instance is

    a.   an implied agent.
    b.   a dual agent.
    c.   a single agent.
    d.   a subagent.

S 27. A transaction broker should disclose his or her agency relationship to prospective buyers and sellers

    a.   upon first substantive communication.
    b.   upon completion of the listing agreement.
    c.   immediately following completion of any offer.
    d.   immediately prior to closing.

S 28. A transaction facilitator in a residential transaction represents

    a.   the seller.
    b.   the buyer.
    c.   both seller and buyer.
    d.   neither seller nor buyer.

S 29. A principal instructs an agent to inform minority buyers that the property for lease was just leased an hour ago and is no longer available. The agent refuses to comply. In this case,

    a.   the agent should exercise caution until the listing expires, then decline to renew it.
    b.   the principal has proposed an illegal act, which should not be obeyed.
    c.   the agent is liable for breaching the listing terms.
    d.   the agent may sue the principal for discrimination and misrepresentation.

S 30. The amount of a real estate broker's commission is established by

   a. agreement among competing brokers.
   b. negotiation with clients.
   c. the local Board of Realtors®.
   d. state real estate license law.

S 31. A client revokes an exclusive right-to-sell listing two months prior to expiration. The reason stated: the client is too busy to meet with the agent. In this case,

   a. the client is criminally liable for negligence.
   b. the client may be liable for a commission and marketing expenses.
   c. the agent can sue the client for specific performance, even if no customer had been located.
   d. the agent must accept the revocation without the possibility of damage recovery.

S 32. A protection period clause in an exclusive listing provides that

   a. the owner is protected from all liabilities arising from the agent's actions performed within the agent's scope of duties.
   b. the agent has a claim to a commission if the owner sells or leases to a party within a certain time following the listing's expiration.
   c. agents are entitled to extend a listing agreement's term if a transaction is imminent.
   d. an owner is not liable for a commission if a prospective customer delays in completing an acceptable offer.

S 33. Real estate advertising must conform to regulatory standards and requirements. One requirement is

   a. a broker may only place blind ads in social media outlets.
   b. a broker must have all advertising approved by the local real estate board.
   c. the advertising must not be deceptive.
   d. sales agents may only advertise in their own name.

S 34. The three principal brokerage firms in a market agree to pay sales agents 15% more than any other competitor currently in practice. This is an example of

   a. collusion.
   b. price fixing.
   c. allocation of markets.
   d. steering.

S 35. Two leading agencies jointly agree to raise commissions charged to residential sellers to 7.5% of the sales price. Which of the following is true?

   a. This is a perfectly legitimate business practice.
   b. The brokers have illegally fixed prices.
   c. The brokers have allocated markets.
   d. The brokers have engaged in legal collusion.

S 36. A sale contract contains an open-ended financing contingency: if the buyer cannot obtain financing within a reasonable time, the deal is off. Six months later, the buyer still cannot secure financing. Which of the following is true?

   a. The seller may cancel the contract, since it can be ruled invalid.
   b. The buyer can continue indefinitely to seek financing, and the seller's property must remain off the market, since "reasonable" is not defined.
   c. The escrow agent is entitled to the buyer's deposit.
   d. The seller can force a lender to commit to a loan under fair financing laws.

S 37. In the event of a buyer's default, a provision for liquidated damages in a sale contract enables a seller to

    a.   sue the buyer for specific performance.
    b.   force the buyer to quitclaim equitable title.
    c.   sue the buyer for the broker's marketing expenses.
    d.   claim the deposit as compensated damages for the buyer's failure to perform.

S 38. Which of the following is true of an option-to-buy agreement?

    a.   The potential buyer, the optionee, is obligated to buy the property once the option agreement is completed.
    b.   The optionor must perform if the optionee takes the option, but the optionee is under no obligation to do so.
    c.   The contract can be executed at no cost to the optionee.
    d.   It is a bilateral agreement.

S 39. If a manufacturer that is the major employer in a small city moves its operations to another city, it is reasonable to expect

    a.   a fall in housing demand, but no other changes in the real estate market.
    b.   a decline in demand for all types of real estate in the real estate market.
    c.   an immediate fall in the demand for industrial real estate, but no other changes in the real estate market.
    d.   an immediate decline in the prices for industrial and office real estate, but no impact on the residential market.

S 40. If a commercial real estate market is undersupplied, it is likely that

    a.   rental prices in that market will fall.
    b.   rental prices in that market will rise.
    c.   rental prices will remain stable until equilibrium is reached.
    d.   construction will increase to the point of equilibrium.

S 41. The amount of available property that becomes occupied over a period of time is called

    a.   vacancy.
    b.   absorption.
    c.   equilibrium.
    d.   occupation.

S 42 The roof of a property cost $20,000. The economic life of the roof is 20 years. Assuming the straight-line method of depreciation, what is the depreciated value of the roof after 3 years?

    a. $20,000.
    b. $17,000.
    c. $14,000.
    d. $3,000.

S 43. The income capitalization approach to appraising value is most applicable for which of the following property types?

    a.   Single family homes.
    b.   Apartment buildings.
    c.   Undeveloped land.
    d.   Churches.

S 44. In the income capitalization approach, an appraiser

    a.   estimates gross income and multiplies times the gross income multiplier.
    b.   estimates effective income, subtracts tax, and applies a capitalization rate.
    c.   estimates net income and applies a capitalization rate to it.
    d.   estimates potential income and applies a capitalization rate to it.

S 45. Net operating income is equal to

    a.   potential income minus expenses minus debt service.
    b.   effective gross income minus potential income.
    c.   potential gross income minus vacancy and credit loss minus expenses.
    d.   effective gross income minus vacancy and credit loss.

S 46. If net income on a property is $40,000 and the cap rate is 10%, the value of the property using the income capitalization method is

    a. $100,000.
    b. $400,000.
    c. $1,000,000.
    d. $4,000,000.

S 47. The key feature of an adjustable mortgage loan is that

    a.   the interest rate may vary.
    b.   the monthly payment increases over the life of the loan.
    c.   the principal balance does not amortize.
    d.   the loan term can be shortened or lengthened.

S 48. Why is a wraparound mortgage loan potentially interesting to a home seller as an investment?

    a.   It is a senior loan that can be easily subordinated for additional debt.
    b.   A wraparound lender can profit when the interest rate of the wraparound exceeds that of the underlying mortgage.
    c.   The underlying loan is retired early.
    d.   The second mortgage borrower may make payments directly to the first mortgage lender.

S 49. A builder is required to secure a loan with mortgages on three properties. This is an example of

    a.   a participation mortgage loan.
    b.   a blanket mortgage loan.
    c.   a permanent mortgage loan.
    d.   a bridge loan.

S 50. Which of the following is true of a loan with negative amortization?

    a.   The interest rate on the loan increases as the principal balance decreases.
    b.   Payments are not sufficient to retire the loan.
    c.   The loan balance is diminishing, or going negative.
    d.   Additional interest is being added to the monthly payment.

S 51. The loan-to-value ratio is used as an underwriting mechanism because

    a.   the LTV determines the profitability of the loan.
    b.   the loan amount needs to be less than the property's value.
    c.   borrowers tend to inflate the true value of the property.
    d.   a full-price loan overfinances the borrower.

S 52. In the past, borrowers were often surprised by unexpected or undisclosed borrowing fees and expenses at closing. This phenomenon has been largely corrected through disclosure requirements mandated by which of the following laws?

    a. Equal Credit Opportunity Act
    b. Truth-in-Lending laws
    c. National Disclosure Procedures Act
    d. Federal Fair Housing Laws

S 53. Which of the following is an important function of the secondary mortgage market?

    a. Participants borrow funds from banks so the banks can make more loans.
    b. Participants issue tax certificates and sell them to primary lenders.
    c. Participants purchase pools of defaulted loans from lenders to keep them solvent.
    d. Participants sell mortgage-backed securities in order to buy pools of loans.

S 54. Cash flow is a measure of how much pre-tax or after-tax cash an investment property generates. To derive cash flow it is therefore necessary to exclude

    a. cost recovery expense.
    b. interest expense.
    c. loan principal payments.
    d. net operating income.

S 55. The method for deriving an investor's return on investment, or ROI, is by

    a. dividing net operating income by cash flow.
    b. multiplying the required yield times after-tax cash flow.
    c. dividing net income by the price paid for the property.
    d. multiplying cash flow times the price paid for the property.

S 56. Which of the following items would affect a homeowner's adjusted basis?

    a. Installing a higher capacity air conditioning and purifying system.
    b. Replacing a washing machine.
    c. Stripping and staining hardwood floors.
    d. Replacing a broken picture window.

S 57. Which of the following is true with respect to real property taxation by the federal government?

    a. It imposes ad valorem property taxes and capital gain tax.
    b. It may not impose property taxes or tax liens.
    c. There are no federal ad valorem taxes on real property.
    d. It imposes ad valorem tax, but not capital gain tax.

S 58. Ad valorem taxes are based on

    a. the replacement value of property.
    b. the assessed value of property.
    c. the millage value of property.
    d. the broker's estimate of value.

S 59. A retirement facility prohibits ownership of any unit by persons under 55 years of age. The association claims it has made the prohibition properly. Which of the following is true?

    a. They are violating the Civil Rights Act of 1866.
    b. They are violating the Fair Housing Amendments Act of 1988.
    c. They are guilty of age discrimination.
    d. The prohibition may be legal if performed correctly.

S 60. An owner suddenly pulls a property off the market after hearing from the agent on the phone that the agent had received a full-price offer from a minority party. The agent then informs the offeror that the home has been removed from the market and is unavailable. Which party or parties, if any, have violated fair housing laws?

a. The agent only.
b. The owner only.
c. The agent and the owner.
d. Neither agent nor owner.

S 61. Which of the following are examples of closing items not prorated between buyer and seller?

a. Taxes.
b. Inspection fees.
c. Utilities.
d. Condominium assessments.

S 62. Which of the following activities is not allowed under the Real Estate Settlements and Procedures Act?

a. A broker having any business relationship with an insurance company that is involved in the broker's transaction.
b. A broker pre-qualifying a buyer for a mortgage loan.
c. A lender requiring a deposit from a borrower for a tax and insurance escrow account.
d. A lender paying a fee to a broker for referring a borrower to the lender.

S 63. Which of the following communication records must (as opposed to should) be kept?

a. Notes on every conversation.
b. Copies of required communications to principals.
c. Notes from company training sessions.
d. Business cards of licensees one meets at open houses.

S 64. To minimize the risk of violating fair housing laws, a licensee should

a. refuse to use terms that refer to or describe any of the classes of persons protected by the laws.
b. avoid working in neighborhoods that are predominantly occupied by a single ethnic group.
c. make discriminatory or derogatory remarks in conversation only, never in writing.
d. give better service to members of a protected class than is standard for other clients or customers.

S 65. What are "tenant improvements?"

a. Modifications to a rental suite to conform to a tenant's usage specifications
b. Marketing programs that yield a higher quality of tenant
c. Increased revenue resulting from a rise in rental rates
d. Increased occupancy resulting from a population increase in the market area

S 66. For the proper handling of client and owner monies, a property manager is generally required to

a. deposit all funds every month in the management firm's central operating account.
b. employ a notary to witness and record every deposit or payment received.
c. maintain a special trust account in a qualified financial depository.
d. disburse all funds to their legal owners on a weekly basis.

S 67. Jennifer advised her clients they needed to paint their living room before showing the property. The walls of these rooms were all 8' high. The wall lengths were 14', 18', 16', and 18'. If a gallon of paint covers 200 SF, how many whole gallons would the homesellers have to buy?

a. 1
b. 2
c. 3
d. 6

S 68. An investor just purchased a rectangular 2-acre retail lot for $250 a frontage foot. If she paid $100,000 total, what was the depth of the lot?

a. 400'
b. 250
c. 871'
d. 218'

S 69. Andra can afford to spend $5,000 in closing costs to refinance her home. The lender quotes closing costs of $800 plus 2 points. The house appraised out at $240,000, and she can get an 80% loan. Can Annika afford to refinance?

a. No, she is short by $64.
b. No, she is short by $1,600.
c. Yes, with $360 left over.
d. Yes, she in fact breaks even.

S 70. A lender offers an investor a maximum 70% LTV loan on the appraised value of a property. If the investor pays $230,000 for the property, and this is 15% more than the appraised value, how much will the investor have to pay as a down payment?

a. $93,150
b. $79,350
c. $90,000
d. $69,000

S 71. A house is being appraised using the sales comparison approach. The house has three bedrooms, two bathrooms, and a patio. The appraiser selects a comparable house that has three bedrooms, 2.5 bathrooms, and no patio. The comparable house just sold for $100,000. A half-bath is valued at $5,000, and a patio at $1,000. Assuming all else is equal, what is the adjusted value of the comparable?

a. $100,000
b. $104,000
c. $96,000
d. $106,000

S 72. A family purchased a $90,000 lot to build a custom home. At the date of closing, the lot was assessed at $84,550 and the tax rate was $1.91 / $100 assessed valuation. When they completed the home, the assessment increased by $235,000 to include the new construction. If the monthly tax escrow is based on the assessed value, what will the monthly tax escrow be?

a. $517
b. $6096
c. $508
d. $367

S 73. The James family purchased a home for $180,000 five years ago and obtained an 80% LTV loan. Now the property has appreciated 25%. In addition, the loan has been paid down $11,000. What is the James's current equity in the home?

    a. $47,000
    b. $81,000
    c. $45,000
    d. $92,000

S 74. George and Mary have owned a rental house for 10 years. They bought it for $240,000 and estimated the land value @ 25%. If the property is depreciated on a 39-year schedule, and appreciation totals 50% over the period, what is their gain if they sell the property today?

    a. $159,230
    b. $166,150
    c. $181,538
    d. $120,000

S 75. Adelpha's home is valued at $250,000. She has insurance coverage of $160,000 with an 80% co-insurance clause. If Adelpha has a damage claim amounting to $100,000, how much will she receive from her policy?

    a. $32,000
    b. $60,000
    c. $80,000
    d. $100,000

S 76. Bank teller Barbara refers Bruce and Jackie West to real estate agent Albert. The Wests buy one of Albert's listings. Which of the following is true?

    a. Albert has violated the license laws.
    b. Barbara is practicing real estate without a license.
    c. The Wests may be required to pay a referral fee.
    d. Albert violates license law if he pays Barbara a referral fee.

S 77. To obtain a North Carolina provisional broker license, applicants must

    a. pass a 60-hour prelicense class.
    b. be at least 18 years old; pass a 75-hour prelicense class; pass the state examination; and demonstrate sufficient moral character.
    c. be at least 18 years old, pass a 165-hour prelicense class, and pass the state examination.
    d. submit an application; pass the state examination; and demonstrate sufficient moral character.

S 78. If an unlicensed employee of an active broker performs an act in violation of the NC license law, which of the following will occur?

    a. The NCREC will discipline the broker.
    b. The NCREC will discipline the employee.
    c. Both parties will be disciplined by the NCREC.
    d. Nothing; the NCREC has no jurisdiction in this case.

S 79. If a licensee changes his or her name or address, the licensee must

    a. notify the Real Estate Commission in writing within 10 days.
    b. notify the Real Estate Commission in writing within 45 days.
    c. notify his or her broker-in charge.
    d. receive prior approval from the Administrator of the Real Estate Commission.

S 80. A provisional brokers who must take the 90-hour postlicensing courses may be granted an extension of time to complete the requirement _____ if the licensee is able to prove to the Commission that he or she had an incapacitating illness or other circumstance for a significant portion of the year.

    a. for the first year's 30-hour requirement only
    b. for the first and second year's requirements only
    c. for any of the three year's requirements
    d. none of the above

S 81. According to NCREC, a provisional broker is

    a. a broker whose license may be cancelled if the broker fails to complete the continuing education requirement.
    b. a broker awaiting approval to be a broker-in-charge.
    c. a broker who must be supervised by a broker-in-charge until the provisional status is removed.
    d. a salesperson who has completed the 24-hour broker transition course.

S 82. Michelle receives her broker's license and begins practicing real estate in January. Her deadline for completing the NC continuing education requirement is

    a. the following January, one year following her licensure.
    b. before the next license renewal deadline.
    c. before her second renewal.
    d. two years following the date of initial licensure.

S 83. Louis is a salaried employee of a property manager. Which of the following activities is Louis not allowed to perform without a real estate license?

    a. Exhibiting units for lease to prospective tenants.
    b. Giving prospective tenants information about available apartments and accepting applications.
    c. Completing pre-printed form leases and accepting security deposits payable to the owner.
    d. Negotiating the amount of the security deposits or rents.

S 84. Provisional brokers may receive compensation from which of the following parties?

    a. The employing broker or broker-in-charge.
    b. The principal party to the agency agreement.
    c. The cooperating broker.
    d. All of the above.

S 85. The North Carolina Residential Property Disclosure Act (NCRPDA) applies to all of the following properties except

    a. duplexes.
    b. condominiums.
    c. single family homes.
    d. new home sales.

S 86. If a homeseller fails to deliver the property condition disclosure statement in a timely fashion, the buyer may

    a. cancel the contract within seven days following the receipt of the disclosure statement.
    b. cancel the contract within three days following the execution of the sales contract.
    c. cancel the contract within three days following the closing.
    d. cancel the contract within three days following possession.

S 87. As a rule, "first substantial contact" with regard to agency disclosure occurs at the specific point where

    a.   a telephone contact takes place.
    b.   a face-to-face encounter takes place.
    c.   a buyer or seller submits an offer to purchase or lease.
    d.   a buyer or seller begins to disclose his or her specific property needs, wants or desires.

S 88. An ad appears in the classified real estate section which reads "principals only, please call 865-5958." A prospect calls the number and the listing broker answers the phone and proceeds to sell the prospect. In this case, the agent

    a.   has not violated license laws if he is following the seller's instruction forbidding him to cooperate with other brokers.
    b.   has not violated license laws, since the ad is a classified ad.
    c.   must indicate his brokerage identity at the earliest possible opportunity.
    d.   has failed to identify his brokerage in violation of NC license laws.

S 89. Provisional brokers Jim and Frank have a commission dispute involving their respective commission splits. To resolve the dispute, the licensees must

    a.   submit the facts of the case to the North Carolina Real Estate Commission for arbitration.
    b.   submit the facts of the case to the North Carolina Real Estate Commission to initiate hearing proceedings.
    c.   settle the dispute with their broker.
    d.   abide by the commission guidelines of the North Carolina Real Estate Commission.

S 90. A provisional broker specializing in buyer brokerage explains to a walk-in buyer prospect that she would like to exclusively represent the prospect for a trial period of 30 days. At what point must the buyer representation agreement be put in writing?

    a.   Immediately.
    b.   At first substantial contact.
    c.   Prior to any offer.
    d.   Buyer agreements need not be in writing.

S 91. The publication "Working with Real Estate Agents" must be distributed

    a.   to prospective buyers before completion of an offer.
    b.   to prospective sellers prior to completing a listing agreement.
    c.   to prospective buyers immediately following execution of a representation agreement.
    d.   to prospective buyers and sellers upon first substantial contact.

S 92. What are a buyer broker's agency disclosure obligations, if any, following the initial agency disclosure to a seller?

    a.   None. The broker's initial disclosure completes the obligation.
    b.   The broker must provide written disclosure confirmation within 3 days of the initial disclosure.
    c.   The broker must provide written disclosure confirmation on or before delivery of an offer.
    d.   The broker must provide written disclosure confirmation on or before closing.

S 93. A designated agent for the seller may not disclose

    a.   the buyer's motivations for wanting the property.
    b.   what the buyer may pay for the property.
    c.   the seller's motivations or selling terms not established by the seller, unless required by law to disclose them.
    d.   material defects with the property.

S 94. According to guidelines provided by the NC Real Estate Commission, to be included in the home's living area an area must be

    a.   enclosed, finished, and connected to all other living areas.
    b.   under roof, finished, and heated.
    c.   heated, 75% finished, and attached to other living areas.
    d.   heated, finished, and directly accessible from other living areas.

S 95. Persons who feel they have been discriminated against in violation of the NC Fair Housing Act must first

    a.   file a complaint with the North Carolina Civil Rights Board.
    b.   enter a lawsuit in the appropriate court jurisdiction.
    c.   file a complaint with the North Carolina Human Relations Commission.
    d.   notify the NCREC of the violation.

S 96. In North Carolina, if an agent is representing a subdivision developer, the agent

    a.   must disclose the developer's development costs.
    b.   must warrant the marketability of the title.
    c.   must disclose whether the subdivision's streets are public or private.
    d.   may not disclose his agency relationship to a customer.

S 97. John Blake, a carpenter, performed extensive building repairs to Molly Anderson's home. Ms. Anderson, however, refused to pay John. In this case, John may recover his losses by filing a mechanic's lien, provided he

    a.   takes action to enforce the lien within 180 days following completion of the job.
    b.   gains lien priority over any other previously recorded lien.
    c.   files the lien within 30 days following the completion of the work.
    d.   gives the owner a 10-day grace period for payment.

S 98. In North Carolina, if the property manager of an investor's property is a salaried employee of the investor, the manager

    a.   must be licensed as a broker.
    b.   must be licensed as a broker or provisional broker.
    c.   need not be licensed.
    d.   is violating North Carolina license laws.

S 99. Under the Time Share Act, which of the following would be considered a time share?

    a.   The right to use a friend's home in Florida in exchange for the use of one's home in North Carolina.
    b.   A pre-paid reservation for one month in a vacation hotel.
    c.   A vacation home owned by a company for the use of employees.
    d.   The right to occupy an apartment every January for the next ten years.

S 100. According to the North Carolina Marketable Title Act,

    a.   if a person claims an interest in one's property, the claim must be made prior to any title transfer.
    b.   if a title record is free of claims for the past 30 years, the title is free and clear regardless of prior claims.
    c.   claims on title must be made within one year to be enforced.
    d.   clouds on title of any description or age prevent the property from being marketable.

S 101. In a residential transaction, seller Tyler wants to keep a swing set in the yard, and buyer Sasha wants to buy the Tyler's washing machine. What must the parties do in the sales contract to achieve these ends?

    a.   Sasha must list the personal property to be acquired in the contract. The swing set as a fixture must be sold with the property.
    b.   Tyler must list the swing set as an exclusion in the contract, but Sasha must enter into a separate agreement to purchase the washing machine using the Major Appliance Purchase Form.
    c.   The parties may not transact personal property in the sales contract.
    d.   Tyler must exclude the swing set and Sasha include the washing machine in the contract.

S 102. Assume an apartment complex goes into foreclosure. Under North Carolina law, if a tenant has a lease, what happens to the tenant as a result of the proceedings?

    a.   The tenant may be compelled to vacate, but the owner must pay the tenant's relocation expenses.
    b.   The lender and foreclosure buyer must honor the lease and all of its terms.
    c.   The tenant must vacate the premises following the closing and upon the demand of the new owner.
    d.   The tenant may forestall the proceedings via a duly filed injunction.

S 103. Neighboring owners may not cause an owner's land to shift, collapse or erode. This is best known as the right to

    a.   littoral support.
    b.   bundle.
    c.   subjacent support.
    d.   riparian support.

S 104. What is a critical distinction between a modular home and a manufactured home?

    a.   The modular home is considered and taxed as real property once assembled.
    b.   The manufactured home does not qualify for hurricane insurance whereas modular homes do.
    c.   Manufactured housing is considered real property while modular homes are personal property until affixed.
    d.   Once affixed, the manufactured dwelling remains personal property while the modular home becomes real property.

S 105. In the context of land use restrictions, licensees have a duty to disclose to clients and customers

    a.   that a property is rumored to be haunted.
    b.   that a new bridge is being constructed in the immediate vicinity.
    c.   the last time a tornado formed within five miles of the property.
    d.   that there may be a possible encroachment by abutting property owners.

Section VII: Answer Key

NATIONAL TEST 1: Rights; Interests and Estates; Ownership

1.1 (a) Wells, driveways, and signs on a parcel of land.
The legal concept of real estate encompasses land and all man-made structures that are "permanently" attached to the land. The phrase "permanently attached" refers primarily to one's intention in attaching the item. Obviously, very few if any man-made structures can be permanently attached to the land in the literal sense. But if a person constructs a house with the intention of creating a permanent dwelling, the house is considered real estate. By contrast, if a camper affixes a tent to the land with the intention of moving it to another camp in a week, the tent would not be considered real estate.

1.2 (c) A chicken coop permanently attached to land.
Improvements to real estate include such things as fences, streets, buildings, wells, sewers, sidewalks and piers. Modifications to land or a developer's preparations of a parcel of land can include such activities as grading or clearing, neither of which are considered to be "improvements" in this sense of the word.

1.3 (b) The center of the earth and infinite space above the earth.
The legal concept of land encompasses the surface area of the earth; everything beneath the surface of the earth extending downward to its center; all natural things permanently attached to the earth; and the air above the surface of the earth extending outward to infinity. Land, therefore, includes minerals beneath the earth's surface, water on or below the earth's surface, and the air above the surface.

1.4 (a) enjoyed by the owner of a property.
This group of rights includes the right to Possess, Use, Transfer, Encumber, and Exclude others from using the property. (Remember: "PUTEE") Transfer rights include the right to sell, rent, donate, assign, or bequeath. The owner may also encumber the item by mortgaging it as collateral for debt.

1.5 (b) Any item of property that is not definable as real property.
Personal property is any owned item which is not real estate, and the rights associated with owning the personal property item. Items of personal property are also called chattels or personalty.

1.6 (b) pledge the property as collateral for debt..
The right to encumber the property essentially means the right to mortgage the property as collateral for debt. There may be restrictions to this right, such as a spouse's right to limit the degree to which a homestead may be mortgaged.

1.7 (a) transfer of a portion of the bundle of rights.
An ordinary lease is a common example of the transfer of a portion of one's bundle of rights. The owner relinquishes the right to possess portions of the surface, perhaps a building, in return for rent. The tenant enjoys the rights to possess and use the building over the term of the lease, after which these rights revert to the landlord. During the lease term, the tenant has no rights to the property's subsurface or airspace other than what the building occupies. Further, the tenant does not enjoy any of the other rights in the bundle of rights: he or she cannot encumber the property or transfer it. To a limited degree, the tenant may exclude persons other than the legal owner from the property.

1.8 (d) Yes. The drones infringe on his air rights.
Air rights apply to the space above the surface boundaries of the parcel, as delineated by imaginary vertical lines extended to infinity. Since the advent of aviation, property owners' air rights have been curtailed to allow aircraft to fly over one's property provided the overflights do not interfere with the owner's use and enjoyment of the property. The issue of violation of air rights for the benefit of air transportation is an ongoing battle between aircraft owners, airlines, airports, and nearby property owners.

1.9 (c) Navigable lakes, seas, and oceans.
Littoral rights concern properties abutting bodies of water that are not moving, such as lakes and seas. Owners of properties abutting a navigable, non-moving body of water enjoy the littoral right of use, but do not own the water nor the land beneath the water. The legal premise underlying the definition of littoral

rights is that a lake or sea is a navigable body of water, therefore, public property owned by the state. By contrast, a body of water entirely contained within the boundaries of an owner's property is not navigable. In such a case, the owner would own the water as well as unrestricted rights of usage.

1.10 (a) the high water mark of the body of water at the shoreline.
Ownership extends to the high-water mark of the body of water. The low water mark would imply that the owner owned the water itself at times of high water levels!

1.11 (d) They transfer with the property when the property is sold.
Littoral rights attach to the property. When the property is sold, the littoral rights transfer with the property to the new owner.

1.12 (c) Streams and rivers.
Riparian rights concern properties abutting moving water such as streams and rivers. If a property abuts a stream or river, the owner's riparian rights are determined by whether the water is navigable or not navigable. If the property abuts a non-navigable stream, the owner enjoys unrestricted use of the water and owns the land beneath the stream to the stream's midpoint. If the waterway in question is navigable, the waterway is considered to be a public easement. In such a case, the owner's property extends t the water's edge as opposed to the midpoint of the waterway.

1.13 (b) An item of personal property that has been converted to real property.
A personal property item that has been converted to real property by attachment to real estate is called a fixture. Typical examples are chandeliers, toilets, water pumps, septic tanks, and window shutters. The owner of real property inherently owns all fixtures belonging to the real property. When the owner sells the real property, the buyer acquires rights to all fixtures.

1.14 (a) the owner originally intended to remove it after a period of time.
One's original intention can override the test of movability in determining whether an item is a fixture or not. If someone attached an item to real property, yet intended to remove it after a period of time, the article may be deemed personal property. If a person intended an article to be a fixture, even though the item is easily removable, the article may be deemed a fixture. For example, an apartment renter installs an alarm system, fully intending to remove the system upon lease expiration. Here, the alarm system would be considered personal property.

1.15 (c) Fifty percent of the estate consisting of the indivisible whole of the real property.
An undivided interest is an owner's fractional interest in an entire (undivided) estate, but not in a physical portion of the real property itself. An owner who has an undivided equal interest with another cannot exercise exclusive rights over a portion of the real estate, which is an indivisible whole.

1.16 (a) an estate in land.
Interests are principally distinguished by whether they include possession. If the interest-holder enjoys the right of possession, the party is considered to have an estate in land, or, familiarly an estate. Freehold and leasehold estates in land are further distinguished by whether the duration of the owner's rights can be determined.

1.17 (a) a public interest.
Public entities may own or lease real estate, in which case they enjoy an estate in land. However, government entities also have non-possessory interests in real estate which act to control land use for the public good within the entity's jurisdiction. The prime example of public interest is police power, or the right of the local or county government to zone. Another example of public interest is the right to acquire ownership through the power of eminent domain.

1.18 (c) a freehold estate.
In a freehold estate, the duration of the owner's rights cannot be determined: the rights may endure for a lifetime, for less than a lifetime, or for generations beyond the owner's lifetime. By contrast, leasehold estates have expirations.

1.19 (d) that the estate is limited by a lease term.
A leasehold estate is distinguished by its specific duration, as represented by the lease term. Further, leasehold tenants only enjoy limited property rights: use; temporary possession, and limited exclusion.

1.20 (d) Fee simple defeasible.
The defeasible fee estate is perpetual, provided the usage conforms to stated conditions. Essential characteristics are that the property must be used for a certain purpose or under certain conditions, and, if the use changes or if prohibited conditions are present, the estate reverts to the previous grantor of the estate.

1.21 (c) An ordinary life estate.
A life estate is limited in duration to the life of the owner or other named person. Upon the death of the owner (ordinary life estate) or other named individual (pur autre vie life estate), the estate passes to the original owner (a reversionary interest) or another named party (a remainder interest). Thus with the life estate, the owner enjoys full ownership rights during the estate period, and holders of the future interest own either a reversionary or a remainder interest.

1.22 (b) a legal life estate.
Homestead, dower, and curtesy are legal life estates. A legal life estate is created by state law as opposed to being created by a property owner's agreement. The focus of a legal life estate is defining and protecting the property rights of surviving family members upon the death of the husband or wife.

1.23 (b) The boat, house, and motorcycle.
Separate property consists of: property owned by either spouse at the time of the marriage; property acquired by either spouse through inheritance or gift during the marriage; property acquired with separate-property funds; and income from separate property. Community property consists of all other property earned or acquired by either party during the marriage. A spouse owns separate property free and clear of claims by the other spouse. He or she can transfer it without the other spouse's signature. Upon the death of the separate property owner, the property passes to heirs by will or laws of descent. Community property cannot be transferred or encumbered without the signatures of both spouses. Upon the death of either spouse, half of the deceased's community property passes to the surviving spouse, and the other half passes to the decedent's heirs.

1.24 (d) The right to possess and use the premises.
Leasehold tenants are entitled to possess and use the leased premises during the lease term in the manner prescribed in the lease. They also have restricted rights to exclusion.

1.25 (a) the tenant makes, and landlord accepts, regular rent payments.
In an estate from period-to-period, also called a periodic tenancy, the tenancy period automatically renews as long as the tenant pays rent in a timely manner and the landlord accepts it. At the end of a tenancy period, if the landlord accepts another regular payment of rent, the leasehold is considered to be renewed for another period. A conveyance of leased property does not cancel a leasehold interest.

1.26 (c) terminates on the death of lessor or lessee.
The estate at will, also called a tenancy at will, has no definite expiration date and hence no "renewal" cycle. The landlord and tenant agree that the tenancy will have no specified termination date, provided rent is paid on time and other lease conditions are met. For example, a son leases a house to his father and mother "forever," or until they want to move. The estate at will is terminated by proper notice, or by the death of either party.

1.27 (a) an estate at sufferance.
In an estate at sufferance, a tenant occupies the premises without consent of the landlord or other legal agreement with the landlord. Usually such an estate involves a tenant who fails to vacate at the expiration of the lease, continuing occupancy without any right to do so. For example, a tenant violates the provisions of a lease and is evicted. The tenant protests and refuses to leave despite the eviction order.

1.28 (b) Estate from period to period.
In an estate from period-to-period, also called a periodic tenancy, the tenancy period automatically renews for an indefinite period of time, subject to timely payment of rent. At the end of a tenancy period, if the landlord accepts another regular payment of rent, the leasehold is considered to be renewed for another period.

1.29 (a) tenancy in severalty.
If a single party owns the fee or life estate, the ownership is a tenancy in severalty. Synonyms are sole ownership, ownership in severalty, and estate in severalty.

1.30 (c) tenancy in common.
The tenancy in common, also known as the estate in common, is the most common form of co-ownership when the owners are not married (though tenants in common can be married). The defining characteristics are: two or more owners; identical rights; interests individually owned; electable ownership shares; no survivorship; and no unity of time. With "identical rights", co-tenants share an indivisible interest in the estate, i.e., all have equal rights to possess and use the property subject to the rights of the other co-tenants.

1.31 (a) Parties must acquire respective interests at the same time.
To create a joint tenancy, all owners must acquire the property at the same time, use the same deed, acquire equal interests, and share in equal rights of possession. These are referred to as the four unities.

1.32 (b) cannot will their interest to a party outside the tenancy. The survivorship feature of joint tenancy presents an advantage to tenancy in common, in that interests pass without probate proceedings. On the other hand, joint tenants relinquish any ability to will their interest to parties outside of the tenancy.

1.33 (c) Legal life estate.
A legal life estate is created by state law as opposed to being created by a property owner's agreement. The focus of a legal life estate is defining and protecting the property rights of surviving family members upon the death of the husband or wife.

1.34 (a) A homestead interest cannot be conveyed by one spouse.
A homestead is one's principal residence. Homestead laws protect family members against losing their homes to general creditors attempting to collect on debts. Homestead laws generally provide that: the homestead interest cannot be conveyed by one spouse; both spouses must sign the deed conveying homestead property.

1.35 (a) sell or transfer his interest without the consent of the other tenants in common.
All tenants in common have distinct and separable ownership of their respective interests. Co-tenants may sell, encumber, or transfer their interests without obstruction or consent from the other owners. A co-tenant may not, however, encumber the entire property.

1.36 (c) Income derived from community property
If an income-producing property has been defined as community property, the revenue accruing from the investment is likewise community property.

1.37 (c) The beneficiary
A land trust allows the trustor to convey the fee estate to the trustee and to name himself or herself the beneficiary. The land trust applies only to real property, not to personal property. The agreement, or deed in trust, grants the beneficiary the rights to possess and use the property, and to exercise control over the actions of the trustee.

1.38 (c) The Buick and the second property
Community property laws define property rights of legal spouses before, during, and after their marriage, as well as after the death of either spouse. Community property law distinguishes real and personal property into categories of separate and community property. Separate property belongs to one spouse; community property belongs to both spouses equally. Separate property is that property which is acquired prior to the marriage, by gift or inheritance during the marriage, property acquired by separate-property funds, or income from separate property.

1.39 (a) A cooperative may hold an owner liable for the unpaid operating expenses of other tenants.
Since the corporation owns an undivided interest in the cooperative property, debts and financial obligations apply to the property as a whole, not to individual units as in a condominium.

1.40 (b) The owners enjoy an indivisible interest.
The tenancy in common, also known as the estate in common, is the most common form of co-ownership when the owners are not married (though tenants in common can be married). The defining characteristics are: two or more owners; identical rights; interests individually owned; electable ownership shares; no

survivorship; and no unity of time. With "identical rights," co-tenants share an indivisible interest in the estate, i.e., all have equal rights to possess and use the property subject to the rights of the other co-tenants.

1.41 (a) sell her interest to a third party without the consent of Robert
All tenants in common have distinct and separable ownership of their respective interests. Co-tenants may sell, encumber, or transfer their interests without obstruction or consent from the other owners. A co-tenant may not, however, encumber the entire property.

1.42 (d) It passes by probate to the deceased tenant's heirs.
A deceased co-tenant's estate passes by probate to the decedent's heirs and devisees rather than to the other tenants in common. Any number of heirs can share in the ownership of the willed tenancy.

1.43 (c) The tenants have an equal and indivisible ownership interest.
In a joint tenancy, two or more persons collectively own a property as if they were a single person. Rights and interests are indivisible and equal: each has a shared interest in the whole property which cannot be divided up. Joint tenants may only convey their interests to outside parties as tenant-in-common interests. One can not convey a joint tenant interest.

1.44 (a) there is a single title to the property.
Whereas tenants in common hold separate title to their individual interests, joint tenants together hold a single title to the property. This is referred to as unity of ownership.

1.45 (a) the new owner becomes a tenant in common with the other owners, who continue to hold a joint tenancy with each other and a tenancy in common with the new owner.
A joint tenant may transfer his or her interest in the property to an outside party, but only as a tenancy in common interest. Whoever acquires the interest co-owns the property as a tenant in common with the other joint tenants. The remaining joint tenants continue to own an undivided interest in the property, less the new co-tenant's share.

1.46 (d) It passes to the surviving joint tenants.
In most states, joint tenants enjoy rights of survivorship: if a joint tenant dies, all interests and rights pass to the surviving joint tenants free from any claims of creditors or heirs. When only one joint tenant survives, the survivor's interest becomes an estate in severalty, and the joint tenancy is terminated.

1.47 (c) If they are married.
Tenancy by the entireties is a form of ownership reserved exclusively for husband and wife. It features survivorship, equal interests, and limited exposure to foreclosure. In some states it now applies to same-sex couples.

1.48 (c) The trustee.
In an estate in trust, a fee owner-- the grantor or trustor-- transfers legal title to a fiduciary-- the trustee-- who holds and manages the estate for the benefit of another party, the beneficiary. The trust may be created by a deed, will, or trust agreement.

1.49 (a) sell or mortgage the unit without impediment from individual owners of neighboring units.
Condominium units can be individually sold, mortgaged, or otherwise encumbered without interference from other unit owners. An owner may not sell interests in the apartment separately from the interest in the common elements. Unit owners exclusively possess their apartment space, but must share common areas with other owners.

1.50 (b) the unit's pro rata share of the property value as defined in the declaration.
The unit's pro rata share of the property's ownership as defined in the declaration determines the amount of a unit owner's assessment. For example, if a unit represents a 2% share of the property value, that unit owner's assessment will be 2% of the property's common area expenses.

1.51 (a) shares in a corporation or association and a proprietary lease in a physical unit.
In a cooperative, or co-op, one owns shares in a non-profit corporation or cooperative association, which in turn acquires and owns an apartment building as its principal asset. Along with this stock, the shareholder acquires a proprietary lease to occupy one of the apartment units.

1.52 (d) the corporate entity of the cooperative association.
The corporate entity of the cooperative association is the only party in the cooperative with a real property interest. The association's interest is an undivided interest in the entire property. There is no ownership interest in individual units, as with a condominium.

1.53 (a) undivided interests in the property as tenants in common.
In a freehold time-share, or interval ownership estate, tenants in common own undivided interests in the property. Expense prorations and rules governing interval usage are established by separate agreement when the estate is acquired.

NATIONAL TEST 2: Encumbrances; Liens; Title Transfer and Recording; Leases

2.1 (c) A third party's interest in a real property that limits the interests of the freehold property owner.
An encumbrance is an interest in and right to real property that limits the legal owner's freehold interest. In effect, an encumbrance is another's right to use or take possession of a legal owner's property, or to prevent the legal owner from enjoying the full bundle of rights in the estate.

2.2 (a) They involve the property that contains the easement and a non-owning party. An easement is an interest in real property that gives the holder the right to use portions of the legal owner's real property in a defined way. One cannot own an easement over one's own property. Easement rights may apply to a property's surface, subsurface, or airspace, but the affected area must be defined. An easement may be affirmative, allowing a use, such as a right-of-way, or negative, prohibiting a use, such as an airspace easement that prohibits one property owner from obstructing another's ocean view.

2.3 (d) An easement appurtenant.
An easement appurtenant gives a property owner a right of usage to portions of an adjoining property owned by another party. The property enjoying the usage right is called the dominant tenement, or dominant estate. The property containing the physical easement itself is the servient tenement, since it must serve the easement use.

2.4 (c) easement by necessity.
An easement by necessity is an easement appurtenant granted by a court of law to a property owner because of a circumstance of necessity, most commonly the need for access to a property. Since property cannot be legally landlocked, or without legal access to a public thoroughfare, a court will grant an owner of a landlocked property an easement by necessity over an adjoining property that has access to a thoroughfare.

2.5 (b) an unauthorized physical intrusion of one property into another.
An encroachment is the unauthorized, physical intrusion of one owner's real property into that of another. Examples of encroachments are: a tree limb extending into the neighbor's property, violating his or her airspace; a driveway extending beyond the lot line onto the neighbor's land; and a fence built beyond the property line.

2.6 (c) a trespasser has been using an owner's property for a certain period with the owner's knowledge but without permission.
If someone uses another's property as an easement without permission for a statutory period of time and under certain conditions, a court order may give the user the easement right by prescription, regardless of the owner's desires. For a prescriptive easement order to be granted, the following circumstances must be true: the use has been occurring without permission or license; the owner knows or is presumed to have known of the use; and the use has been generally uninterrupted over the statutory prescriptive period.

2.7 (d) how a property may be used and what improvements may be built on it.
A deed restriction is a limitation imposed on a buyer's use of a property by stipulation in the deed of conveyance or recorded subdivision plat. A deed restriction may apply to a single property or to an entire subdivision. A developer may place restrictions on all properties within a recorded subdivision plat. Subsequent re-sales of properties within the subdivision are thereby subject to the plat's covenants and conditions.

2.8 (c) the creditor's claim against the property as collateral security for the loan.
A lien is a creditor's claim against personal or real property as security for a debt of the property owner. If the owner defaults, the lien gives the creditor the right to force the sale of the property to satisfy the debt. For example, a homeowner borrows $5,000 to pay for a new roof. The lender funds the loan in exchange for the borrower's promissory note to repay the loan. At the same time, the lender places a lien on the property for $5,000 as security for the debt. If the borrower defaults, the lien allows the lender to force the sale of the house to satisfy the debt.

2.9 (d) An equitable interest.
A lienor generally has an equitable interest in the property, but not legal ownership. The exception is a mortgage lien on a property in a title-theory state. In these states, the mortgage transaction conveys legal title to the lender, who holds it until the mortgage obligations are satisfied. During the mortgage loan period, the borrower has equitable title to the property.

2.10 (a) Payment of the debt that is the subject of the lien and recording of the satisfaction.
A lien terminates on payment of the debt and recording of documents. Payment of the debt and recording of the appropriate satisfaction documents ordinarily terminate a lien. If a default occurs, a suit for judgment or foreclosure enforces the lien. These actions force the sale of the property.

2.11 (d) involuntary general lien.
A general lien is one placed against any and all real and personal property owned by a particular debtor. An example is an inheritance tax lien placed against all property owned by the heir. A specific lien attaches to a single item of real or personal property and does not affect other property owned by the debtor. In addition, judgment liens are junior, involuntary liens.

2.12 (a) Real estate tax lien.
The category of superior, or senior, liens ranks above the category of inferior, or junior, liens, meaning that superior liens receive first payment from the proceeds of a foreclosure. The superior category includes liens for real estate tax, special assessments, and inheritance tax. Other liens, including income tax liens, mortgage liens and judgment liens, are inferior.

2.13 (d) subordinate the lien.
A lienor can change the priority of a junior lien by voluntarily agreeing to subordinate, or lower, the lien's position in the hierarchy. This change is often necessary when working with a mortgage lender who will not originate a mortgage loan unless it is senior to all other junior liens on the property. The lender may require the borrower to obtain agreements from other lien holders to subordinate their liens to the new mortgage.

2.14 (c) A proceeding to enforce a lien by forcing the sale or transfer of a secured property.
All liens can be enforced by the sale or other transfer of title of the secured property, whether by court action, operation of law, or through powers granted in the original loan agreement. The enforcement proceedings are referred to as foreclosure. Note that lienors already possess equitable title, so they do not need to undertake a legal proceeding to establish this.

2.15 (b) file a foreclosure suit.
Judicial foreclosure occurs in states that use a two-party mortgage document (borrower and lender) that does not contain a "power of sale" provision. Lacking this provision, a lender must file a foreclosure suit and undertake a court proceeding to enforce the lien.

2.16 (a) strict foreclosure. Strict foreclosure is a court proceeding that gives the lender title directly, by court order, instead of giving cash proceeds from a public sale. On default, the lender gives the borrower official notice. After a prescribed period, the lender files suit in court, whereupon the court establishes a period within which the defaulting party must repay the amounts owed. If the defaulter does not repay the funds, the court orders transfer of full, legal title to the lender.

2.17 (d) A license, which terminates upon the owner's death.
A license is a personal right that a property owner grants to another to use the property for a specific purpose (to reach the kindergarten school bus). Unlike a personal easement in gross, which terminates only

on the death of the grantee (Betty Luanne, in this instance), a license is revocable at any moment, is not transferable and does not attach to the land. It ceases on the death of either party, or on the sale of the property.

2.18 (d) Dominant tenement.
An easement appurtenant gives a property owner a right of usage to portions of an adjoining property owned by another party. The property enjoying the usage right is called the dominant tenement, or dominant estate. The property containing the physical easement itself is the servient tenement, since it must serve the easement use.

2.19 (b) a deed restriction.
A private party who wants to control the quality and standards of a property can establish a deed restriction. Deed restrictions take precedence over zoning ordinances if they are more restrictive.

2.20 (a) It involves a monetary claim against the value of a property.
A lien is a creditor's claim against personal or real property as security for a debt of the property owner. If the owner defaults, the lien gives the creditor the right to force the sale of the property to satisfy the debt. Liens do not necessarily alter the property value. Liens can be involuntary as well as voluntary. Finally, liens attach to the property, but so do other encumbrances.

2.21 (d) It is knowledge received or imparted through direct experience.
The term "notice" is synonymous with "knowledge." A person who has received actual notice has actual knowledge of something. Receiving actual notice means learning of something through direct experience or communication. Thus, a document in itself cannot be actual notice. It is the seeing of the document that makes it actual notice.

2.22 (b) It is knowledge one could have or should have obtained.
Constructive notice, or legal notice, is knowledge of a fact that a person could have or should have obtained. The foremost method of imparting constructive notice is by recordation of ownership documents in public records, specifically, title records. Since public records are open to everyone, the law generally presumes that when evidence of ownership is recorded, the public at large has received constructive notice of ownership.

2.23 (a) grant, deed, and will.
Voluntary transfer, or voluntary alienation, is an unforced transfer of title by sale or gift from an owner to another party. If the transferor is a government entity and the recipient is a private party, the conveyance is a public grant. If the transferor is a private party, the conveyance is a private grant. A living owner makes a private grant by means of a deed of conveyance, or deed. A private grant that occurs when the owner dies is a transfer by will.

2.24 (c) It gives constructive notice of ownership.
Recording is not necessary to make a deed valid. However, it is in the grantee's best interests to do so. Recording the deed gives the public constructive notice of the grantee's ownership.

2.25 (b) granting clause.
The granting, or premises, clause is the only required clause. It contains the conveyance intentions; names the parties; describes the property; and indicates a nominal consideration.

2.26 (a) general warranty deed.
The general warranty deed, or warranty deed for short, contains the fullest possible assurances of good title and protection for the grantee. The deed is technically a bargain and sale deed in which the grantor promises to defend against any and all claims to the title. The overall general warranty covenant is: "I own and will defend."

2.27 (d) To have an encumbrance removed if the lienholder cannot prove its validity.
Where there is a possibility that prior errors in deeds or other recorded documents might cloud (encumber) the title, the relevant parties execute a quitclaim deed to convey "any and all" interest to the grantee. If a party responsible for encumbering title refuses to quitclaim the interest, the owner may file a quiet title suit. This requires the lienor to prove the validity of an interest. If the defendant is unable to do so, the court removes the cloud by decree.

2.28 (a) A transfer tax based on the price of the property being conveyed.
State law usually requires payment of a documentary stamp tax on a conveyance of real property. The tax is based on the actual price of the property conveyed, thus enabling taxing authorities to ascertain current market value for ad valorem tax purposes. Payment of the tax is evidenced on the deed.

2.29 (b) probate.
A court proceeding called probate generally settles a decedent's estate, whether the person has died testate (having left a valid will) or intestate (having failed to do so).

2.30 (a) It will escheat to the state or county.
If an intestate decedent has no heirs, the estate escheats, or reverts, to the state or county after all claims and debts have been validated and settled.

2.31 (d) Eminent domain.
Various government and public entities can transfer private property to the public sphere by the power of eminent domain. The transfer is involuntary, even though the owner receives compensation. For example, a city government wants to widen a highway to accommodate growth. The government uses eminent domain to condemn and purchase all properties abutting the thoroughfare in order to complete the construction project.

2.32 (a) openly possessing and claiming the property without the owner's consent.
To claim legal title, the adverse possessor must be able to show a claim of right or color of title as reason for the possession; have notorious possession, which is possession without concealment; maintain a consistent claim of hostile possession, which is a claim to ownership and possession regardless of the owner's claims or consent; occupy the property continuously for a statutory period of time; in some states, pay taxes.

2.33 (c) The buyer.
Title records protect the buyer by revealing whether a property has marketable title, one free of undesirable encumbrances. The buyer is legally responsible for knowing the condition of title, since it is a matter of public record.

2.34 (a) a clouded title.
Chain of title refers to the succession of property owners of record dating back to the original grant of title from the state to a private party. If there is a missing link in the chronology of owners, or if there was a defective conveyance, the chain is said to be broken, resulting in a clouded title to the property.

2.35 (b) standard owner's title insurance policy.
An owner's policy may have standard coverage or extended coverage. Standard coverage protects against title defects such as incompetent grantors, invalid deeds, fraudulent transaction documents, and defects in the chain of title. Extended coverage protects against liabilities that may not be of public record, including fraud, unrecorded ownership claims, unintentional recording errors, and unrecorded liens.

2.36 (a) voluntary alienation.
Voluntary alienation is an unforced transfer of title by sale or gift from an owner to another party.

2.37 (d) A quitclaim deed.
A quitclaim deed transfers real and potential interests in a property, whether an interest is known to exist or not. The grantor makes no claim to any interest in the property being conveyed and offers no warrants to protect the grantee. Where there is a possibility that prior errors in deeds or other recorded documents might cloud (encumber) the title, the relevant parties execute a quitclaim deed to convey "any and all" interest to the grantee.

2.38 (a) pass to the heirs by the laws of descent and distribution.
In this circumstance, the estate, including real property, will pass to lawful heirs according to the state's laws of descent and succession or distribution. These laws apportion the estate without regard to the wishes of the heirs or the intentions of the decedent. Escheat, by which the state takes the property, applies only if there are no legal heirs.

2.39 (d) declined because possession was secretive.
One of the preconditions for a claim of ownership based on adverse possession is notorious possession, or possession without concealment. Even if the length of possession in this case meets the statutory requirement, the drifter's secretiveness would invalidate the claim.

2.40 (b) free of undisclosed defects and encumbrances.
Marketable title is, by definition, one that is free and clear of undesirable and unknown encumbrances, claims, clouds, or other defects. Attorney's abstracts and title certificates do not guarantee that a title is marketable.

2.41 (c) Estate at will.
Three of the four principal types of leasehold estate are: the estate for years, which has a specific lease term; the estate from period-to-period, where the lease term of a specific period automatically renews; and the estate at will, which has no specified lease term. The fourth principal type, the estate at sufferance, is a tenancy without consent that therefore also has no specific term.

2.42 (b) for specified reasonable purposes.
A tenant has the sole right to occupy and use the premises without interference from outside parties, including the landlord. The landlord may enter the premises for specified purposes such as inspections, but the interference must be reasonable and limited. In addition, the landlord can do nothing outside of the lease's express provisions that would impair the tenant's enjoyment of income deriving from use of the premises.

2.43 (a) compliance with the rules and regulations of the building.
The lease defines the tenant's obligations, which principally are to pay the rent on time; maintain the property's condition; and comply with the rules and regulations of the building.

2.44 (b) providing required building support and services.
The lease defines the landlord's obligations, which principally are to provide the necessary building support and services, and maintain the condition of the property. It is the tenant's responsibility to obtain insurance and to determine the fairness of the rent.

2.45 (d) the tenant's estate is still obligated under the lease.
A valid lease creates obligations that survive the death of the landlord or tenant, with certain exceptions. A tenant's estate remains liable for payment of rent if the tenant dies; the landlord's estate remains bound to provide occupancy despite the landlord's death.

2.46 (a) The remaining tenant is responsible for the full rent obligation.
Multiple tenants who sign a single lease are jointly and severally responsible for fulfilling lease obligations. Thus, if one renter abandons an apartment, the other renters remain liable for rent.

2.47 (c) sublease.
Subletting (subleasing) is the transfer by a tenant, the sublessor, of a portion of the leasehold interest to another party, the sublessee, through the execution of a sublease. The sublease spells out all of the rights and obligations of the sublessor and sublessee, including the payment of rent to the sublessor. The sublessor remains primarily liable for the original lease with the landlord. The subtenant is liable only to the sublessor.

2.48 (d) net lease.
A net lease requires a tenant to pay for utilities, internal repairs, and a proportionate share of taxes, insurance, and operating expenses in addition to rent. In effect, the landlord "passes through" actual property expenses to the tenant rather than charging a higher rent level. Net leases vary as to exactly what expenses the tenant is responsible for. The purest form of net lease requires tenants to cover all expenses, including major repairs and property taxes.

2.49 (a) gross lease.
A gross lease, or full service lease, requires the landlord to pay the property's operating expenses, including utilities, repairs, and maintenance, while the tenant pays only rent. Rent levels under a gross lease are higher than under a net lease, since the landlord recoups expense outlays in the form of added rent.

2.50 (b) An owner-developer wants to retain ownership of the land portion of the improved real property.
Ground leases are primarily used when an owner wishes to lease raw land to an agricultural or mining interest; when unimproved property is to be developed and the owner wants to retain ownership of the land; when the developer or future users of the property do not want to own the land; or when the owner of an improved property wishes to sell an interest in the improvements while retaining ownership of the underlying land.

2.51 (a) either party giving proper notice.
In the absence of an explicit term with beginning and ending date, a court will generally construe the lease to be a tenancy at will, cancelable upon proper notice.

2.52 (b) a tenancy from period-to-period.
URLTA sets standards for improving oral, vague, or unbalanced lease agreements. In the case of an unclear lease expiration date, the lease is generally deemed to be a periodic tenancy.

2.53 (a) a hotel.
State laws based on URLTA generally do not apply to transient occupancies, such as hotel and motel rentals, proprietary leases in cooperatives, or to occupancy in a residence that is under a contract for deed.

2.54 (c) a temporary possessory interest.
A lease is both an instrument of conveyance and a contract between principal parties to uphold certain covenants and obligations. As a conveyance, a lease conveys an interest, called the leasehold estate, but does not convey legal title to the property. For this reason, a leasehold is also called a less-than-freehold estate.

2.55 (d) A leased fee estate.
In conveying the leasehold estate, the landlord acquires a leased fee estate, which entails the rights to: receive rent; re-possess the property following the lease term; and monitor the tenant's obligations to maintain the premises.

2.56 (c) occupy the property.
The legal essence of a valid lease is that it conveys an exclusive right to use and occupy a property for a limited period of time in exchange for rent and the return of the property after the lease term is over.

2.57 (a) The buyer acquires title subject to the lease, which remains in effect.
The landlord may sell, assign, or mortgage the leased fee interest. However, transferring and encumbering the leased property do not extinguish the obligations and covenants of a lease. Buyers and creditors, therefore, must take their respective interests subject to the terms of the lease.

2.58 (c) When either party gives proper notice.
In the absence of an explicit term with beginning and ending date, a court will generally construe the lease to be a tenancy at will, cancelable upon proper notice.

2.59 (c) a five-year lease must be in writing to be enforceable.
Generally, a lease for a period exceeding one year cannot be oral but must be in writing to be enforceable because of the statute of frauds.

2.60 (b) The original tenant retains primary responsibility for performance of the original lease contract.
In a sublease-- a transfer of a portion of the leasehold-- the sublessor (original tenant) remains primarily liable for the original lease with the landlord. The subtenant is liable only to the sublessor.

NATIONAL TEST 3: Land Use Regulation & Control; Legal Descriptions; Contract Law

3.1 (d) Zoning ordinances are a primary means of keeping land use in harmony with the master plan.
The master plan fuses state and regional land use laws with local land use objectives that correspond to the municipality's social and economic conditions. The completed plan becomes the overall guideline for creating and enforcing zones, building codes, and development requirements.

3.2 (c) specify usage for every parcel within the zoning authority's jurisdiction.
The intent of zoning ordinances is to specify land usage for every parcel within the jurisdiction. In some areas, state laws permit zoning ordinances to apply to areas immediately beyond the legal boundaries of the city or county.

3.3 (b) To separate land uses so that they do not interfere with each other.
One of the primary applications of zoning power is the separation of residential properties from commercial and industrial uses. Proper design of land use in this manner preserves the aesthetics and value of neighborhoods and promotes the success of commercial enterprises through intelligently located zones. Six common types of zone are: residential; commercial; industrial; agricultural; public; and planned unit development (PUD).

3.4 (c) The public interest
The principal forms of exceptions to a conforming use is legal nonconforming use (grandfathered in); variance based on hardship; and special exception based on the public interest.

3.5 (d) The area of a commercial or industrial facility in relation to the size of the site.
Commercial zoning regulates intensity of usage by limiting the area of store or office per site area. Intensity regulation is further achieved by minimum parking requirements, setbacks, and building height restrictions.

3.6 (c) It requires that multiple tracts of land be developed according to a single design.
Planned unit development zoning restricts use to development of whole tracts that are designed to use space efficiently and maximize open space. A PUD zone may be for residential, commercial, or industrial uses, or combinations thereof.

3.7 (a) A homeowner in a residential zone converts her residence to a private school.
A legal nonconforming use can be illustrated as follows. A motel is situated in a residential area that no longer allows commercial activity. The zoning board rules that the motel may continue to operate until it is sold, destroyed or used for any other commercial purpose. An illegal nonconforming use is one that conflicts with ordinances that were in place before the use commenced. For instance, if the motel in the previous example is sold, and the new owner continues to operate the property as a motel, the motel is now an illegal, nonconforming use.

3.8 (b) A variance is granted by the zoning board if the owner has a justifiable reason.
A nonconforming use is one that clearly differs from current zoning and is subject to change upon conveyance. A zoning variance allows a use that differs from the applicable ordinance for a variety of justifiable reasons.

3.9 (c) certificate of occupancy.
Building inspectors inspect a new development or improvement for code compliance. If the work complies, the municipality or county issues a certificate of occupancy which officially clears the property for occupation and use.

3.10 (c) It conveys legal title to the acquiring entity.
Eminent domain allows a government entity to purchase a fee, leasehold, or easement interest in privately owned real property for the public good, regardless of the owner's desire to sell or otherwise transfer any interest. In exchange for the interest, the government pays the owner a "just" compensation. To acquire a property, the public entity initiates a condemnation suit. Transfer of title extinguishes all existing leases,

liens, and other encumbrances on the property.

3.11 (d) parties responsible for improper disposal of hazardous waste could be charged for the cleanup costs.
Under CERCLA and the Superfund Amendment of 1986, current landowners as well as previous owners of a property may be held liable for environmental violations, even if "innocent" of a violation. Sellers often carry the greatest exposure, and real estate licensees may be held liable for improper disclosure.

3.12 (a) Individual property rights and the public's interest.
The optimum management of real property usage must take into account both the interests of the individual and the interests of the surrounding community. While maintaining the value of an individual estate is important, the owner of an estate must realize that unregulated use and development can jeopardize the value not only of the owner's estate but of neighboring properties.

3.13 (c) police power.
At the local level, county and city governments control land use through the authority known as police power. The most common expressions of police power are county and municipal zoning.

3.14 (d) The owner must sell the property in exchange for market-value compensation.
Eminent domain allows a government entity to purchase a fee, leasehold, or easement interest in privately owned real property for the public good, regardless of the owner's desire to sell or otherwise transfer any interest. In exchange for the interest, the government pays the owner a "just" compensation.

3.15 (a) reasonably promote community health, safety and welfare.
Local planners do not have unlimited authority to do whatever they want. Their zoning ordinances must be clear in import, apply to all parties equally, and promote health, safety, and welfare of the community in a reasonable manner.

3.16 (d) To ensure that improvements comply with codes.
Local governments enforce zoning ordinances by issuing building permits to those who want to improve, repair, or refurbish a property. To receive a permit, the project must comply with all relevant ordinances and codes.

3.17 (b) To regulate the density of dwellings in the residential zone.
Residential zoning regulates density, by limiting the number and size of dwelling units and lots in an area.

3.18 (a) a special exception.
A special exception grant authorizes a use that is not consistent with the zoning ordinance in a literal sense, yet is clearly beneficial or essential to the public welfare and does not materially impair other uses in the zone.

3.19 (c) a legal nonconforming use.
An illegal nonconforming use is one that conflicts with ordinances that were in place before the use commenced. For instance, if a motel that was allowed as a legal nonconforming use is sold, and the new owner continues to operate the property as a motel, the motel is now an illegal, nonconforming use.

3.20 (b) a plat of subdivision.
In addition to complying with zoning ordinances, a developer of multiple properties in a subdivision must meet requirements for subdivisions, including submission of a plat of subdivision.

3.21 (a) accurately identifies the boundaries of the property as distinct from all other properties.
A legal description of real property is one which accurately locates and identifies the boundaries of the subject parcel to a degree acceptable by courts of law in the state where the property is located. The general criterion for a legal description is that it alone provides sufficient data for a surveyor to locate the parcel. A legal description identifies the property as unique and distinct from all other properties.

3.22 (c) reference points, angles, and distances.
A metes and bounds description identifies the boundaries of a parcel of real estate using reference points, distances, and angles. The description always identifies an enclosed area by starting at an origination point, called point of beginning, or POB, and returning to the POB at the end of the description.

3.23 (b) two consecutive common meridians.
The "vertical" area between consecutive meridians is called a range. A range is identified by its relationship to the principal meridian. All ranges are six miles wide.

3.24 (c) two consecutive parallels.
The "horizontal" area between two parallels is called a tier, or a township strip. A tier is identified by its relationship to the base parallel. All tiers are six miles wide.

3.25 (b) Six miles by six miles, or 6 miles square.
A township is the area enclosed by the intersection of two consecutive meridians and two consecutive parallels. Since the parallels and meridians are six miles apart, a township is a square with six miles on each side. Its area is therefore 36 square miles. Remember to differentiate square miles from miles square: 4 square miles is a measure of area (2 miles x 2 miles); 4 miles square is a representation of the sides of a square (4 miles by 4 miles).

3.26 (d) 1/64.
The size in acres of a subsection of a township is a fraction of 640 acres, since there are 640 acres in a section. Thus ten acres is 10/640, or 1/64th of a section.

3.27 (d) properties in a subdivision.
The recorded plat method, also called the lot and block system, is used to describe properties in residential, commercial, and industrial subdivisions. Under this system, tracts of land are subdivided into lots. The entire group of lots comprises the subdivision. In a large subdivision, lots may be grouped together into blocks for ease of reference.

3.28 (c) Metes and bounds.
A metes and bounds description identifies the point of beginning and describes the distance and direction from that point to the first monument, and thence to subsequent monuments and back to the beginning to define the property's enclosed perimeter.

3.29 (d) Thirty-six.
The rectangular survey system divides a township into thirty-six sections.

3.30 (a) 640.
Each side of a section is one mile in length. Thus the area of a section is one square mile, or 640 acres.

3.31 (c) something of value traded in exchange for something of value.
A contract must contain a two-way exchange of valuable consideration as compensation for performance by the other party. The contract is not valid or enforceable if just one party provides consideration. Valuable consideration may be something of tangible value, such as money, or something the party promises to do. It may also be something intangible that a party must give up.

3.32 (a) contain a legal description of the property.
In addition to satisfying the requirements of a valid contract in general, a contract that conveys an interest in real estate must be in writing, contain a legal description of the property, and be signed by one or more of the parties.

3.33 (d) A reasonable time, or until the expiration date on the offer.
If an offer contains an expiration date and the phrase "time is of the essence," the offer expires at exactly the time specified. In the absence of a stated time period, the offeree has a "reasonable" time to accept an offer.

3.34 (b) The buyer's death terminated the offer.
Any of the following actions or circumstances can terminate an offer: acceptance; rejection; revocation; lapse of time; counteroffer; or death or insanity of either party.

3.35 (c) A contract for the sale of undeveloped land.
A real estate contract that is not a personal contract for services can be assigned to another party unless the terms of the agreement specifically prohibit assignment. Listing agreements, for example, are not

assignable, since they are personal service agreements between agent and principal. Sales contracts, however, are assignable, because they involve the purchase of real property rather than a personal service.

3.36 (b) the parties act is if there is a contract.
An implied contract is an unstated or unintentional agreement that may be deemed to exist when the actions of any of the parties suggest the existence of an agreement.

3.37 (b) A sale contract before closing.
An executory contract is one in which performance is yet to be completed. A sales contract prior to closing is executory: while the parties have agreed to buy and sell, the buyer has yet to pay the seller and the seller has yet to deed the property to the buyer.

3.38 (a) both parties promise to do something in exchange for the other party's performance.
A bilateral contract is one in which both parties promise to perform their respective parts of an agreement in exchange for performance by the other party. An example of a bilateral contract is an exclusive listing: the broker promises to exercise due diligence in the efforts to sell a property, and the seller promises to compensate the broker when and if the property sells.

3.39 (c) The broker may have a claim for marketing expenses expended during the listing term.
The damaged party may elect the following legal remedies: rescission; forfeiture; suit for damages; or suit for specific performance. However, the broker must show that the seller has breached the contract.

3.40 (d) the failure of a party to perform according to the terms of the contract.
A breach of contract is a failure to perform according to the terms of the agreement.

3.41 (b) The act of declaring that a contract is no longer in effect for a given party.
Parties to a contract may rescind a contract by mutual consent, or a damaged party may rescind the contract unilaterally. This act of rescission cancels the contract and returns the parties to their pre-contract condition, including the refunding of any monies already transferred.

3.42 (a) reflect a mutual understanding or agreement.
Mutual consent, also known as offer and acceptance and meeting of the minds, requires that a contract involve a clear and definite offer and an intentional, unqualified acceptance of the offer.

3.43 (c) unenforceable.
A valid contract that is in writing is enforceable within a statutory time period. A valid contract that is made orally is also generally enforceable within a statutory period, with the exception that some contracts are enforceable only if they are in writing. These laws apply in particular to the transfer of interests in real estate. A void or voidable contract was not a truly valid contract.

3.44 (b) is possibly valid and enforceable.
Incompetent parties, or parties of "unsound mind," may not enter into enforceable contracts. However, during the period of one's incompetency, a court may appoint a guardian who may act on the incompetent party's behalf with court approval.

3.45 (c) a counteroffer.
By changing any of the terms of an offer, the offeree creates a counteroffer, and the original offer is void. At this point, the offeree becomes the offeror, and the new offeree gains the right of acceptance. If accepted, the counteroffer becomes a valid contract provided all other requirements are met.

3.46 (d) valuable consideration.
Valuable consideration can be something of tangible value, such as money, or something a party promises to do or not do. For example, a home builder may promise to build a house for a party as consideration for receiving money from the home buyer.

3.47 (c) is void.
The content, promise, or intent of a contract must be lawful. A contract that proposes an illegal act is void.

3.48 (a) must act within a statutory period.
The statute of limitations restricts the time period for which an injured party in a contract has the right to

rescind or disaffirm the contract. A party to a voidable contract must act within the statutory period.

3.49 (b) require certain conveyance-related contracts to be in writing.
The statute of frauds requires that certain contracts must be in writing to be enforceable. Real estate contracts that convey an interest in real property fall in this category, with the exception that a lease of one year's duration or less may be oral.

3.50 (b) The buyer has no obligations to the seller whatsoever.
The mutual consent required for a valid contract is reached through the process of offer and acceptance. If the offeree accepts all terms without amendment, the offer becomes a contract. The exact point at which the offer becomes a contract is when the offeree gives the offeror notice of the acceptance. If an offer contains an expiration date and the phrase "time is of the essence," the offer expires at exactly the time specified.

NATIONAL TEST 4: Agency; Listing Agreements

4.1 (b) the laws of agency, or in some states, by statute.
In every state, a body of law, generally called the law of agency, defines and regulates the legal roles of this relationship. While the relationship is subject to contract law, agency law dictates how the relationship will achieve its purposes, regardless of what the listing contract states.

4.2 (c) The relationship is independent of any compensation arrangement.
It is important to understand that the agency relationship does not require compensation or any form of consideration. Nor does compensation define an agency relationship: a party other than the principal may compensate the agent.

4.3 (c) The defaulting party may have a financial consequence.
Involuntary termination of the relationship may create legal and financial liability for a party who defaults or cancels. For example, a client may renounce an agreement but then be held liable for the agent's expenses or commission.

4.4 (b) present all offers to the principal regardless of their amount.
A conventional listing agreement does not authorize an agent to obligate the client to contracts, and it does not allow the agent to conceal offers to buy, sell, or lease coming from a customer or another agent. Further, since a client relies on a broker's representations, a broker must exercise care not to offer advice outside of his or her field of expertise.

4.5 (c) confidentiality.
The confidentiality standard is one of the duties that extends beyond the termination of the listing: at no time in the future may the agent disclose confidential information.

4.6 (d) comparable to that of other practitioners in the area.
The agent is hired to do a job, and is therefore expected to do it with diligence and reasonable competence. Competence is generally defined as a "standard of practice" equal to the level of real estate marketing skills and knowledge of other practitioners in the area.

4.7 (c) disclose the information to the seller.
An agent has the duty to inform the client of all material facts, reports, and rumors that might affect the client's interests in the property transaction. This includes: the agent's opinion of the property's condition; information about the buyer's motivations and financial qualifications; discussions between agent and buyer regarding the possibility of the agent's representing the buyer in another transaction.

4.8 (a) the Andersons.
Since Gerry executed an agency agreement with the Andersons, they become the client and the Lincolns the customer, regardless of who pays the commission.

4.9 (c) a broker who has an agency relationship with a client.
In a subagency, a broker or licensed salesperson works as the agent of a broker who is the agent of a client.

Subagents might include a cooperating licensed broker, that broker's licensed salespeople, and the listing broker's licensed salespeople, all of whom agree to work for the listing broker on behalf of the client.

4.10 (b) One agent represents both sides in a transaction.
Dual agency means representing both principal parties to a transaction. The agent represents both buyer and seller or tenant and owner.

4.11 (c) disclosing material facts that affect the value of the property to both parties.
In the role of facilitator, the broker's only fiduciary duties and standards of conduct are those of accounting; skill, care, and diligence; honesty and fair dealing; and disclosure to both parties of all material facts in residential sale transactions affecting the property's value. Some states do not allow for this form of relationship in a real estate transaction.

4.12 (a) The agent is showing the client's property to a prospective buyer.
Agency disclosure must occur upon "substantive contact" between the listing agent and a customer. Examples of substantive contact include: showing the prospect a property; eliciting confidential information from a prospect regarding needs, motivation, or financial qualification; and executing a contractual offer to sell or lease.

4.13 (d) trust, confidence, and good faith.
The essence of the agency relationship is trust, confidence, and mutual good faith. The principal trusts the agent to exercise the utmost skill and care in fulfilling the authorized activity, and to promote the principal's best interests. The agent undertakes to strive in good faith to achieve the desired objective, and to fulfill the fiduciary duties.

4.14 (b) general.
In a general agency, the principal delegates to the agent ongoing tasks and duties within a particular business or enterprise. Such delegation may include the authority to enter into contracts.

4.15 (b) special.
Under a special agency agreement, the principal delegates authority to conduct a specific activity, after which the agency relationship terminates. In most cases, the special agent may not bind the principal to a contract. Real estate brokerage is commonly based on a special agency.

4.16 (c) a party creates an agency relationship outside of an express agreement.
An agency relationship can arise by implication, intentionally or unintentionally. Implication means that the parties act as if there were an agreement. For example, if an agent promises a buyer to do everything possible to find a property at the lowest possible price, and the buyer accepts the proposition, there may be an implied agency relationship even though there is no specific agreement.

4.17 (a) Condemnation of the property
An agency relationship may terminate contrary to the wishes of the parties by reason of: death or incapacity of either party; abandonment by the agent; condemnation or destruction of the property; renunciation; breach; bankruptcy; or revocation of the agent's license.

4.18 (a) The agent has violated the duty of confidentiality.
An agent may not disclose any information that would harm the client's interests or bargaining position, or anything else the client wishes to keep secret. The confidentiality standard is one of the duties that extends beyond the termination of the listing: at no time in the future may the agent disclose confidential information.

4.19 (b) the agent has not violated fiduciary duty.
Since it is illegal to refuse to show buyers the property based on where the buyers live, the agent has not violated fiduciary duty. The duty of obedience only applies to legal activities.

4.20 (d) inform the seller.
An agent has the duty to inform the client of all material facts, reports, and rumors that might affect the client's interests in the property transaction.

4.21 (a) prior to completing a listing agreement.
An agent who intends to represent a seller or owner must disclose the import of the proposed agency relationship in writing before the listing agreement is executed.

4.22 (c) Whenever substantive communication is made beyond casual conversation.
A listing agent must disclose in writing to a buyer or tenant that the agent represents the owner in the transaction. This disclosure must occur before or at the first "substantive contact" with the customer prospect. In some states, buyer representatives must disclose the agency relationship to sellers or their agents upon initial contact.

4.23 (b) upon initial contact.
A buyer agent must disclose the agency relationship to the seller or seller's agent on first contact. Substantive contact is assumed to occur immediately in this circumstance.

4.24 (a) may not represent one party's interests to the detriment of the other.
A dual agent's first duty is to disclose the agency relationship to both principal parties or to withdraw from one side of the duality. After disclosing, the agent must obtain the written consent of both parties. If both parties accept the dual agency, the agent owes all the fiduciary duties to both parties except full disclosure, undivided loyalty, and exclusive representation of one principal's interests.

4.25 (d) practicing law without a license.
An agent should not act or speak outside the agent's area of expertise. A customer may rely on anything an agent says, and the agent will be held accountable. For example, an agent represents that a property will appreciate. The buyer interprets this as expert investment advice and buys the property. If the property does not appreciate, the buyer may hold the agent liable.

4.26 (a) Fiduciary and contractual obligations with the client.
A listing agreement establishes an agency relationship between agent and client that commits the agent to the full complement of fiduciary duties to the client in fulfilling the agreement.

4.27 (d) market, sell and show the property.
Special agency limits the scope of the broker's authority to specific activities, generally those which generate customers and catalyze the transaction. A special agency agreement usually does not authorize a broker to obligate the client to a contract as a principal party. Normally, principals do not delegate the authority to negotiate price to an agent in a residential transaction.

4.28 (b) An implied agency may have been created, with obligations to perform for both seller and agent.
Clients and agents may also create an implied agency listing based on substantive actions rather than on an express agreement. For example, if a seller allows a broker to undertake certain activities toward effecting a transaction without a specific authorization, but with full knowledge and consent, an implied agency may have been created.

4.29 (a) The agent cannot assign the listing agreement.
Since a listing agreement is a personal service contract, it is not assignable. In particular, a broker cannot assign a listing to another broker.

4.30 (b) exclusive right to sell.
The exclusive right to sell listing, or "exclusive," gives the agent the most control over the property and the greatest likelihood of being compensated for his or her marketing efforts.

4.31 (c) A listing that is entered in a multiple listing service to enable cooperation with member brokers.
Though not a distinct type of listing agreement, multiple listing is a significant feature of brokerage practice. Multiple listing is an authorization to enter a listing in a multiple listing service.

4.32 (b) The customer must be legally competent to undertake the transaction.
Effecting a completed transaction means finding a customer who is not only ready, willing, and able, but one who makes an acceptable offer. A ready, willing, and able customer is one who is: amenable to the terms of the transaction (ready and willing), and is financially capable of paying the price and legally

capable of completing the transaction (able).

4.33 (a) obtain and distribute compensation.
In the normal course of business, a listing broker delegates marketing responsibilities to salespeople. A salesperson may not, however, seek compensation directly from a client. Only the broker can obtain and disburse the compensation.

4.34 (c) Perry, since he found the customer.
The two principal determinants of procuring cause are being first to find the customer, and being the one who induces the customer to complete the transaction.

4.35 (d) It may be terminated against the agent's will.
A listing may terminate on grounds of: performance; infeasibility; mutual agreement; revocation; abandonment; breach; lapse of time; invalidity of the contract; incapacitation of either party; destruction of the property; or, in this case; involuntary title transfer.

4.36 (b) Sue the broker for money damages.
If the broker cancels the listing or otherwise defaults, the client may sue the broker for money damages.

4.37 (b) exclusive agency agreement.
An exclusive agency listing authorizes a single broker to sell the property and earn a commission, but leaves the owner the right to sell the property without the broker's assistance, in which case no commission is owed.

4.38 (c) open listing.
An open listing is a non-exclusive authorization to sell or lease a property. The owner may offer such agreements to any number of brokers in the marketplace. With an open listing, the broker who is the first to perform under the terms of the listing is the sole party entitled to a commission.

4.39 (d) net listing.
A net listing is one in which an owner sets a minimum acceptable amount to be received from the transaction and allows the broker to have any amount received in excess as a commission, assuming the broker has earned a commission according to the other terms of the agreement.

4.40 (a) the client.
Generally, buyer and tenant representation agreements are subject to the same laws and regulations as those applying to owner listings. The only difference is the client and his or her transaction expectations.

4.41 (a) To list the owner's property in a multiple listing service.
A multiple listing is not a distinct listing contract but rather a provision in an exclusive listing authorizing the broker to place the listing into a multiple listing service. A multiple listing service is an organization of member brokers who agree to cooperate in the sale of properties listed by other brokers in exchange for a share of the broker's resulting commission.

NATIONAL TEST 5: Brokerage Business; Sale Contracts

5.1 (d) Non-profit corporation.
A non-profit corporation is a corporate entity which is not legally entitled to generate profit. A non-profit organization may not broker real estate.

5.2 (c) are properly licensed.
A joint venture is a partnership formed to complete a specific business endeavor, such as a real estate development. Individuals, general and limited partnerships, and corporations may participate. A joint venture may broker real estate, provided the co-venturers are duly licensed.

5.3 (b) a single employing broker who has an active broker's license.
Only a broker with an active broker's license can hire and employ a licensed salesperson. A licensed salesperson may work only for the employing broker and may not work for or receive direct compensation from any other broker.

220

5.4 (c) Offer a property for lease on behalf of the employing broker.
A sales agent is only authorized to represent a broker and carry out such duties as the broker may legitimately delegate. Thus a sales agent does not directly represent the client in a transaction but is rather the agent of the broker and subagent of the client.

5.5 (d) The employing broker.
Agents can only receive compensation from their employing brokers. Co-op commissions, referral fees, and other compensations always flow through the broker to the sales agent.

5.6 (d) $4,940.
First calculate the total commission, then the co-brokerage splits, then the agent-broker split. Thus: $380,000 x 6.5% = $24,700 total commission. ($24,700 x 50%) = $12,350 total listing broker share. ($12,350 x 40% = $4,940 agent's share.

5.7 (c) $4,278.
The total commission is ($245,000 x 3%) = $7,350. The agent gets (65% x $7,350) - $500, which equals $4,278.

5.8 (c) complete the signing of the listing.
Once the seller signs the listing, the next critical task is to get it signed, thereby making the listing a contract. Some states allow a salesperson to do this and in other states, the listing must be given to the broker for signing. This result will set in motion the process of marketing the property. The agency disclosures must take place prior to the execution of the agreement.

5.9 (b) Present the offer to the seller at the earliest possible moment.
When a buyer or tenant makes an offer, the agent must present it to the seller or landlord at the earliest possible moment. If the terms of the offer are unacceptable, the agent may assist the seller in developing a counteroffer.

5.10 (c) The broker has illegally converted security funds for business use.
Conversion is the act of misappropriating escrow funds for the broker's business or personal use. Conversion carries serious consequences, including license revocation.

5.11 (d) Never.
All advertising must reveal the identity of the broker; licensed brokers and agents may not use blind ads that conceal their identities.

5.12 (a) fair trade and anti-trust laws.
Brokerage companies, like other businesses, are subject to anti-trust laws designed to prevent monopolies and unfair trade practices. In real estate brokerage, the primary manifestations of unfair trade practice are collusion, price fixing and market allocation. In this instance the brokers are price fixing.

5.13 (b) Outside brokers assist a listing agent in procuring a buyer.
Most listing agreements provide for brokerage cooperation in the multiple listing clause. A transaction involving a cooperating subagent is called co-brokerage. In a co-brokered transaction, the listing broker splits the commission with the "co-broker," typically on a 50-50 basis.

5.14 (d) Only members of the National Association of Realtors®.
The term Realtor® is a protected trade name of the National Association of Realtors®. Only members of this organization may use the term to refer to themselves.

5.15 (a) represent their employing broker in procuring clients and customers.
Agents may only act on behalf of their broker. They may not assume responsibilities for other listings since listings are not transferable.

5.16 (a) The IC is responsible for his or her own taxes; the broker does not withhold.
Generally, a broker has limited control over the actions of a contractor. Specifically: a broker can require performance results, but is limited in demanding how a contractor performs the work; and the broker does not take responsibility for a contractor's income and social security taxes.

5.17 (b) competitive conditions.
Commission structures are negotiated between the agent and employing broker as a function of competitive market conditions.

5.18 (c) avoid disclosing what price the owner will accept.
An agent must be extremely careful at this point to abide by fiduciary obligations to the client, whoever that party may be. Discussions of price are particularly delicate: whether the client is buyer or seller, the agent's duty is to uphold the client's best interests. Thus it is not acceptable to suggest to a customer what price the client will or will not accept.

5.19 (d) mixing escrow funds with the broker's operating funds.
Commingling, a prohibited activity, is the act of mixing the broker's personal or business funds with escrow funds.

5.20 (a) There is insufficient evidence of anything other than a normal business practice.
Charging identical commission rates in itself is legitimate. Price-fixing occurs when competitors have in fact colluded together to set prices.

5.21 (c) all the obligations and promises are performed and the transaction is closed.
An executory contract is one for which the signatories have yet to perform their respective obligations and promises. Upon closing, the sale contract is fully performed and no longer exists as a binding agreement.

5.22 (a) Use a standard contract promulgated by a state agency or a real estate board.
It is advisable, and legally required in most states, for a broker to use a standard contract form promulgated by state agencies or real estate boards, as such forms contain generally accepted language. This relieves the broker of the dangers of creating new contract language, which can be construed as a practice of law for which the broker is not licensed.

5.23 (b) be written.
A contract for the sale of real estate is enforceable only if it is in writing. A buyer or seller cannot sue to force the other to comply with an oral contract for sale, even if the contract is valid.

5.24 (a) The contract has been legitimately cancelled and is null and void.
To be valid, a contract must meet the criteria of: competent parties, voluntary act of good faith, mutual consent, legal purpose, and valuable consideration. The buyer broke the mutual consent requirement by opting out before being told of the seller's acceptance. Thus, there is no valid contract.

5.25 (c) An offer and acceptance.
A contract of sale is created by full and unequivocal acceptance of an offer. Offer and acceptance satisfy the mutual consent requirement for a valid contract. The offeree must accept the offer without making any changes whatsoever.

5.26 (d) Equitable title.
A sale contract gives the buyer an interest in the property that is called equitable title, or ownership in equity. If the seller defaults and the buyer can show good faith performance, the buyer can sue for specific performance, that is, to compel the seller to transfer legal title upon payment of the contract price.

5.27 (b) a condition that, if unmet, renders the contract unenforceable.
A contingency is a condition that must be met before the contract is enforceable. If one party cannot meet a contingency condition by a specified deadline, the other party may cancel the contract.

5.28 (c) The buyer may be able to have the contract canceled.
The termite inspection clause is a contingency clause. If one party cannot meet a contingency condition by a specified deadline, the other party may cancel the contract. Did the clause state that the inspector had to be properly licensed? If so, the buyer has a good case for cancellation.

5.29 (a) Until the seller communicates acceptance of the offer.
An offeror may revoke an offer for any reason prior to communication of acceptance by the offeree.

5.30 (b) Fred has entered into contracts with both Jack and Sally to sell the same property.
Jack's acceptance of Fred's offer creates a valid contract, just as Fred's acceptance of Sally's offer creates a valid contract. Fred should have revoked his offer to Jack before accepting Sally's offer.

5.31 (d) agency relationships and property condition.
It is common for the seller to disclose the property condition requiring the buyer to acknowledge receipt of the disclosure. The broker discloses the applicable agency relationships in the transaction and names the party who must pay the brokerage commission.

5.32 (b) valuable consideration and a right to buy.
An option-to-buy is an enforceable contract in which a potential seller, the optionor, grants a potential buyer, the optionee, the right to purchase a property before a stated time for a stated price and terms. In exchange for the right of option, the optionee pays the optionor valuable consideration.

5.33 (a) Schmidt must sell to Carboy for $10,000.
Mary's option-to-buy contract is enforceable, assuming she paid a consideration for it.

5.34 (d) It is always assignable unless the contract prohibits assignment.
A real estate contract that is not a personal service contract can be assigned to another party unless the terms of the agreement specifically prohibit assignment. An option-to-buy is therefore assignable in the absence of such a prohibiting clause.

5.35 (c) At the end of the contract period, the vendor conveys legal title, provided the vendee has fulfilled all obligations.
A contract for deed is a bilateral agreement between a seller, the vendor, and a buyer, the vendee, in which the vendor defers receipt of some or all of the purchase price of a property over a specified period of time. At the end of the period, the buyer completes payment to the vendor of the full purchase price and the vendor deeds legal title to the vendee.

5.36 (b) the parties have completed a verbal, executory contract.
As a sale contract created by an offer and acceptance, the parties have an executory contract: the parties have yet to perform their respective obligations and promises. However, as a contract for the sale of real estate, this verbal contract is not enforceable. An enforceable real estate sale contract must be in writing.

5.37 (c) The assignor has completed a legal action.
Either party to a sale transaction can assign the sale contract to another party, subject to the provisions and conditions contained in the agreement.

5.38 (d) any conveyance may trigger an acceleration of any loans secured by the property.
The mortgage agreement may or may not state that the seller's loan will be accelerated by the lender and called due on sale. The due-on-sale clause in the sale contract merely stipulates that the buyer and seller recognize the possibility that loans that survive the closing may be called due.

5.39 (d) The option is expired, and the tenant has no rightful claim to money paid for the option.
The option automatically expires at the end of the option period. The landlord has no obligation, either to sell the property or to return the consideration, after the expiration date.

5.40 (c) the seller retains legal title while the buyer makes partial payments until the contract is fully executed.
In a contract for deed, the seller, or vendor, defers receipt of some or all of the purchase price of a property over a specified period of time. During the period, the vendor retains legal title and the vendee acquires equitable title. At the end of the period, the buyer pays the vendor the full purchase price and the vendor deeds legal title to the vendee.

NATIONAL TEST 6: Economics; Appraisal

6.1 (b) demand for the item is increasing in relation to supply of the item.
In a market economy, the primary interactions between supply, demand and price are: if supply increases

relative to demand, price decreases; if supply decreases relative to demand, price increases; if demand increases relative to supply, price increases; and if demand decreases relative to supply, price decreases.

6.2 (d) Supply and demand are equal, and price and value are equal.
A market tends toward a state of equilibrium in which supply equals demand, and price, cost, and value are identical. According to this principle, market demand moves to meet supply, and supply moves to meet demand. If there is an extreme shortage of an item for which there is normally a strong demand, suppliers will rush to increase production to close the gap. If inventories of an item are very high, suppliers will stop production until the oversupply has been depleted.

6.3 (c) the uniqueness of every parcel.
In comparison with other economic products and services, real estate has certain unique traits. Traits of real estate include: inherent product value; uniqueness of every property; demand must come to the supply; illiquidity; slow to respond to changes; and a decentralized local market.

6.4 (d) Prices rise.
If demand is increasing and a moratorium slows supply, demand will begin to outpace supply, forcing prices to rise as the product becomes scarcer in relation to demand.

6.5 (b) an increase in demand for all types of real estate.
New businesses will arise to support the new company. They will hire new employees, some from out of town. The new employees will need housing. Hence the demand for residential real estate, as well as for commercial and industrial, will intensify, and it will also stimulate new construction.

6.6 (d) The number of available units that become occupied over a period of time.
Absorption is the amount of available property that becomes occupied over a period of time.

6.7 (a) rising prices.
Within the business cycle of real estate, declining vacancy indicates a combination of increasing demand which "fills up" supply which in turn decreases. As space becomes scarcer, rents for available space increase.

6.8 (b) desire, utility, scarcity, and purchasing power.
The value of something is based on the answers to four questions: how much do I desire it; how useful is it; how scarce is it; and am I able to pay for it.

6.9 (b) will increase.
If there is no longer a supply to meet the increasing demand of a growing population, prices for existing supply will rise.

6.10 (d) the market tending toward equilibrium.
A market tends toward a state of equilibrium in which supply equals demand, and price, cost, and value are identical. Thus if supply is scarce, construction will increase to stabilize the imbalance.

6.11 (c) the market is over-supplied.
Falling prices indicate an oversupply of commercial properties in relation to demand. In this case, construction of new supply will also slow down.

6.12 (a) have been increasing.
A rise in prices is a market signal that there is an undersupply of product in relation to demand. As the market moves toward equilibrium, builders construct more buildings to meet the unmet demand.

6.13 (c) It is often difficult to convert to cash.
Since real estate is often a large, long-term investment that has no exact duplicate, the process of a buyer's evaluating and choosing the right property is long and complex; hence, finding a buyer at a desired price can take a long time.

6.14 (b) The number of persons employed in base industries in an area
Base employment is the number of persons employed in the base industries that represent the economic foundation of an area. It is the driving component of total employment, which includes secondary and

support industries, and which creates demand for all types of real estate.

6.15 (d) The total existing space of a certain type that is unoccupied at a given time
Vacancy is the amount of total real estate inventory of a certain type that is unoccupied at a given time. It is often stated as a percentage of total inventory, the vacancy rate for that property type.

6.16 (a) local government influencing the real estate market, regardless of demand.
Local governments sometimes declare a moratorium on new construction because of present or projected inadequacies of the infrastructure—water, sewer, power, roads, etc.—or because of the desire to conform to a master plan. The result may be to drive up prices, as supply cannot freely increase to meet demand.

6.17 (c) In- and out-migrations of major employers
Changes in employment numbers in a local market area, especially in major industries, have a direct impact on real estate demand in the area. Money supply, interest rates, and trade imbalances also have an impact, but they are regional or national factors rather than strictly local.

6.18 (b) Vacancy rises and prices fall.
New construction generally occurs to meet an excess of demand. By adding supply, it tends to increase vacancy and lower prices until supply-demand equilibrium is achieved.

6.19 (d) Residential
While all types of users may have these needs, they are most prominent for residential users because of concerns for family comfort and safety. Retail users are more concerned with competitive features of the trade area; office users care more about occupancy costs and suitability for the business; industrial users care more about such features as functionality, accessibility, and the labor pool.

6.20 (c) its susceptibility to swings in the local economy.
Because a real property cannot be transferred to a large, central real estate marketplace, its marketability is closely tied to local conditions. Investors and users must come to the product, unlike other types of economic product that can be moved to a place in search of greater demand.

6.21 (b) anticipation.
Anticipation is the value principle that a buyer will pay a price based on the benefits the buyer expects to derive from a property over a holding period. For example, if an investor anticipates an annual rental income from a leased property to be one million dollars, this expected sum has a direct bearing on what the investor will pay for the property.

6.22 (b) A homeowner adds a third bathroom to a house and thereby increases the appraised value by $10,000.
The principle of contribution focuses on the degree to which a particular improvement affects market value of the overall property. In essence, the contribution of the improvement is equal to the change in market value that the addition of the improvement causes. For example, adding a bathroom to a house may contribute an additional $15,000 to the appraised value. Thus the contribution of the bathroom is $15,000.

6.23 (a) assemblage.
Assemblage, or the conjoining of adjacent properties, sometimes creates a combined value that is greater than the values of the unassembled properties. The excess value created by assemblage is called plottage value.

6.24 (d) Market value is an estimate; market price is the price at which a property sold.
Market value is an estimate of the price at which a property will sell at a particular time. The market price, as opposed to market value, is what a property actually sells for. Market price should theoretically be the same as market value if all the conditions essential for market value are present. Market price, however, may not reflect the analysis of comparables and of investment value that an estimate of market value includes.

6.25 (d) define the appraisal problem and the purpose of the appraisal.
The first step in the process is to define the appraisal problem and the purpose of the appraisal. This involves identifying the subject property by legal description; specifying the interest to be appraised; specifying the purpose of the appraisal; specifying the date for which the appraisal is valid; and identifying

the type of value to be estimated.

6.26 (c) weighing the applicability of the approaches and considering the quality of data supporting each approach.
The final step in the appraisal process is to reconcile the value estimates produced by the three approaches to value into a final value estimate. To do this, an appraiser must weigh the appropriateness of a particular approach to the type of property being appraised and take into account the quality and quantity of data obtained in each method.

6.27 (b) Make dollar adjustments to the sale prices of comparable properties to account for competitive differences with the subject. The sales comparison approach consists of comparing sale prices of recently sold properties that are comparable with the subject, and making dollar adjustments to the price of each comparable to account for competitive differences with the subject. After identifying the adjusted value of each comparable, the appraiser weights the reliability of each comparable and the factors underlying how the adjustments were made. The weighting yields a final value range based on the most reliable factors in the analysis.

6.28 (d) takes into account the competitive value of specific amenities of the subject property.
The sales comparison approach is widely used because it takes into account the subject property's specific amenities in relation to competing properties. In addition, because of the currency of its data, the approach incorporates present market realities.

6.29 (a) adds value to a comparable that is inferior to the subject property.
If the comparable is inferior to the subject in some characteristic, an amount is added to the price of the comparable. If the comparable is better than the subject in some characteristic, an amount is deducted from the sale price of the comparable. This neutralizes the comparable's competitive advantage or disadvantage in an adjustment category. For example, a comparable has a swimming pool and the subject does not. To equalize the difference, the appraiser deducts an amount, say $6,000, from the sale price of the comparable.

6.30 (b) requires the fewest and smallest adjustments.
As a rule, the fewer the total number of adjustments, the smaller the adjustment amounts, and the less the total adjustment amount, the more reliable the comparable.

6.31 (c) $195,000.
Since the comparable has an extra bath, it is adjusted downward to equalize with the subject. Conversely, since it has no patio, the appraiser adds value to the comparable. Thus, $200,000 minus $7,000 plus $2,000 equals $195,000.

6.32 (d) Add the estimated land value and cost of improvements and subtract the accrued depreciation of the improvements.
The cost approach consists of estimating the value of the land "as if vacant;" estimating the cost of improvements; estimating and deducting accrued depreciation; and adding the estimated land value to the estimated depreciated cost of the improvements.

6.33 (b) is very accurate for a property with new improvements that represent the highest and best use.
The strengths of the cost approach are that it: provides an upper limit for the subject's value based on the undepreciated cost of reproducing the improvements. It is also very accurate for valuing a property with new improvements which are the highest and best use of the property.

6.34 (c) a property loses the same increment of value each year over the economic life of the property.
All property improvements have an economic life, which becomes incrementally shorter year after year as physical deterioration takes its toll. The property as a whole does not lose value, since land itself does not depreciate. Similarly, an improvement can regain value if it is repaired or updated. Finally, not all properties lose value from economic obsolescence.

6.35 (d) $115,000.
To appraise value using the cost approach, add the land value to the value of the depreciated improvement. Thus you have $30,000 + ($95,000 - 10,000), or $115,000.

6.36 (b) Divide the income a property generates by a rate of return.
An appraiser obtains an indication of value from the income capitalization method by dividing the estimated net operating income for the subject by the rate of return, or capitalization rate. The formula is: NOI / Cap rate = Value.

6.37 (c) uses a method that is also used by investors to determine how much they should pay for an investment property.
The strength of the income approach is that it is used by investors themselves to determine how much they should pay for a property. Thus, in the right circumstances, it provides a good basis for estimating market value. The approach, however, does not project what an income property's future income will be. Moreover, it is not an applicable method for estimating value if the subject is a non-income producing property.

6.38 (a) $370,000.
First, identify net income by subtracting out vacancy and expenses. Then divide by the capitalization rate. Thus, ($60,000 –3,000 – 20,000) ÷ 10% = $370,000.

6.39 (d) 150.
The monthly gross rent multiplier for a property is equal to the price divided by the monthly rent. Thus, ($450,000 ÷ $3,000) = 150.

6.40 (c) $203,000.
Multiply the monthly gross income times 12 to derive annual income. Multiply annual income times the gross income multiplier to derive the estimate of price. Thus, $1,200 times 12 equals $14,400. This times 14.1 equals $203,040, or $203,000 rounded.

6.41 (c) the state in which the appraiser operates.
A state-certified appraiser is one who has passed the necessary examinations and competency standards as established by each state in conformance with the federal standards.

6.42 (a) The Financial Institutions Reform, Recovery and Enforcement Act (FIRREA).
Title XI of FIRREA requires that competent individuals whose professional conduct is properly supervised perform all appraisals used in federally-related transactions. As of January 1, 1993, such federally-related appraisals must be performed only by state-certified appraisers.

6.43 (a) if two similar properties are for sale, a buyer will purchase the cheaper of the two.
According to the principle of substitution, a buyer will pay no more for a property than the buyer would have to pay for an equally desirable and available substitute property. For example, if three houses for sale are essentially similar in size, quality and location, a potential buyer is unlikely to choose the one that is priced significantly higher than the other two.

6.44 (a) is physically and financially feasible, legal, and the most productive.
This valuation principle holds that there is, theoretically, a single use for a property that produces the greatest income and return. A property achieves its maximum value when it is put to this use. The use must however be legal.

6.45 (d) $200,000. Market value is an opinion of the price that a willing seller and willing buyer would probably agree on for a property at a given time if: the transaction is for cash; the property is exposed on the open market for a reasonable period; buyer and seller have full information about market conditions ; there is no abnormal pressure on either party; it is an "arm's length" transaction; title is marketable; and the price does not include hidden influences such as special financing deals. The amount Lynne actually paid is the market price. The previous listing price and Ken's offer might be interesting data for the appraiser, but the appraisal must also consider other market data, such as comparable sales.

6.46 (a) there may be no recent sale price data in the market.
The sales comparison approach is limited in that every property is unique. As a result, it is difficult to find good comparables, especially for special-purpose properties. In addition, the market must be active; otherwise, sale prices lack currency and reliability.

6.47 (c) selects comparable properties, adjusts the comparables, and estimates the value.
The steps are to first identify comparable sales; then compare comparables to the subject and make adjustments to comparables; then, finally, weigh values indicated by adjusted comparables for the final value estimate of the subject.

6.48 (b) the seller offers below-market seller financing.
The principal factors for comparison and adjustment are time of sale, location, physical characteristics, and transaction characteristics. An adjustment may be made for such differences as mortgage loan terms, mortgage assumability, and owner financing.

6.49 (b) weights the comparables.
The last step in the approach is to perform a weighted analysis of the indicated values of each comparable. The appraiser, in other words, must identify which comparable values are more indicative of the subject and which are less indicative. However, all comparables are taken into account, not simply the nearest comparable.

6.50 (b) market value is not always the same as what the property cost.
The limitations of the cost approach are that: the cost to create improvements is not necessarily the same as market value; and depreciation is difficult to measure, especially for older buildings.

6.51 (b) replacement cost.
Reproduction cost is the cost of constructing, at current prices, a precise duplicate of the subject improvements. Replacement cost is the cost of constructing, at current prices and using current materials and methods, a functional equivalent of the subject improvements.

6.52 (d) functional obsolescence.
Functional obsolescence occurs when a property has outmoded physical or design features which are no longer desirable or acceptable to current users.

6.53 (b) incurable economic obsolescence.
Economic (or external) obsolescence is the loss of value due to adverse changes in the surroundings of the subject property that make the subject less desirable. Since such changes are usually beyond the control of the property owner, economic obsolescence is considered an incurable value loss.

6.54 (c) depreciation.
Depreciation is the loss of value in an improvement over time. The loss of an improvement's value can come from any cause, such as deterioration, obsolescence, or changes in the neighborhood.

6.55 (a) estimates depreciation, subtracts depreciation from cost, and adds back the land value.
The steps in the costs approach are: (1) estimate land value; (2) estimate reproduction or replacement cost of improvements; (3) estimate accrued depreciation; (4) subtract accrued depreciation from reproduction or replacement cost; and (5) add land value to depreciated reproduction or replacement cost.

NATIONAL TEST 7: Finance

7.1 (b) A state in which a mortgagee has equitable title to a secured property.
States differ in their interpretation of who owns mortgaged property. Those that regard the mortgage as a lien held by the mortgagee (lender) against the property owned by the mortgagor (borrower) are called lien-theory states. Those that regard the mortgage document as a conveyance of ownership from the mortgagor to the mortgagee are called title-theory states.

7.2 (d) It is evidence of the borrower's debt to the lender.
A valid mortgage or trust deed financing arrangement requires a note as evidence of the debt.

7.3 (a) trust deed or mortgage.
The mortgage or trust deed is evidence of the collateral pledge of the purchased property as security for the loan.

7.4 (b) mortgagor.
The mortgagor is the borrower and the mortgagee is the lender. As a memory aid, notice that "lender" and "mortgagee" both have two "e"s. "Mortgagor" and "borrower" both have two "o"s.

7.5 (d) $1,000.
Multiply the rate times the loan amount and divide by 12 to calculate monthly interest. Thus, ($200,000 x 6%) ÷ 12 = $1,000.

7.6 (b) $100,000.
The equation for the loan amount is (annual interest divided by the interest rate) = loan amount. Thus, ($500 x 12) ÷ .06 = $100,000.

7.7 (a) 7.5%.
The equation for the interest rate is (annual payment / loan amount) = interest rate. Thus ($3750 / $50,000) = 7.5%.

7.8 (b) $2,000.
A discount point is one percent of the loan amount. Thus, one point on a $100,000 loan equals ($100,000 x 2%) or ($100,000 x .02), or $2,000.

7.9 (b) Part of each periodic payment is applied to repayment of the loan balance in advance and part is applied to payment of interest in arrears.
In an amortizing loan, part of the principal is repaid periodically along with interest, so that the principal balance decreases over the life of the loan. The annual interest is never the same, since the principal balance to which the interest rate applies changes every year. Interest on a loan is always paid in arrears, not in advance.

7.10 (b) private mortgage insurance.
Mortgage insurance protects the lender against loss of a portion of the loan (typically 20-25%) in case of borrower default. Private mortgage insurance generally applies to loans that are not backed by the Federal Housing Administration (FHA) or Veterans Administration (VA) and that have a down payment of less than 20% of the property value. The FHA has its own insurance requirement for loans with a down payment of less than 20%.

7.11 (d) The fraction of the appraised value of the property offered as collateral which the lender is willing to lend.
The relationship of the loan amount to the property value, expressed as a percentage, is called the loan-to-value ratio, or LTV. If the lender's loan to value ratio is 80%, the lender will lend only $80,000 on a home appraised at $100,000. The difference between what the lender will lend and what the borrower must pay for the property is the amount the borrower must provide in cash as a down payment.

7.12 (c) buyer's down payment.
Price less loan is the down payment. This is also the buyer's initial equity.

7.13 (a) refusing a loan because the borrower does not match the lender's target market.
The Equal Credit Opportunity Act (ECOA) requires a lender to evaluate a loan applicant on the basis of that applicant's own income and credit rating, unless the applicant requests the inclusion of another's income and credit rating in the application. In addition, ECOA has prohibited a number of practices in mortgage loan underwriting, including refusing a loan based on an applicant's demographic characteristics.

7.14 (b) $1680.
Monthly income qualification is derived by multiplying monthly income by the income ratio. Thus (72,000 / 12) x .28 = $1680. Remember to first derive the monthly income.

7.15 (b) adjust the applicant's debt ratio calculation and lower the loan amount.
Since a lender lends only part of the purchase price of a property according to the lender's loan-to-value ratio, a lender will verify that a borrower has the cash resources to make the required down payment. If someone is lending an applicant a portion of the down payment with a provision for repayment, a lender will consider this another debt obligation and adjust the debt ratio accordingly. This can lower the amount

a lender is willing to lend.

7.16 (c) All loans secured by a residence.
Regulation Z applies to all loans secured by a residence. It does not apply to commercial loans or to agricultural loans over $25,000. Its provisions cover the disclosure of costs, the right to rescind the credit transaction, advertising credit offers, and penalties for non-compliance with the act.

7.17 (d) the borrower has a limited right to cancel the transaction within a certain period.
A borrower has a limited right to cancel the credit transaction, usually within three days of completion of the transaction. The right of rescission does not apply to "residential mortgage transactions," that is, to mortgage loans used to finance the purchase or construction of the borrower's primary residence. It does, however, apply to refinancing of mortgage loans, and to home equity loans. State law may require a rescission period and notice on first mortgage loan transactions as well.

7.18 (b) ask the buyer/borrower about his/her religion or national origin.
ECOA prohibits discrimination in extending credit based on race, color, religion, national origin, sex, marital status, age, or dependency upon public assistance. A creditor may not make any statements to discourage an applicant on the basis of such discrimination or ask any questions of an applicant concerning these discriminatory items. A real estate licensee who assists a seller in qualifying a potential buyer may fall within the reach of this prohibition.

7.19 (d) not FHA-insured or VA-guaranteed.
A conventional mortgage loan is a permanent long-term loan that is not FHA-insured or VA-guaranteed. FNMA does not "back" loans; FHA only insures FHA loans; and the VA, not GNMA guarantees loans.

7.20 (b) limited by when the loan was originated.
Rules for assumability vary according to when the FHA-insured loan was originated and whether the original loan was for an investment property or an owner-occupied principal residence. Loans originated before December 1, 1986, are generally assumable without restriction. Loans originated after December 1, 1986, require that the assumer show creditworthiness. Some mortgages executed from 1986 through 1989 contain language that is not enforced as a result of later Congressional action. Mortgages from that period are now freely assumable, despite any restrictions stated in the mortgage.

7.21 (c) how much of a loan the VA will guarantee.
A veteran must apply for a Certificate of Eligibility to find out how much the VA will guarantee in a particular situation.

7.22 (d) Zero.
If a loan is fully amortizing, its loan balance is zero at the end of the loan term.

7.23 (b) The buyer gives the seller a mortgage and note as part of the purchase price of the property.
With a purchase money mortgage, the borrower gives a mortgage and note to the seller to finance some or all of the purchase price of the property. The seller in this case is said to "take back" a note, or to "carry paper," on the property.

7.24 (c) hypothecation.
The process of securing a loan by pledging a property without giving up ownership of the property is called hypothecation.

7.25 (a) The borrower gives the lender a note and a mortgage in exchange for loan funds.
When a borrower gives a note promising to repay the borrowed money and executes a mortgage on the real estate for which the money is being borrowed as security, the financing method is called mortgage financing.

7.26 (c) The trustor conveys title to a trustee in exchange for loan funds from the beneficiary.
A deed of trust conveys title to the property in question from the borrower (trustor) to a trustee as security for the loan. The trustee is a third party fiduciary to the trust. While the loan is in place, the trustee holds the title on behalf of the lender, who is the beneficiary of the trust.

7.27 (a) title-theory state.
States that regard the mortgage document as a conveyance of ownership from the mortgagor to the mortgagee are called title-theory states.

7.28 (b) usury.
Many states have laws against usury, which is the charging of excessive interest rates on loans. Such states have a maximum rate that is either a flat rate or a variable rate tied to an index such as the prime lending rate.

7.29 (c) $1,200.
A point is one percentage point of a loan amount. Thus, 2 points on a $60,000 loan equal (.02 x $60,000), or $1,200.

7.30 (a) an amortized loan is paid off over the loan period.
Amortized loans retire the principal balance over the loan period. If a loan does not do this, one must make a balloon payment at the end of the loan term to complete the loan payoff.

7.31 (c) it is a negotiable instrument.
A promissory note is a negotiable instrument, which means the payee may assign it to a third party. The assignee would then have the right to receive the borrower's periodic payments.

7.32 (d) may be required to execute a release of mortgage document.
Lenders may be required to release the mortgage or trust document to the borrower when the borrower has paid off the loan and all other sums secured by the document. The release clause, also known as a defeasance clause, may specify that the mortgagee will execute a satisfaction of mortgage (also known as release of mortgage and mortgage discharge) to the mortgagor.

7.33 (a) an appraisal report.
Loan underwriting is the process of assessing the lender's risk in giving a loan. Mortgage underwriting includes: evaluating the borrower's ability to repay the loan; appraising the value of the property offered as security; and determining the terms of the loan.

7.34 (c) the ability to re-pay, the value of the collateral, and the profitability of the loan.
A lender assesses risks by examining, or qualifying, both borrower and property. In qualifying a borrower, an underwriter weighs the ability of the borrower to repay the loan. In qualifying a property, an underwriter assesses the ability of the property value to cover potential losses. In this evaluation, a lender requires that the appraised value of the property be more than adequate to cover the contemplated loan and costs. Finally, the loan must make money for the lending organization as a basic business precept.

7.35 (b) they want to ensure there is more than enough collateral to cover the loan amount.
Without an ample difference between the property value and the loan amount, a drop in property values could cause the loan balance to exceed the collateral itself. This greatly increases the risk of a loan loss should the borrower default since the balance could not be completely recovered in a foreclosure sale.

7.36 (b) consider the income of a spouse in evaluating a family's creditworthiness.
The Equal Credit Opportunity Act (ECOA) requires a lender to evaluate a loan applicant on the basis of that applicant's own income and credit rating, unless the applicant requests the inclusion of another's income and credit rating in the application. In such a case, a lender may not discount or disregard income from part-time work, a spouse, child support, alimony, or separate maintenance.

7.37 (a) insure the buyer has the earning power to make the loan payments.
Both the income and debt ratios in borrower qualification quantify how much a borrower can safely afford to pay on a mortgage loan. The income ratio focuses on the borrower's earning power.

7.38 (d) debt payments divided by gross income.
The debt ratio formula is (debt obligations) ÷ (income).

7.39 (c) the parties complete all loan origination documents and the loan is funded.
Closing of a mortgage loan normally occurs with the closing of the real estate transaction. At the real estate closing, the lender typically has deposited the funded amount with an escrow agent, along with

instructions for disbursing the funds. The borrower deposits necessary funds with the escrow agent, executes final documents, and receives signed copies of all relevant documents.

7.40 (b) Truth-in-Lending laws and Regulation Z.
Regulation Z, which implements the Truth-in-Lending Act, applies to all loans secured by a residence. It does not apply to commercial loans or to agricultural loans over $25,000. It prescribes requirements to lenders regarding the disclosure of costs, the right to rescind the credit transaction, advertising credit offers, and penalties for non-compliance with the Truth-in-Lending Act.

7.41 (a) The Equal Credit Opportunity Act.
ECOA prohibits discrimination in extending credit based on race, color, religion, national origin, sex, marital status, age, or dependency upon public assistance.

7.42 (c) the Real Estate Settlement and Procedures Act.
RESPA is a federal law which aims to standardize settlement practices and ensure that buyers understand settlement costs. RESPA applies to purchases of residential real estate (one- to four-family homes) to be financed by "federally related" first mortgage loans. In addition to imposing settlement procedures, RESPA provisions prohibit lenders from paying kickbacks and unearned fees to parties who may have helped the lender obtain the borrower's business.

7.43 (b) Buying securities, changing the discount rate, and controlling banking reserves.
The Federal Reserve System regulates the money supply by means of three methods: selling or re-purchasing government securities, primarily Treasury bills, changing the reserve requirement for member banks; changing the interest rate, or discount rate, the system charges member institutions for borrowing funds from the Federal Reserve System.

7.44 (a) It cycles funds back to primary lenders so they can make more loans.
Secondary mortgage market organizations buy pools of mortgages from primary lenders and sell securities backed by these pooled mortgages to investors. By purchasing loans from primary lenders, the secondary market returns funds to the primary lenders, thereby enabling the primary lender to originate more mortgage loans.

7.45 (a) Fannie Mae, Freddie Mac, and Ginnie Mae.
As major players in the secondary market, the Federal National Mortgage Association (FNMA, "Fannie Mae"), Government National Mortgage Association (GNMA, "Ginnie Mae), and Federal Home Loan Mortgage Corporation (FHLMC, "Freddie Mac") tend to set the standards for the primary market. FHA, VA, and the Federal Reserve are not organizations in the secondary mortgage market.

7.46 (c) It purchases FHA-backed and VA-backed loans.
Fannie Mae buys conventional, FHA-backed and VA-backed loans; gives banks mortgage-backed securities in exchange for blocks of mortgages; and sells bonds and mortgage-backed securities. It does not guarantee, insure, or originate loans.

7.47 (b) It insures loans made by approved lenders.
The Federal Housing Administration (FHA) does not lend money, but insures permanent long-term loans made by others. The lender must be approved by the FHA, and the borrower must meet certain FHA qualifications.

7.48 (a) It guarantees loans made by approved lenders.
The Veterans Administration (VA) offers loan guarantees to qualified veterans. The VA partially guarantees permanent long-term loans originated by VA-approved lenders on properties that meet VA standards. The VA's guarantee enables lenders to issue loans with higher loan-to-value ratios than would otherwise be possible.

7.49 (c) the loan payments gradually increase.
Graduated payment mortgages allow for smaller initial monthly payments which gradually increase. The interest rate remains fixed as does the loan term.

7.50 (b) the borrower pays additional interest at the onset in order to obtain a lower interest rate.
A buydown loan entails a prepayment of interest on a loan. The prepayment effectively lowers the interest

rate and the periodic payments for the borrower. Buydowns typically occur in a circumstance where a builder wants to market a new development to a buyer who cannot quite qualify for the necessary loan at market rates.

NATIONAL TEST 8: Investments; Taxation; Ethics

8.1 (b) negative leverage.
Leveraging is borrowing funds in order to make an investment that is larger than your own resource permits you to do directly. In negative leverage situations, your cost of borrowing funds to make the investment becomes greater than the income the investment returns to you.

8.2 (b) income properties.
Cost recovery, or depreciation, allows the owner of income property to deduct a portion of the property's value from gross income each year over the life of the asset. Principal residences cannot be depreciated (unless portions are treated as a home office.) Further, land cannot be depreciated.

8.3 (c) 19.5 %.
Appreciation amount is the current value of the property minus the original cost. The total appreciation rate is derived by dividing the appreciation amount by the original cost. Subtract the estimated current market value from the price originally paid (239,000 - 200,000 = 39,000) and then divide the result by the original price (39,000 / 200,000 = . 195 or 19.5%).

8.4 (d) a deduction for mortgage interest.
Deducting mortgage interest is a significant tax advantage of owning one's residence. Depreciation and cost-deductions do not apply to a non-income producing residence. Appreciation is a benefit, but not a tax benefit.

8.5 (d) $232,900.
The figure for net proceeds from sale is expressed by the formula: sale price - costs of sale = net proceeds. Thus $250,000 - (6% x 250,000) – 600 – 1,500 = $232,900.

8.6 (b) $157,000.
The beginning basis is the cost of acquiring a property. Basis is increased by capital improvements and decreased by depreciation. The basic formula for adjusted basis is Beginning basis ($150,000) + capital improvements ($3,000 + $4,000) - depreciation ($0) = adjusted basis ($157,000).

8.7 (c) $34,000.
The gain on sale (capital gain) of a primary residence is represented by the basic formula: amount realized (net sales proceeds, $210,000) - adjusted basis ($176,000) = gain on sale ($34,000). Note the purchase price of the second house is irrelevant.

8.8 (a) There is no taxable gain.
There is no taxable gain because the gain falls under the exclusion limit of $250,000. As of August 5, 1997, tax law provides an exclusion of $250,000 for an individual taxpayer and $500,000 for married taxpayers filing jointly on the gain from sale of a principal residence. The seller must have owned the property for at least two years during the five years preceding the date of sale; used the property as principal residence for a total of two years during that five-year period; and have waited two years since the last use of the exclusion for any sale.

8.9 (c) direct investment.
Individuals, corporations, or other investor entities may invest as active investors in a property by buying it directly and taking responsibility for managing and operating the property. This investment mode is called direct investment.

8.10 (a) $2,100.
Annual gross operating income ($1,500 x 12 = $18,000) - annual operating expenses ($500 x 12 = $6,000) = annual net operating income ($12,000); annual net operating income ($12,000) - cost recovery expense ($5,000) = taxable income ($7,000); taxable income ($7,000) x tax rate (30%) = tax liability ($2,100).

8.11 (b) the more the investor stands to gain, the greater the risk that the investor may lose.
The general rule in investments is that the safer the investment, the more slowly it gains in value. The more you want it to gain, and the more quickly, the more you must risk losing it. Reward in investing corresponds directly to the degree of risk.

8.12 (a) income and tax benefits.
The basic financial rewards of an investment include income, appreciation in asset value, positive borrowing leverage, and tax benefits.

8.13 (d) relatively illiquid.
Real estate is by nature more difficult to convert to cash than many other types of investment. Compare the selling of a home with the ease of drawing money out of a bank account or selling a stock.
8.14 (b) a more management-intensive investment.

Real estate tends to require a high degree of investor involvement in management of the investment. Even raw land requires some degree of maintenance to preserve its value. Improved properties often require extensive management, including repairs, maintenance, onsite leasing, tenant relations, security, and fiscal management.

8.15 (a) a general partnership.
A general partnership is a syndicate in which all members participate equally in managing the investment and in the profits or losses it generates.

8.16 (d) gross income minus expenses minus building depreciation.
Taxable income from investment real estate is the gross income received minus any expenses, deductions or exclusions that current tax law allows. Depreciation of land is not allowed.

8.17 (c) deduct interest payments from income.
Taxable income is net operating income minus all allowable deductions. The interest portion of debt service is allowed and is deducted from Net Operating Income as interest expense. Principal repayment is not an allowable deduction on investment properties. Capital gain derivation does not involve interest or principal payments.

8.18 (d) The owner may be able to avoid capital gain tax when the property is sold.
Provided the owner meets certain ownership and use tests, there is no capital gain tax on sale of the property unless the gain exceeds $250,000 for a single taxpayer or $500,000 for married taxpayers who file jointly. Since the property is not used for business, deductions for expenses against income are not allowed.

8.19 (c) may be deducted from the sale price for gains tax purposes.
Selling costs include such expenses as brokerage commissions, relevant advertising, legal fees, seller-paid points and other closing costs. These costs are deducted from the selling price to get the amount realized, which is reduced by the adjusted basis to calculate gain on sale for gains tax purposes.

8.20 (b) the difference between amount realized and adjusted basis.
The formula for gain tax is Taxable Gain on Sale x the owner's marginal tax bracket. The formula for gain on sale is: Amount Realized - Adjusted Basis = Gain on Sale. The formula for Amount Realized is: Selling Price - Selling costs = Amount Realized. Therefore, the gain tax = (Amount Realized - Adjusted Basis) x tax rate.

8.21 (c) A tax district.
Real estate property taxes are imposed by "taxing entities" or "taxing districts" at county and local levels of government. States may legally levy taxes on real property, but most delegate this power to counties, cities, townships and local taxing districts. The federal government does, however, tax income derived from real property and gains realized on the sale of real property.

8.22 (b) properties owned by a government agency.
Certain types of property are exempt from property taxes. Certain classes of property owner may also be

exempted or have a reduced liability. Exemptions include government-owned properties, real properties owned by churches, and properties owned by other non-profit organizations.

8.23 (c) It adjusts assessments in a locality to make them more consistent with an average level for the state or other higher level jurisdiction.
Equalization factors level out the unevenness of valuations for groups of properties. For instance, if assessed values of properties in one county are consistently ten percent below the average for other counties, an equalization board may multiply each assessed value in that county by a factor of 110% to raise them to the average level for the state.

8.24 (c) $2,000,000,000.
The mill rate = (tax requirement / the tax base). A mill is one one-thousandth of a dollar ($.001). To solve for the tax base, reconfigure this formula to be: Base = Tax Requirement / Mill Rate. Thus the Base = $20,000,000 / .010, or $2,000,000,000.

8.25 (d) $441.
The library tax is ($1.00 x 147) and the fire district tax is ($2.00 x 147). Thus the tax is $441.

8.26 (b) $5,700.
Special assessments are based on the cost of the improvement and apportioned on a pro rata basis among benefiting properties according to the value that each parcel will receive from the improvement. Here, Mary's share is 38 / 200, or 19%. 19% x $30,000 = $5,700.

8.27 (a) A conveyance instrument for a property that is sold to enforce a tax lien.
A tax deed is a legal instrument for conveying title when a property is sold for non-payment of taxes. The application for a tax deed causes the taxing agency to institute a tax sale or tax foreclosure.
8.28 (d) a statutory right of redemption.
If the taxpayer can redeem the property after the tax sale, this right is known as a statutory right of redemption. In this case, the taxpayer must pay the amount paid by the winning bidder at the tax sale, plus any charges, additional taxes, or interest that may have accumulated.

8.29 (b) the total of all assessed values of properties minus exemptions.
The tax base of an area is the total of the appraised or assessed values of all real property within the area's boundaries, excluding partially or totally exempt properties such as those owned by the government or non-profit organizations.

8.30 (c) multiplying each district's tax rate times the taxable value of the property.
Each property owner's tax bill is determined by multiplying the tax rate for each taxing district times the taxable value of the property. Taxable value is the assessed value after all exemptions and adjustments have been taken into account.

8.31 (a) Civil Rights Act of 1866.
The original fair housing statute, the Civil Rights Act of 1866, prohibits discrimination in housing based on race. The prohibition relates to selling, renting, inheriting, and conveying real estate.

8.32 (c) race, color, religion, and national origin.
Title VIII of the Civil Rights Act of 1968, known today as the Fair Housing Act, prohibits discrimination in housing based on race, color, religion, or national origin.

8.33 (c) Advertising a property as available to individuals of a particular race. The prohibition against discriminatory advertising states that an agent may not advertise residential properties in such a way as to restrict their availability to any prospective buyer or tenant.

8.34 (c) An agent persuades a family to put their house on the market because ethnic minority families are beginning to move into the neighborhood.
Blockbusting, a prohibited activity, is the practice of inducing owners in an area to sell or rent to avoid an impending change in the ethnic or social makeup of the neighborhood that will cause values to go down.

8.35 (a) The Home Mortgage Disclosure Act.
The Home Mortgage Disclosure Act requires lenders involved with federally guaranteed or insured loans

to exercise impartiality and non-discrimination in the geographical distribution of their loan portfolio. In other words, the act is designed to prohibit redlining, the practice of restricting loans by geographical are(a)

8.36 (c) privately owned single-family residences listed with a broker.
Among the circumstances where the Fair Housing Act might allow for an exemption is: a privately owned single-family home where no broker is used, with certain additional conditions. In other words, as soon as a broker is used in the sale, the law applies.

8.37 (a) illegal, because the agent changed the terms of the sale to discourage this particular couple.
The Fair Housing Act prohibition against discriminatory misrepresentation states that an agent may not conceal available properties, represent that they are not for sale or rent, or change the sale terms for the purpose of discriminating.

8.38 (d) The owner of a duplex who resides in one of the units refuses to rent the other unit to a non-Christian.
The Fair Housing Act would exempt the owner in this situation because it involves rental of an apartment in a 1-4 unit building where the owner is also an occupant and there is no discriminatory advertising.

8.39 (b) File a complaint with HUD and/or file suit against the offending parties in a state or federal court within the prescribed time period.
The Fair Housing Amendments Act of 1988 prohibits discrimination based on sex. If May feels she has been discriminated against in this way, she may file a complaint with the Office of Fair Housing and Equal Opportunity (OFHEO) in HUD within one year or file suit in a federal or state court within two years of the alleged violation.

8.40 (a) Inform Scott that the condition is illegal and that she cannot comply with it.
Scott is not allowed to discriminate based on race, color, religion, national origin, sex, family status, or handicap. If an agent goes along with a client's discriminatory act, the agent is equally liable for violation of fair housing laws. It is thus imperative to avoid complicity with client discrimination. Further, an agent should withdraw from any relationship where client discrimination occurs.

8.41 (c) require families without children to pay the same security deposit that families with children must pay.
Fair housing laws prohibit discriminatory advertising, discrimination on the basis of national origin, discrimination based on age in dwellings of more than four units, and discrimination against families with children. The fact that the owner is requiring the same deposit from tenants with and without children does not discriminate against families with children but actually favors them.

8.42 (d) It is a single-family house, and the owner owns only one other rental home in addition to his own residence.
Federal fair housing laws do not prohibit age and family status discrimination in residential dwellings of four units or less and in single family houses if sold or rented by owners who have no more than three houses.

8.43 (c) the Fair Housing Amendments Act of 1988.
The Fair Housing Amendments Act of 1988 prohibited discrimination based on sex and discrimination against handicapped persons and families with children. Executive Order 11063 concerned racial discrimination in housing where federal funding was involved; the Civil Rights Act of 1968 concerned discrimination based on race, color, religion, and national origin; Jones v Mayer concerned racial discrimination.

8.44 (c) steering.
Steering is the illegal practice of limiting customers' choices by encouraging or discouraging them about the suitability of an area and directing them only to areas the agent deems suitable for them.

8.45 (a) providing unequal services.
The agent may be illegally providing unequal services by altering the nature or quality of brokerage services to a party based on race, color, sex, national origin, or religion.

8.46 (a) discriminatory misrepresentation by omission.
Discriminatory misrepresentation is the concealing of available properties, representing that they are not for sale or rent, or changing the sale terms for the purpose of discriminating.

NATIONAL TEST 9: Closings; Risk Management; Property Management

9.1 (c) returns funds to the buyer.
If for any reason the transaction cannot be completed, the escrow instructions usually provide a mechanism for reconveying title to the seller and funds to the buyer. In such a case, both parties return to their original status as if no sale had occurred.

9.2 (d) disclose in writing any business relationships they have with other parties involved in the transaction.
Business relationships and affiliations among real estate firms, mortgage brokers, title insurance firms and other such companies that are involved in a transaction are permitted, provided the relationships are disclosed in writing to the consumer, the consumer is free to go elsewhere for the relevant service, and the companies do not exchange fees for referrals.

9.3 (a) The item must be prorated and recorded as a debit to one party and a credit to the other party for the same amount.
An income or expense item that affects both parties is apportioned, or prorated, to each party to reflect the proper amount that each owes or should receive. A prorated item is treated as a debit to one party and a credit to the other party for the same amount.

9.4 (b) at some time after the expense is incurred.
Items paid in arrears are paid after the expense has been incurred.

9.5 (d) A debit to the seller and credit to the buyer for $580.
For income the seller received in advance, the buyer receives a credit and the seller receives a debit. In effect, the seller has received some of the buyer's income, and the seller must pay this share to the buyer. Therefore the seller is debited and the buyer is credited the $580 the buyer is entitled to earn as the new owner.

9.6 (b) A debit to the seller and credit to the buyer for $43.
For an item the buyer will pay in arrears, the buyer receives a credit and the seller receives a debit. In effect, the seller has incurred some of the expenses that the buyer will be paying for after closing. Thus the seller must pay the buyer the used portion of the expense, or $43.

9.7 (b) $546.00.
The daily tax expense, first, is ($2,190 ÷ 365) or $6.00. Since the buyer will pay the taxes after closing, the seller will owe the buyer his or her portion of the tax bill, which is the 91 days from the beginning of the year through closing. Therefore, credit the buyer and debit the seller ($6.00 x 91), or $546.00.

9.8 (d) $191.67.
This method assumes all months are 30 days and the year is 360 days. The daily proration is therefore $375 ÷ 360, or $1.04. The closing occurs on the 184th day of the year. Thus, ($1.04 x 184) = $191.67. Note that if the day of closing is the buyer's, there would be 183 day's worth of prorated expense.

9.9 (d) $735.34.
Assuming a 365 day year, the daily tax expense is ($1,100 ÷ 365), or $3.013. As taxes are paid in arrears, the buyer will be paying the annual bill. Thus, he will be owed a credit for the seller's share of the bill, which is $3.013 x 244 days, or $735.34.

9.10 (a) $116.03.
The buyer's share is the unused portion, or (365 days – 244 days), or 121 days. The daily expense is ($350 ÷ 365), or $.9589. ($.9589 x 121) = $116.03. The seller receives this amount as a credit and the buyer a debit.

9.11 (a) $507.50.
If the buyer pays $525 interest for 30 days, the daily expense is ($525 ÷ 30), or $17.50. If there are 29 days of pre-paid expense, the buyer's charge is ($17.50 x 29), or $507.50.

9.12 (c) $1,775.
$88,750 x .02 = $1,775. Remember, one point = 1% of the loan amount.

9.13 (d) $11,250.
$187,500 x 6% = $187,500 x .06 = $11,250.

9.14 (d) the buyer must pay the expense.
Explicit agreements in the sale contract supercede traditional expense-payment responsibilities which can vary from state to state.

9.15 (a) the excess of the buyer's debits over the buyer's credits.
To determine how much money the buyer owes at closing, the buyer's debits are totaled and compared with the total of the buyer's credits. The excess of debits over credits is the amount the buyer must bring to the closing.

9.16 (d) negligence, error or omission in carrying out professional services.
A standard E&O policy provides coverage for "damages resulting from any negligent act, error or omission arising out of Professional Services." It does not cover dishonest or illegal acts, including environmental violations and mishandling of funds.

9.17 (a) Failing to inform and disclose properly.
Agency risks commonly concern the requirement to inform and disclose. Most states require agency relationships to be in writing and to be disclosed to all parties to a transaction. In states that do not use agency, there is still the obligation to explain and disclose the nature of the relationship.

9.18 (b) failing to disclose known adverse facts.
Depending on the state, the licensee may have no further duty to disclose property condition after properly informing parties of their rights and obligations. However, the licensee may still be subject to legal action for failing to disclose adverse facts the licensee knew about or should have known about.

9.19 (d) avoid creating a false impression that the licensee is a certified appraiser.
Misuse of such terms as "appraisal" and "value" could lead to a charge of misrepresenting oneself as an appraiser.

9.20 (b) exceeding the authority of the agreement.
Licensees must stay within the bounds of the authority granted by the agency agreement and avoid doing anything requiring permission without first getting that permission in writing.

9.21 (a) use a checklist of all items, contingencies, dates and responsibilities that must be met.
One way to reduce risk in the contracting process is to use a checklist that covers all the contract items, such as inclusions and exclusions, contingency periods, documents, forms, data checking, and milestone dates.

9.22 (d) the principals may make changes as long as they sign or initial each change.
Real estate professionals who are not attorneys are usually limited to filling in blanks or making deletions on a preprinted contract form prepared by a lawyer. While a licensee may make deletions, additions to a form should be drafted by an attorney. The principals themselves can make changes as long as each change is signed or initialed by all signers.

9.23 (b) obtain education in the content and intent of the laws.
The risk of violating fair housing laws can be minimized through ongoing education that addresses both the intent of the laws and their current content..

9.24 (a) being present at a conversation where the setting of commission rates is discussed.
Antitrust laws forbid brokers to band together to set a price on their services in listing and selling property. Even being overheard discussing commission rates or being present at such a conversation can lead to charges of *price fixing*.

9.25 (a) License discipline, fines, and possible incarceration.
Intentional misrepresentation, as a type of fraud, is a criminal act that may result in fines and incarceration, in addition to discipline from state regulators and professional organizations.

9.26 (c) stating that a client should seek legal counsel.
Unintentional misrepresentation occurs when a licensee *unknowingly* gives a consumer inaccurate information concerning a property, financing or agency service. Information that the licensee, as a professional, should have known to be false or inaccurate may be included in the definition. Telling a client that legal counsel would be advisable is not misrepresentation and, in fact, is often an important risk management technique.

9.27 (d) avoid speculative statements in all reports.
Progress reports should be accurate, timely, in writing, and free of speculation. Speculation may encourage the consumer to believe the agent has expertise that in fact is non-existent. If a consumer has a question about the meaning of something in an inspection report, the licensee should refer the consumer to the person who wrote the report rather than trying to explain it.

9.28 (b) It reduces the chance of presenting an offer from an unqualified buyer.
Using a lender to qualify the buyer protects the agent against leading a seller to believe a purchaser is fully qualified when this may not be the case. Also, lenders and loan agents are better able to look into the buyer's qualifications than a real estate licensee is. If it is necessary to show a property to a potential buyer who has not been qualified by a lender, the licensee can gain some protection by performing an informal qualification and documenting the fact that it was based on the information provided by the buyer.

9.29 (c) the agency relationship.
Maintaining the confidentiality of any information that would harm the client's interests or bargaining position or anything else the client wishes to keep secret, unless the law requires disclosure, is one of the primary duties of agency. The duty to maintain confidentiality generally survives the termination of a listing agreement into perpetuity.

9.30 (a) performing a comparative market analysis.
In preparing a Comparative Market Analysis, licensees should guard against using the terms "appraisal" and "value," which are reserved for the use of certified appraisers. Misuse of these terms could lead to a charge of misrepresenting oneself as an appraiser.

9.31 (d) make a substantial misrepresentation.
The license laws of most states list as illegal advertising activities subject to discipline such actions as making any substantial and intentional misrepresentation, making false promises, and making misleading or untruthful statements in any advertising.

9.32 (c) fiduciary
The management agreement creates an agency relationship between the manager and the principal. This is a fiduciary relationship and, in general, the agent is charged with producing the greatest possible net return on the owner's investment while safeguarding the value of the investment for the owner/investor.

9.33 (b) financial reporting to the principal.
Financial reporting to the principal is a fundamental responsibility of the property manager. Reports may be required monthly, quarterly, and annually. Required reports typically include operating budget, cash flow, profit and loss, and budget comparison statements.

9.34 (d) revenue from all sources minus losses from uncollected rents, vacancies, and evictions.
The total of scheduled rents plus revenues from such sources as vending services, storage charges, late fees, utilities, and contracts is the potential gross income. Subtracting losses caused by uncollected rents, vacancies and evictions gives effective gross income.

9.35 (a) cost per tenant prospect generated per lease.
The efficiency of marketing activities can be judged in terms of how many prospects per completed lease they generate. The lower the cost per prospect per lease, the more effective and efficient the program.

9.36 (b) raise rental rates.
Vacancy rates are directly related to demand and competitive supply in the market. If vacancy rates in the managed property are too high, the manager may have to lower rates or identify problems in the property or its management that are contributing to vacancy level. On the other hand, if the property's vacancy rate is significantly lower than market rates, the manager may conclude that higher rental rates are called for.

9.37 (b) Routine, preventive, and corrective
The foremost maintenance objective is generally to preserve the value of the physical asset for the owner over the long term. Three general types of maintenance are required to keep a property in serviceable condition: routine (day-to-day), preventive (scheduled), and corrective (repairs and replacements).

9.38 (a) ensure that disabled employees have the same level of access to facilities that all employees have.
Employers with at least fifteen employees must follow nondiscriminatory employment and hiring practices and make reasonable accommodations to enable disabled employees to perform essential functions of their jobs. Modifications to the physical components of the building may be necessary to provide the required access to tenants and their customers. Existing barriers must be removed when the removal is "readily achievable," that is, when cost is not prohibitive.

9.39 (a) replacement value.
The amount of coverage provided by certain types of policies may be based on whether the property is insured at depreciated value or current replacement value. Depreciated value is original value minus the loss in value over time. Current replacement value, which is more expensive, is the amount it would cost to rebuild or replace the property at current rates. Commercial policies include coinsurance clauses requiring the insured to bear a portion of the loss. Fire and hazard policies usually require the coverage to be in an amount equal to at least 80 percent of the replacement value.

9.40 (b) cash for the management firm's operating expenses.
Managers are responsible for proper handling of monies belonging to other parties (trust funds) that come into the manager's hands in the course of doing business. For property managers, such trust funds include rents collected from tenants, security deposits, and capital contributions from the property owner. Funds belonging to the management firm must not be commingled with those of the client

9.41 (c) General
Property managers are usually considered to be general agents empowered to perform some or all of the ongoing tasks and duties of operating the property, including the authority to enter into contracts.

9.42 (b) The tenant pays a fixed rent, and the landlord pays all operating expenses.
In a gross lease, the tenant pays an established, fixed rent, and the landlord pays all property operating expenses, such as taxes, insurance, utilities, and other services. This is the arrangement commonly used in residential leases. If the tenant pays some of the operating expenses, the lease is a form of net lease.

9.43 (d) the property manager does not have to maintain it.
The lease should set forth items that are excluded or included in the leased property. For instance, a residential lease may include built-in appliances such as dishwashers but exclude freestanding ones, such as refrigerators. At issue for the landlord is the cost of maintenance. If a refrigerator is not included, it does not have to be maintained by the property manager.

9.44 (b) deliver a habitable property.
The landlord (by way of the property manager), is expected to deliver a property that is habitable. This means keeping heating, plumbing, cooling, and electrical systems in good repair as well as maintaining serviceability of floors, stairways, railings, roofs, and windows.

9.45 (c) A tenant declares a landlord in default and vacates the leased premises.
A constructive eviction occurs when a tenant vacates the leased premises and declares the lease void, claiming that the landlord's actions have made the premises unfit for the purpose described in the lease. The

tenant must prove that it was the landlord's actions that were responsible and may be able to recover damages.

9.46 (a) the competitive market for the property.
In preparing a management plan, a manager must consider the owner's objectives, including financial goals; the competitive market for the property, both local and regional, depending on the property type; and the features of the particular property. The plan will also include a budget and indications of what the manager intends to do with the property to meet the owner's objectives.

NATIONAL TEST 10: Real Estate Math

10.1 (a) $.023 / SF
5/6ths of an acre = (5 x 43,560 SF) / 6, or 36,300 SF. Her commission was (.06 x $28,000) x .50, or $840. $840 / 36,300 SF = $.023 / SF.

10.2 (b) $370,170
The land costs $.50 x 43,560 SF/ac. x 1.5 ac, or $32,670. The home will cost $135 / SF x 2,500, or $337,500. The total property will cost $370,170.

10.3 (a) 12%
The lot measures 43,560 / 4, or 10,890 SF. The tennis court will take up 9,600 SF, leaving 1,290 SF. This amount is 11.8% of the total lot area.

10.4 (c) 40
The total area available for lots is 11.2 acres (16 acres x 70% for houses), or 487,872 SF (11.2 x 43,560). Dividing this area by 12,000 SF / lot = 40.66. Thus he can have a 40-lot subdivision.

10.5 (a) 6
First, the requirement = 2(13'x 9') +2 (18'x 9') =558 SF. Each roll is 2'x 50', or 100 SF. Thus she will need 6 rolls.

10.6 (d) 1,376 SF
First figure the area to be mulched. If the home is 40 x 30, the flower area adds 8' to each side of the house. Thus the outside perimeter of the flowered area is (40+8+8) by (30+8+8), or 46' by 56'. The area of the flowered area is (46' x 56') minus the house area of 1,200 SF. This is 1,376 SF.

10.7 (b) 40 acres
First, remember that a section contains 640 acres. The area in question is a forth of a half of a half of the total section. So divide 640 by (4 x 2 x 2). 4 x 2 x 2 is 16 and 640/16= 40 acres.

10.8 (c) 10 acres
This key to this question is to recall that a section has 640 acres. Theresa's property only is a ¼ of a ¼ of a ¼ of the entire section. Multiply 4 x 4 x 4 which equals 64. Savannah owns 1/64 of the section. Divide 640 by 64 and you get the answer of 10 acres.

10.9 (a) $38,955
Their fixed rent is (1,800 SF x $1.40/SF) x 12 months, or $30,240. The percentage rent is ($41,500 x .0175) x 12, or $8,715. Total rent is ($30,240 + 8,715), or $38,955.

10.10 (a) 5.04%
First, convert to decimals: 2 2/3 % = 2.67%; 5 1/5% = 5.2%; 7 1/4% = 7.25%. Thus total appreciation = (2.67% + 5.2% + 7.25%), or 15.12%. Divide by 3 to derive the average: 15.12% / 3 = 5.04%

10.11 (c) 29 %.
Appreciation as a per cent can be estimated by (1) subtracting the estimated current market value from the price originally paid (239,000 - 185,000 = 54,000) and (2) dividing the result by the original price (54,000 / 185,000 = . 29 or 29%).

10.12 (c)   94%
To find the percent of listing price the offer is, divide the offer by the listing price. In this question the
offer is $290,000 and the listing price is $308,000. $\dfrac{\$290,000}{\$308,000} = 94\%$

10.13 (a) $206,000.
Remember the formula V = I / R where V is value, I is annual income, and R is the cap rate. Variations of
this are: R = I / V in solving for the cap rate, and I = V x R in solving for income. Here, first identify net
income by subtracting out vacancy and expenses. Then divide by the capitalization rate. Thus, ($30,000 –
1,500 – 10,000) / 9% = $205,555, or $206,000 rounded.

10.14 (b) $375,000.
Value = Income / Cap rate. Thus, V= $30,000 / .08 = $375,000.

10.15 (b) $13,600.
First derive the annual depreciation which is the cost divided by the economic life. Then multiply annual
depreciation times the number of years to identify total depreciation. Remember to subtract depreciation
from the original cost if the question asks for the ending value. Thus, ($16,000 / 20 years x 3 years) =
$2,400 total depreciation. The ending value is $16,000 –2,400, or $13,600.

10.16 (a) $1,077
First, Lee's depreciable basis, without the land, is $280,000 x 75%, or $210,000. The annual depreciation
for the entire home is ($210,000 / 39 years), or $5,384.61. Second, his office is 20% of the house (500 sf /
2,500 sf). Therefore Lee can take annual depreciation of ($5,384.61 x 20%), or $1,076.92.

10.17 (d) $188,000.
Cost Approach formula: Land + (Cost of Improvements + Capital Additions – Depreciation) = Value.
Thus you have $40,000 + ($175,000 - 27,000), or $188,000.

10.18 (c) $475,000
Use the same Cost Approach formula: Land + (Cost of Improvements + Capital Additions – Depreciation)
= Value. The land is worth (100,000 x 125%), or $125,000. Remember, you cannot depreciate the land,
only the cost of the improvements. Therefore, annual depreciation is ($400,000 / 40), or $10,000. Total
depreciation is ($10,000 x 5 years), or $50,000. Thus the value is ($125,000 + 400,000 – 50,000), or
$475,000.

10.19 (d)   125.
Use the formula: GRM = Price / Monthly Rent. Thus, $400,000 / $3,200 = 125.

10.20 (c) $194,000.
Use the formula: GIM = Price / Annual Income. To solve for price convert the formula to Price = GIM x
Annual Income. Thus, ($1,100 x 12) equals $13,200 annual income. ($13,200 x 14.7 GIM) = $194,040, or
$194,000 rounded.

10.21 (d) $750
The loan amount is $200,000 x .75, or $150,000. The first month interest equals ($150,000 x 6%) / 12
months, or $750.

10.22 (b) $179,000.
The equation for the loan amount is (annual interest divided by the interest rate) = loan amount. Thus,
($790 x 12) / .053 = $178,868 or $179,000 rounded.

10.23 (a)   4.82%.
The equation for the interest rate is (annual payment / loan amount) = interest rate. Thus ($1,000 x 12) /
$249,000 = 4.82%.

10.24 (b) $1,456.95
In the first month they pay interest of ($280,000 x 6.25%) / 12, or $1,458. If their fixed payment is $1,724, they paid down the principal by $266 ($1,724 - 1,458). Now they must pay 6.25% interest on the new principal balance of $279,734. This equals (279,734 x .0625) / 12, or $1,456.95.

10.25 (b) The second option, by 150.
The first option's interest total is (6.5% x $60,000) x 5 years, or $19,500. The second option will charge (6.25% x $60,000) x 5 years, plus $600, or a total of $19,350. The 2nd option is $150 cheaper.

10.26 (b) 1.67 points
A discount point is one percent of the loan amount. Jose's loan is ($410,000 x 90%), or $369,000. If he paid $6,150, he paid 1.67% of the loan amount ($6,150 / 369,000), or 1.67 points.

10.27 (c) $4,875.
$325,000 x .015 = $4,875. Remember, one point = 1% of the loan amount.

10.28 (c) $162,500
Use the formula: Price x LTV Ratio = Loan. Then plug in the figures and calculate: Price x .80 = $130,000. Therefore, Price = $130,000 / .80 = $162,500.

10.29 (c) $379,259
First, the annual interest paid is $1,600 x 12, or $19,200. The interest rate is 6.75%. Using the formula (Loan = Interest / Rate), the loan amount is $19,200 / 6.75%, or $284,444. As this is 75% of the price, the price is ($284,444 / .75), or $379,259.

10.30 (b) $1,900.
Monthly income qualification is derived by multiplying monthly income by the income ratio. Thus (76,000 / 12) x .30 = $1,900. Remember to first derive the monthly income.

10.31 (a) $253,846
Total depreciation on this property = ($600,000 / 39 years) x 10 years, or $153,846. His adjusted basis is therefore ($680,000 original price – 153,846 depreciation taken), or $526,154. The gain is then ($780,000 – 526,154), or $253,846.

10.32 (b) $257,000.
Adjusted basis = beginning basis ($250,000) + capital improvements ($2,000 + $5,000) – depreciation (0) = adjusted basis ($257,000).

10.33 (c) $34,000.
Capital gain = amount realized (net sales proceeds, $265,000) - adjusted basis ($231,000) = ($34,000).

10.34 (d) $125,000.
The basic formula for adjusted basis is: Beginning Basis + Capital Improvements - Exclusions and Credits = Adjusted Basis. Debra's adjusted basis is therefore $120.000 + $5,000 = $125,000. The financing terms and subsequent selling price are not relevant.

10.35 (c) $15,000 overpriced.
Use the same formula V = I / R where V is the price and R is the rate of return. Then plug in the numbers to solve for V. The NOI of this property is ($60,000 - $22,000), or $38,000. The return is 11%. Therefore, the value to get this return must be $38,000 / .11, or $345,455. Since the price is $360,000, the price exceeds the amount needed for an 11% return by approximately $15,000 ($360,000 - $345,455 = $14,545).

10.36 (b) Yes, since he will yield 8.375%
Use the same formula R = I / V where V is the $2 million price, and R is the cap rate or rate of return. To identify income: (25,000 SF x $10/SF) = $250,000 gross income, minus 5% vacancy (.05 x $250,000), or $12,500, minus expenses of $70,000 = $167,500 net income. ($250,000 – 12,500 – 70,000) Now divide net income of $167,500 by $2,000,000 to derive the return of 8.375%.

10.37 (a) $1,680.
Annual gross operating income ($1,650 x 12 = $19,800) - annual operating expenses ($600 x 12 = $7,200) = annual net operating income ($12,600); annual net operating income ($12,600) - cost recovery expense ($7,000) = taxable income ($5,600); taxable income ($5,600) x tax rate (30%) = tax liability ($1,680).

10.38 (c) $10,640
The basic formula for tax liability is: Taxable Income x Tax Rate = Tax Liability. Taxable Income is Net Operating Income - Interest Expense - Cost Recovery Expense. Therefore, the annual tax is $150,000 (NOI) - $105,000 (Interest Expense) - $7,000 (Cost Recovery Expense) x 28% = $10,640. Note that the principal payment is not deductible in calculating taxable income.

10.39 (d) 31.4%
The formula for profit % is (profit / initial investment). The profit made was ($23,000 x 4) – 70,000 initial investment, or $22,000. Dividing this by the amount invested derives a profit percent of 31.4%.

10.40 (c) $1,000,000,000.
The mill rate = (tax requirement / the tax base). A mill is one one-thousandth of a dollar ($.001). To solve for the tax base, reconfigure this formula to be: Base = Tax Requirement / Mill Rate. Thus the Base = $10,000,000 / .010, or $1,000,000,000.

10.41 (a) $1,495
First, always use the assessed valuation, not the market value. Subtract out the homestead exemption to derive taxable value, or $140,000 – 25,000 = $115,000. As a shortcut to calculating the tax bill, simply add up all the mills, multiply them times .001 to convert mills to decimals, then multiply this number times the taxable value. Thus (7 + 3 + 2 + 1) x .001 x $115,000 = $1,495.

10.42 (b) 2.13%
The rate = budget / tax base. Thus, $8,000,000 / (400,000,000 – 25,000,000) = 2.13%

10.43 (d) $1,778.
First calculate the total commission, then the co-brokerage splits, then the agent-broker split. Thus: $127,000 x 7% = $8,890 total commission. ($8,890 x 50%) = $4,445 total listing broker share. ($4,445 x 40% = $1,778 agent's share.

10.44 (a) $6,866
Figure the total commission, then the co-brokerage splits, then the broker-agent splits. Thus, ($325,000 x 6.5%) = $21,125. ($21,125 x 50%) = $10,563. ($10,563 x .65) = $6,866.

10.45 (c)   A credit to the buyer and debit to the seller for $785.34.
The daily tax expense, first, is ($3,150 / 365) or $8.63. Since the buyer will pay the taxes after closing, the seller must pay the buyer his or her portion of the tax bill at closing, which is the 91 days from the beginning of the year through closing. Therefore, credit the buyer and debit the seller ($8.63 x 91), or $785.34.

10.46 (a) $507.50.
If the buyer pays $525 interest for 30 days, the daily expense is ($525 / 30), or $17.50. If there are 29 days of pre-paid expense, the buyer's charge is ($17.50 x 29), or $507.50.

10.47 (d)   Credit buyer $712.26.
For the monthly proration using the 365-day method, solve first for the daily rent amount: ($1,380 / 31), or $44.52. Since the landlord received the rent and owes the buyer portions of the rent, the buyer will be credited. The owed amount is for the 16th through the 31st, or 16 days, since the closing day belongs to the buyer. Therefore, credit the buyer and debit the seller ($44.52 x 16),or $712.26.

10.48 (d) $86,372
First calculate the transfer tax: ($322,600 / 500) = 645.2 units of $500. Round this up to 646, then multiply times $1.00 to get $646 transfer tax cost. Next figure the commission @ ($322,600 x .07), or $22,582. Next, the seller's real estate tax proration charge will be $2,000. Then, add up the expenses: ($646 transfer

tax + 450 title + 550 attorney + 22,582 commission + 210,000 loan payoff + 2,000 tax proration) = $236,228. Subtracting this from the sale price = $86,372.

10.49 (d) $5,848.
Be careful here. Since the net price is $5,000, the taking price (TP) minus the commission must equal the net price. In other words, the net price is 90% of the taking price. Since TP x 90% = Net, TP = Net / 90%. So the taking price is $5,556 ($5,000 / .9). Apply the same logic to deriving the asking price: the taking price is 95% of the list price, therefore the list price = (taking price / 95%), or $5,848. Now work backwards to prove your answer: (5,848 x 95% margin x .90 net of commission) = $5,000

10.50 (d) $468,750
Use the formula: (Percent of insurable property value carried / 80% replacement cost) x claim = recovery, where the insurable property value variable excludes the land value and is valued at replacement cost. Here, the insurable portion of the property is ($740,000 - 25% land value), or $555,000. The Wildes are carrying insurance to cover 75% of the replacement cost of the entire property. Their recovery amount is therefore (75% / 80%) x $500,000, or $468,750.

10.51 (c) $140,000
Use the formula: (Percent of insurable property value carried / 80% replacement cost) x claim = recovery. Thus, (75% / 80% x $150,000) = $140,625. However, the face value of the policy is the maximum they can receive, which is $140,000

STATE TEST 11: Licensing & Regulation

11.1 (b) will have his or her license converted to inactive status.
"When a provisional broker fails to complete all 90 hours of required postlicensing education within three years following initial licensure, the broker's license shall be placed on inactive status. The broker's license shall not be returned to active status until he or she has satisfied such requirements as the Commission may by rule require. " §93A-4(a1).

11.2 (d) It is active immediately upon filing unless the NCREC fails to acknowledge within 30 days from the date on the activation form.
"Upon the mailing or delivery of this (prescribed) form, the broker may engage in real estate brokerage activities requiring a license; however, if the broker does not receive from the Commission a written acknowledgment of the license activation within 30 days of the date shown on the form, the broker shall immediately terminate his or her real estate brokerage activities pending receipt of the written acknowledgment from the Commission." Subchapter 58A.0504(d)

11.3 (c) complete a 90-hour postlicensing education requirement within 3 years of initial licensure.
"A provisional broker as described in G.S. 93A- 4(a1) or G.S. 93A-4.3(d) must satisfactorily complete at least one of the 30-hour courses during each of the first three years following the date of his or her initial licensure as a broker in order to retain his or her eligibility to actively engage in real estate brokerage." 58A.1902(a)

11.4 (c) nine members, seven appointed by the Governor, two by the General Assembly.
"The Commission shall consist of nine members, seven members to be appointed by the Governor, one member to be appointed by the General Assembly upon the recommendation of the President Pro Tempore of the Senate in accordance with G.S. 120-121, and one member to be appointed by the General Assembly upon the recommendation of the Speaker of the House of Representatives." §93A-3(a)

11.5 (b) She will be on inactive status and lose her BIC status at the end of the license period.
"A broker's broker-in-charge eligibility and, if currently designated as a broker-in-charge, his or her broker-in-charge designation shall be terminated upon the occurrence of any of the following events: (3) the broker fails to complete the Broker-In-Charge Update Course"
58A.0110(l) .

11.6 (d) A person who buys, sells, or manages real estate on behalf of others
A real estate broker is "any person, partnership, corporation, limited liability company, association, or other business entity who for a compensation or valuable consideration or promise thereof lists or offers to list,

sells or offers to sell, buys or offers to buy, auctions or offers to auction (specifically not including a mere crier of sales), or negotiates the purchase or sale or exchange of real estate, or who leases or offers to lease, or who sells or offers to sell leases of whatever character, or rents or offers to rent any real estate or the improvement thereon, for others. " §93A-2(a)

11.7 (b) He must notify the Commission of the change.
A broker-in-charge shall notify the Commission in writing that he or she no longer is serving as broker-in-charge of a particular office within 10 days following any such change. 58A.0110(n)

11.8 (c) has completed the CE requirement and any postlicensing if required.
"If the provisional broker is on inactive status at the time of associating with a broker or brokerage firm, the provisional broker and broker-in-charge shall also file... the provisional broker's statement that he or she has satisfied the continuing education requirements prescribed by Rule .1703 of this Subchapter, and the postlicensing education requirements, if applicable, prescribed by Rule .1902 of this Subchapter, 58A.1711(2)." 58A.0506(c)

11.9 (a) have a broker's license, two years' full-time experience or its equivalent within the 5 prior years and satisfy an educational requirement.
"To qualify to serve as a broker-in-charge, a broker shall not be a provisional broker and shall possess at least two years of full-time real estate brokerage experience or equivalent part-time real estate brokerage experience within the previous five years or real estate education or experience in real estate transactions that the Commission finds equivalent to such experience. (The broker must also) complete the Commission's 12- classroom hour broker-in-charge course either within three years prior to designation as a broker-in-charge or within 120 days following designation as a broker-in-charge." 58A.0110(g)

11.10 (c) A professional negotiator assists clients in obtaining the best price for their properties.
Exemptions from licensure include parties handling their own properties; persons acting as an attorney in fact; services of an attorney; parties acting under court order; and trustees acting under a trust agreement. §93A-2

11.11 (b) The qualifying broker must be a general partner of the partnership.
All licensed business entities must have a duly licensed qualifying broker. "The qualifying broker of a partnership of any kind must be a general partner of the partnership..." Subchapter 58A.0502

11.12 (c) June 30, 2017.
Her first renewal would be on June 30, 2016, but there is no CE requirement for that renewal. Her second renewal would be June 30, 2017 and her license would lapse on that date if the CE requirement has not been fulfilled by June 10th, 2017. " In order to renew a broker license on active status, the person requesting renewal of a license shall, upon the second renewal of such license following initial licensure, and upon each subsequent annual renewal, have completed, within one year preceding license expiration, eight classroom hours of real estate continuing education in courses approved by the Commission as provided in Subchapter 58E." Subchapter 58A.1702

11.13 (b) a material fact was either misstated or omitted.
Licensees are prohibited from making or omitting material facts to clients and customers in the course of transacting business. Omission may be purposeful or negligent where the licensee should have known and disclosed the material fact. §93A-6

11.14 (c) The partnership license is terminated and the corporation must apply for a new license.
Whenever the business entity changes, the new entity must apply for a new license. Subchapter 58A.0502

11.15 (d) at least three licensed brokers and at least two individuals who are not involved in real estate.
"At least three members of the Commission shall be licensed real estate brokers. At least two members of the Commission shall be persons who are not involved directly or indirectly in the real estate or real estate appraisal business." §93A-3

11.16 (d) Yes, she is guilty of willful omission.
Dorothy has committed willful omission. The issue is material; she knew about the potential problem; and

she intentionally failed to disclose the failure rate. The duty to disclose is not limited to clients. NCREC's License Law and Rule Comments on 93A-6

11.17 (b) Follow the procedure for a licensee whose license has been expired for more than 6 months.
"Reinstatement of a revoked license may be considered upon the submission of a complete and accurate application and payment of a thirty dollar ($30.00) fee. Applicants must satisfy the same requirements as those prescribed in Paragraph (b) of this Rule for reinstatement of licenses expired for more than six months." Subchapter 58A.0505

11.18 (a) is subject to license suspension, revocation, censure or reprimand by the Real Estate Commission.
"The Commission has power to suspend or revoke at any time a license issued under the provisions of this Chapter, or to reprimand or censure any licensee, if, following a hearing, the Commission adjudges the licensee to be guilty of ... (listed offenses)". §93A-6

11.19 (c) may take the 4-hour general update course and an elective, or complete two approved 4-hour electives.
"A nonresident licensee may, within one year preceding license expiration, complete the Commission-prescribed Update course plus four classroom hours of instruction in one Commission-approved continuing education elective courses course, or complete two Commission-approved continuing education elective courses." 58A.1711(2) .

11.20 (c) It reverts to inactive status.
" A firm's license shall be assigned by the Commission to inactive status when the firm does not have a qualifying broker with an active license in good standing." Subchapter 58A.0504(b)

11.21 (a) It is assigned an inactive status.
"Except for persons licensed under the provisions of Section .1800 of this Subchapter, a broker shall also be assigned to inactive status if, upon the second renewal of his or her license following initial licensure, or upon any subsequent renewal, he or she has not satisfied the continuing education requirement described in Rule .1702 of this Subchapter." Subchapter 58A.0504(b)

11.22 (a) not engage in any real estate activity requiring a license.
"The holder of a license on inactive status may not engage in any activity requiring a real estate license, including the referral for compensation of a prospective seller, buyer, landlord or tenant to another real estate licensee or any other party." Subchapter 58A.0504(a)

11.23 (a) on June 30th following issuance of the license.
"All licenses issued by the Commission under the provisions of this Chapter shall expire on the 30th day of June following issuance or on any other date that the Commission may determine and shall become invalid after that date unless reinstated." §93A-4(c)

11.24 (c) three years.
"Members of the Commission shall serve three-year terms, so staggered that the terms of three members expire in one year, the terms of three members expire in the next year, and the terms of three members expire in the third year of each three-year period." §93A-3(a)

11.25 (a) complete a 12-hour broker-in-charge course within three years prior to or within 120 days following designation as a broker-in-charge.
"(The broker must also) complete the Commission's 12- classroom hour broker-in-charge course either within three years prior to designation as a broker-in-charge or within 120 days following designation as a broker-in-charge." 58A.0110

11.26 (c) purchase multiple properties from a broker.
If you are buying real property, you do not need a license.

11.27 (a) relates to features of the property; facts about the property; or facts relating to the ability of the principal to complete the transaction.
The materiality of a fact encompasses both the condition of the property and the circumstances surrounding

the client's ability to complete the transaction. NCREC's License Law and Rule Comments on 93A-6

11.28 (d) as soon as the broker-in-charge has mailed or faxed a completed supervision notification form.
A license issued to a provisional broker shall, upon initial licensure.   Subchapter 58A .0504

11.29 (b) must pass the North Carolina portion of the real estate licensing exam.
"Persons applying for a North Carolina broker license who hold a current real estate license that has been on active status within the previous three years in another state of the United States, a United States territory or possession or a Canadian jurisdiction shall meet the licensing requirements prescribed in G.S. 93A-4 except that such persons shall be exempt from the "national" section of the North Carolina real estate license examination, but shall pass the "state" section of that examination." 21 NCAC 58A .0511

11.30 (a) obtain injunctions against non-licensees who may be violating license law.
"The Commission may appear in its own name in superior court in actions for injunctive relief to prevent any person from violating the provisions of this Chapter or rules promulgated by the Commission." §93A-6c

11.31 (d) complete 8 hours of approved instruction every year following the first renewal.
An individual licensed as a real estate broker is required to complete continuing education requirements in an amount not to exceed eight classroom hours of instruction a year during any license renewal period in subjects and at times the Commission deems appropriate. §93A-4A

11.32 (b) Complete the 90-hour postlicensing requirement within the prescribed period of time.
"Upon completion of the postlicensing education program, the provisional status of the broker's license shall be terminated." § 93A-4.

11.33 (c) take a specially-designated 4-hour continuing education course for BIC's, along with a 4-hour elective CE course within each license period.
"The broker may maintain broker-in-charge eligibility by timely annual renewal of his or her broker license and completion each license year of the four hour mandatory continuing education update course for brokers-in-charge known as the "Broker-In-Charge Update Course" described in Rule 58E .0102(b), and any Commission-approved four hour continuing education elective course described in Rule 58E .0305. " 58A.0110 (k)

11.34 (a) negligent misrepresentation.
First, the representation is a material fact contributing to the buyer's decision, so Ken is exposed to liability. Second, Ken manifestly stated something, whether true or false, and therefore the problem is misrepresentation, not omission.   Finally, since Ken did not intentionally deceive, the problem is negligent misrepresentation: he should have checked out the lot's limitations before making his assurances.
NCREC's License Law and Rule Comments on 93A-6

11.35 (a) submit the annual renewal fee to NCREC.
"A person renewing a license on inactive status shall not be required to have obtained any continuing education in order to renew such license; however, in order to subsequently change his or her license from inactive status to active status, the licensee must satisfy the continuing education requirement prescribed in Rule ..1703 or .1711 of this Subchapter."   Subchapter 58A.0503 (c)

11.36 (a) upon the consummation of the transaction or within 5 days of closing.
Causes for disciplinary action: "(14) Failing, at the time the transaction is consummated, to deliver to the seller in every real estate transaction, a complete detailed closing statement showing all of the receipts and disbursements handled by him or her for the seller or failing to deliver to the buyer a complete statement showing all money received in the transaction from the buyer and how and for what it was disbursed at closing but no later than 5 days following closing." § 93A-6

11.37 (a) The requirements for obtaining a license.
"The Commission shall have power to make reasonable bylaws, rules and regulations that are not inconsistent with the provisions of this Chapter and the General Statutes; provided, however, the Commission shall not make rules or regulations regulating commissions, salaries, or fees to be charged by licensees under this Chapter." §93A-3

11.38 (a) an active license.
Brokers who are not provisional brokers receive active licenses upon approval of their application. Subchapter 58A.0504(b)

11.39 (a) failure to deliver a copy of a purchase agreement to a seller within 5 days
It is a violation when a licensee fails to deliver, within a reasonable time, a completed copy of any purchase agreement or offer to buy and sell real estate to the buyer and to the seller. §93A-6(a)
Licensees may use assumed names provided they are registered. Additionally, they are not required to disclose non-material facts. Finally, agents may pay other agents referral fees. §93A-6(a)

11.40 (d) He must wait 5 months, then demonstrate he is supervised by a broker-in-charge and has completed the continuing education requirement.
"When a (provisional broker's) license is suspended by the Commission, the suspended license shall be restored at the end of the period of active suspension provided that any applicable license renewal fees that accrued during the time of the suspension are paid by the licensee. In order for the license to be restored on active status, the provisional broker shall be required to demonstrate that he or she has satisfied the continuing education requirement for license activation prescribed by Rule .1703 of this Subchapter and that the provisional broker is supervised by a broker-in-charge in compliance with the requirements of Rule .0506 of this Section, if applicable." Subchapter 58A.0505(e)

11.41 (a) It becomes inactive.
"If a provisional broker as described in G.S. 93A-4(a1) or G.S. 93A-4.3(d) fails to complete the required postlicensing education described in paragraph (a) of this Rule by the end of either the first or second year following the date of his or her initial licensure as a broker, his or her license shall be placed on inactive status." 58A.1902(b))

11.42 (b) may be guilty of willful misrepresentation.
The agent is liable for willful misrepresentation since it is a material fact that the licensee made intentionally without having actual knowledge of the fact. In other words, the licensee knew that he didn't know, and made the statement anyway. The fact that another agent claimed the property was 4,000 square feet does not constitute actual knowledge. NCREC's License Law and Rule Comments on 93A-6

STATE TEST 12: Brokerage Business and Listing Agreements

12.1 (a) the homeseller is absolved of the duty to disclose a defect of that item.
"If the statement states that an owner makes no representations as to the conditions of the property, then the owner has no duty to disclose those conditions, whether or not the owner should have known of them." Regardless, the seller is not protected from fraudulent misrepresentations. GS 47E-4(c)

12.2 (b) When the broker has obtained a written agreement.
"Every agreement for brokerage services in a real estate transaction and every agreement for services connected with the management of a property owners association shall be in writing." Subchapter 58A.0104(a)

12.3 (b) Have their broker's and the principal's consent and identify the name of the broker or firm in the ad.
"A provisional broker shall not advertise the sale, purchase, exchange, rent or lease of real estate for another or others without his or her broker's consent and without including in the advertisement the name of the broker or firm with whom the provisional broker is associated. 58A.0105
"A licensee shall not advertise or display a "for sale" or "for rent" sign on any real estate without the consent of the owner or his or her authorized agent." 58A.0105

12.4 (a) No, the agreement must terminate at a specific time without prior notice to the seller.
"Every written agreement for brokerage services of any kind in a real estate transaction shall provide for its existence for a definite period of time and shall provide for its termination without prior notice at the

expiration of that period, except that an agency agreement between a landlord and broker to procure tenants or receive rents for the landlord's property may allow for automatic renewal so long as the landlord may terminate with notice at the end of any contract period and any subsequent renewals. ' Subchapter 58A.0104

12.5 (c) Compliance with the North Carolina Fair Housing Act.
"Every listing agreement, written buyer agency agreement or other written agreement for brokerage services in a real estate sales transaction shall contain the following provision: The broker shall conduct all his brokerage activities in regard to this agreement without respect to race, color, religion, sex, national origin, handicap or familial status. The provision shall be set forth in a clear and conspicuous manner which shall distinguish it from other provisions of the agreement." Subchapter 58A.0104

12.6 (a) All trust monies must be maintained in the association's trust account exclusively.
"The funds of a property owners' association, when collected, maintained, disbursed or otherwise controlled by a broker, are trust money and shall be treated as such in the manner required by Rules .0116 and .0117 of this Section. Such trust money shall be deposited into and maintained in a trust or escrow account dedicated exclusively for trust money belonging to a single property owners' association and shall not be commingled with funds belonging to other property owners' associations or other persons or parties." 58A .0118 (a)

12.7 (b) has violated state regulations by obtaining a secret profit from the buyer.
"A licensee shall not receive, either directly or indirectly, any commission, rebate or other valuable consideration of more than nominal value for services which the licensee recommends, procures, or arranges relating to a real estate transaction for any party, without full disclosure to such party..." Subchapter 58A.0109(b)

12.8 (a) must give the deposit to their broker immediately.
"All monies received by a provisional broker shall be delivered upon receipt to the broker with whom he or she is affiliated." Subchapter 58A.0116

12.9 (d) Yes, if neither the principal nor the listing agent has granted her permission.
A licensee shall not advertise or display a "for sale" or "for rent" sign on any real estate without the consent of the owner or his or her authorized agent. Subchapter 58A.0105

12.10 (c) may only employ one broker-in-charge regardless of the number of provisional brokers employed.
"No broker shall be broker-in-charge of more than one office at a time. If a firm shares office space with one or more other firms, one broker may serve as broker-in-charge of each firm at that location. No office or branch office of a firm shall have more than one designated broker-in-charge." Subchapter 58A.0110

12.11 (b) He must cease representing Sarah and become a subagent of the seller if allowed
If Ethan cannot obtain a written agreement prior to the buyer's offer, he has no agency agreement with the buyer and should cease representing her. He would only be able to proceed with seller subagency by disclosing the change of representation to the buyer, including potential confidentiality disclosures that now must be made to the seller, and by obtaining approval of both principals. Subchapter 58A.0104

12.12 (a) is bound by the requirement to retain records of this transaction for three years.
"Licensees shall retain records of all sales, rental, and other transactions conducted in such capacity, whether the transaction is pending, completed or terminated prior to its successful conclusion. The licensee shall retain such records for three years after all funds held by the licensee in connection with the transaction have been disbursed to the proper party or parties or until the successful or unsuccessful conclusion of the transaction, whichever occurs later." Subchapter 58A.0108

12.13 (c) five days.
"...every broker shall immediately, but in no event later than five days from the date of execution, deliver to the parties thereto copies of any required written agency agreement, contract, offer, lease, or option affecting real property." Subchapter 58A.0106(a)

12.14 (d) may not cancel the contract.
Once a transaction has closed or a buyer has taken possession, the right of rescission is terminated. GS

12.15 (a) the tenant.
"The tenant shall keep that part of the premises that the tenant occupies and uses as clean and safe as the conditions of the premises permit and cause no unsafe or unsanitary conditions in the common areas and remainder of the premises that the tenant uses ." In addition, the tenant is responsible for damages. G.S. 42-43(a-1), (a-6)

12.16 (d) Patrick has violated the prohibition of practicing law.
Licensees in North Carolina may not provide legal advice as to the nature of any interest in real estate, or how title should be held. G.S. 84-2.1

12.17 (a) must disclose the condition of their property to a buyer on or before the point at which they receive an offer.
"The owner of the real property shall furnish to a purchaser a residential property disclosure statement. The disclosure statement shall: (1) Disclose those items which are required to be disclosed relative to the characteristics and condition of the property and of which the owner has actual knowledge; or (2) State that the owner makes no representations as to the characteristics and condition of the real property or any improvements to the real property except as otherwise provided in the real estate contract." G.S. 47E-4 (a)

12.18 (d) has acted properly in view of state regulations provided the payment is made to his/her employing broker.
"A licensee shall not receive, either directly or indirectly, any commission, rebate or other valuable consideration of more than nominal value from a vendor or a supplier of goods and services for an expenditure made on behalf of the licensee's principal in a real estate transaction without the written consent of the licensee's principal." Subchapter 58A.0109(a)

12.19 (d) No, not until the agreement is in writing.
"Every agreement for brokerage services between a broker and an owner of the property to be the subject of a transaction must be in writing from the time of its formation." Subchapter 58A.0104

12.20 (a) identify the broker's name or firm.
"A licensee shall not advertise the sale, purchase, exchange, rent or lease of real estate, for another or others, in a manner indicating the offer to sell, purchase, exchange, rent, or lease is being made by the licensee's principal only. Every such advertisement shall conspicuously indicate that it is the advertisement of a broker or brokerage firm and shall not be confined to publication of only a post office box number, telephone number, or street address." 21 NCAC 58A.0105

12.21 (a) the principals approve of the account and agree in writing on who will receive the interest.
"Prior to depositing trust money into a trust or escrow account that bears interest, the broker having custody over such money shall first secure written authorization from all parties having an interest in the money. Such authorization shall specify and set forth in a conspicuous manner how and to whom the interest shall be disbursed." Subchapter 58A.0116(c)

12.22 (b) the licensee limits his preparations to completing an approved, preprinted form.
"A broker or provisional broker acting as an agent in a real estate transaction shall not draft offers, sales contracts, options, leases, promissory notes, deeds, deeds of trust or other legal instruments by which the rights of others are secured; however, a broker or provisional broker may complete preprinted offer, option contract, sales contracts and lease forms in real estate transactions when authorized or directed to do so by the parties." Subchapter 58A.0111(a)

12.23 (d) may not draft or fill in the blanks of printed forms for others.
Unlike offers or sales contracts, agents may not draft or fill in the blanks of any deed or deed of trust on behalf of clients or customers, without exception (G.S. 93A-4(e)); "... it shall be unlawful for any person or association of persons except active members of the Bar... to give legal advice or counsel, perform for or furnish to another legal services, or to prepare directly or through another for another person, firm or corporation, any will or testamentary disposition, or instrument of trust, or ...prepare for another person, firm or corporation, any other legal document." G.S. 84-4

12.24 (c) It must be on pre-printed forms approved by NCREC.
Rules 58A A.0104(a, b) require that agency agreements must expire, may not automatically renew, and must contain a non-discrimination clause.

12.25 (d) Notify the NCREC of the termination within 10 days following her last day.
"Upon the termination of the supervisory relationship between a provisional broker and his or her broker-in-charge, the provisional broker and the broker-in-charge shall provide written notification of the date of termination to the Commission not later than 10 days following said termination." Subchapter 58A.0506(e)

12.26 (c) five days after closing.
"every broker shall immediately, but in no event later than five days from the date of execution, deliver to the parties thereto copies of any required written agency agreement, contract, offer, lease, or option affecting real property." Subchapter 58A.0106(a)

12.27 (d) Eleven; one for each office, including the headquarters office.
"Every real estate firm shall designate a broker to serve as the broker-in-charge at its principal office and a broker to serve as broker-in-charge at any branch office." Subchapter 58A.0110(b)

12.28 (b) To clarify and identify whether the agent will represent the buyer or seller in the transaction.
"In every real estate sales transaction, a broker or provisional broker shall, at first substantial contact directly with a prospective buyer or seller, provide the prospective buyer or seller with a copy of the publication "Working with Real Estate Agents," review it with him or her, and determine whether the agent will act as the agent of the buyer or seller in the transaction." Subchapter 58A.0104

12.29 (a) leave a clear audit trail, including monthly bank reconciliations.
Records of all receipts and disbursements of trust or escrow monies shall be maintained in such a manner as to create an audit trail from deposit tickets and canceled checks to check stubs or journals and to the ledger sheets. Subchapter 58A.0117 (d)

12.30 (a) has acted properly, since she did not pay a kickback.
"Except as provided in (h) of this rule (for travel agents), a licensee shall not undertake in any manner, any arrangement, contract, plan or other course of conduct, to compensate or share compensation with unlicensed persons or entities for any acts performed in North Carolina for which licensure by the Commission is required." This is the prohibition which Vanessa avoided by simply lowering her commission, which is perfectly legal. Subchapter 58A.0109(g)

12.31 (d) if they handle the funds of others
If a practicing broker does not collect or otherwise handle the funds of others, no trust account is required. 58A.0116.

12.32 (a) Maintaining corporate tax and accounting records and the firm's license status.
Principal responsibilities of brokers-in-charge are: retaining and displaying licenses; making proper notifications to NCREC; assuring proper advertising is conducted; maintaining trust account and transaction records; supervising provisional brokers; and assuring agency disclosures are made. Subchapter 58A.0110

12.33 (b) has misapplied trust funds in violation of state regulations.
"A broker shall not convert the money or property of others to his or her own use, apply such money or property to a purpose other than that for which it was paid or entrusted to him or her, or permit or assist any other person in the conversion or misapplication of such money or property." Subchapter 58A.0116(g)

12.34 (b) Mike must designate himself as broker-in-charge in order to conduct business.
"A broker who is a sole proprietor shall designate himself or herself as a broker-in-charge if the broker engages in any transaction where the broker is required to deposit and maintain monies belonging to others in a trust account, engages in advertising or promoting his or her services as a broker in any manner, or has one or more other brokers affiliated with him or her in the real estate business." Subchapter 58A.0110

12.35 (d) has not violated any regulation.
"If the parties propose to delete or change any word or provision in the form, the form must be marked to

indicate the change or deletion made. The language of the form shall not be modified, rewritten, or changed by the broker or provisional broker or their clerical employees unless directed to do so by the parties." Subchapter 58A.0111(b)

12.36 (c) must disclose the developer's intentions prior to making the offer.
The agent may proceed with his intended offer, but only after a full disclosure of the conflict of interest with the seller. G.S. 93A 6(a)

12.37 (b) within three banking days of acceptance of the offer.
"All monies received by a licensee acting in his or her fiduciary capacity shall be deposited in a trust or escrow account maintained by a broker not later than three banking days following acceptance of the offer..."   Subchapter 58A.0116(a)

12.38 (b) The North Carolina Association of Realtors and North Carolina Bar
The North Carolina Bar Association and North Carolina Association of Realtors have approved a standard "Offer to Purchase and Contract" form. The NC Real Estate Commission sets rules for preprinted contract forms, but does not create or approve forms. Principals may amend the form or draft their own.

12.39 (b) If the seller defaults, the buyer may sue for specific performance.
The only true statement is that the buyer can sue for specific performance if the seller defaults. The sales contract must be in writing, there is no legal requirement on the date of closing, and there is no regulation regarding the escrow amount.

12.40 (d) the seller is responsible for the property condition.
The seller is responsible for the property condition. The buyer must wait until closing has been completed before making improvements to the property. The seller does not have to cure reasonable wear and tear; that has typically already been factored into the purchase price. The sales contract does not automatically become void if there is major damage to the property but could become voidable if the damage is severe.

STATE TEST 13: Agency, Property Management and Other NC Laws

13.1 (a) how long the buyer has been living in his present house.
"...'first substantial contact" shall include contacts between a broker and a consumer where the consumer or broker begins to act as though an agency relationship exists and the consumer begins to disclose to the broker personal or confidential information." Subchapter 58A.0104(c)

Thus, when buyers begin to disclose specific needs, their financial capabilities, and information that they may not want a seller to know about, there is substantial contact. While other revelations may be less substantial, the best rule is to disclose as soon as possible.

13.2 (a) the agent has already received confidential information from the seller in the transaction.
"An individual broker shall not be so designated and shall not undertake to represent only the interests of one party if the broker has actually received confidential information concerning the other party in connection with the transaction."   Subchapter 58A.0104(j)

13.3 (b) Prior express approval of both principals obtained upon the formation of the relationship and reduced to writing as required.
"When a firm represents both the buyer and seller in the same real estate transaction, the firm may, with the prior express approval of its buyer and seller clients, designate one or more individual agents associated with the firm to represent only the interests of the seller and one or more other individual brokers associated with the firm to represent only the interests of the buyer in the transaction. The authority for designated agency must be reduced to writing not later than the time that the parties are required to reduce their dual agency agreement to writing in accordance with Paragraph (d) of this Rule."   Subchapter 58A.0104(j)

13.4 (b) When the broker has obtained prior written consent of both parties.
"A real estate broker representing one party in a transaction shall not undertake to represent another party in the transaction without the written authority of each party. Such written authority must be obtained upon the formation of the relationship except when a buyer or tenant is represented by a broker without a written

agreement in conformity with the requirements of Paragraph (a) of this Rule." 58A A.0104(d). Thus, individual brokers may practice dual agency without involving designated agency.

13.5 (d) all of the above.
A broker-in-charge shall not act as a designated agent for a party in a real estate sales transaction when a provisional broker under his or her supervision will act as a designated agent for another party with a competing interest. Subchapter 58A.0104(j)

13.6 (d) may not be practiced without written consent of both parties to the transaction.
"A real estate broker representing one party in a transaction shall not undertake to represent another party in the transaction without the written authority of each party." Subchapter 58A.0104(d)

13.7 (b) a verbal disclosure followed by a written disclosure mailed within three days.
"If the first substantial contact occurs by telephone or by means of other electronic communication where it is not practical to provide written disclosure, the broker shall immediately disclose by similar means whom he represents and shall immediately mail or otherwise transmit a copy of the written disclosure to the buyer. In no event shall the broker mail or transmit a copy of the written disclosure to the buyer later than three days from the date of first substantial contact with the buyer." Subchapter 58A.0104(e)

13.8 (b) if a provisional broker under his or her supervision represents the other party.
"A broker-in-charge shall not act as a designated agent for a party in a real estate sales transaction when a provisional broker under his or her supervision will act as a designated agent for another party with a competing interest." 58A A.0104(j). The BIC may practice designated agency if the authorization is timely and in writing.

13.9 (a) an agent designated to represent either the buyer or seller in a firm's dual agency situation.
"When a firm represents both the buyer and seller in the same real estate transaction, the firm may, with the prior express approval of its buyer and seller clients, designate one or more individual agents associated with the firm to represent only the interests of the seller and one or more other individual brokers associated with the firm to represent only the interests of the buyer in the transaction." Subchapter 58A.0104(j)

13.10 (b) Upon first substantial contact.
"In every real estate sales transaction, a broker working directly with a prospective buyer as a seller's agent or subagent shall disclose in writing to the prospective buyer at the first substantial contact with the prospective buyer that the broker represents the interests of the seller." Subchapter 58A.0104(e)

13.11 (d) provides building standards for local building inspectors to certify properties for occupancy.
The NC Uniform Building Code establishes minimum quality standards for every facet of a building's construction and operating systems. These standards are provided for the benefit of local municipalities in evaluating the habitability of residential and commercial properties. Properties that meet the code are issued a certificate of occupancy, allowing the building to be occupied. G.S. 143-138(c)

13.12 (d) are not required to report square footage, but are advised to be accurate if they do so.
Although real estate licensees are not required to report the square footage of properties offered for sale (or rent), when they do report square footage, it is essential that the information they give prospective purchasers be accurate. At a minimum, information concerning square footage should include the amount of living area in the dwelling. Agents should be prepared to identify, when requested, the standard used.

13.13 (c) $1.00 per each $500 or fractional part thereof, paid by the seller.
"An excise tax is levied on each instrument by which any interest in real property is conveyed to another person. The tax rate is one dollar ($1.00) on each five hundred dollars ($500.00) or fractional part thereof of the consideration or value of the interest conveyed. The transferor must pay the tax to the register of deeds of the county in which the real estate is located before recording the instrument of conveyance." § 105-228.30

13.14 (b) may not discriminate in the sale of his property.
The NCFHA does not exempt homesellers selling their own home without an agent; they must still comply with the discrimination prohibitions. This varies from federal fair housing law which does allow for such an

exemption, provided no agent is used. G.S. 41A-4

13.15 (a) The homeowner is exempt.
The Act exempts homeowners renting a room in their own homes, regardless of whether agents are employed, provided they inhabit the dwelling. G.S. 41A-6(a.2)

13.16 (d) One year following the alleged discriminatory violation
"A complaint under subsection (a) shall be filed within one year after the alleged unlawful discriminatory housing practice occurred." G.S. 41A-7(b)

13.17 (c) the North Carolina Fair Housing Act of 1983
The North Carolina Fair Housing Act of 1983 prohibits the same discriminatory acts as federal fair housing laws. G.S 41A

13.18 (d) title theory state where trustee's take legal title to the property.
In North Carolina, the lender is beneficiary to legal title to the property. The property's title remains in a trust until the mortgage is paid off. When the borrower satisfies the debt, the title is transferred to the borrower. Hence, North Carolina is a title theory state.

13.19 (a) is 65 years of age or totally disabled.
A person may be able to claim a $60,000 homestead exemption if the owner meets all of the following requirements as of January 1 preceding the taxable year for which the benefit is claimed: (1) Is at least 65 years of age or totally and permanently disabled. (2) Has an income for the preceding calendar year of not more than the income eligibility limit ($25,000). (3) Is a North Carolina resident. § 105-277.1

13.20 (a) An FDIC-insured banking institution.
Exempt properties: real property owned by a nonprofit corporation or association exclusively held and used by its owner for educational and scientific purposes as a protected natural area; real or personal property that is used exclusively for recycling or resource recovering of or from solid waste; and real property owned either by a nonprofit corporation or by a bona fide charitable organization and appropriated exclusively for public parks and drives. § 105-275

13.21 (c) Taxes are levied in July; due and payable in September, and delinquent on January 6.
"Each year - not later than the date prescribed by applicable law or, in the absence of specific statutory provisions, not later than the first day of August - the tax levying authorities of counties and municipalities shall levy on property rates of taxes. Taxes levied are due and payable on September 1 of the fiscal year for which the taxes are levied. Taxes are payable at par or face amount if paid before January 6 following the due date." § 105-347, § 105-360

13.22 (d) every eight years.
"Octennial Plan: each county of the State, as of January 1 of the year prescribed in the schedule set out in subdivision (a)(1) and every eighth year thereafter, shall reappraise all real property in accordance with the provisions of G.S. 105-283 and 105-317." § 105-286

13.23 (a) protect and preserve the state's coastal and estuary regions.
"In the implementation of the coastal area management plan, the public's opportunity to enjoy the physical, esthetic, cultural, and recreational qualities of the natural shorelines of the State shall be preserved to the greatest extent feasible; water resources shall be managed in order to preserve and enhance water quality and to provide optimum utilization of water resources; land resources shall be managed in order to guide growth and development and to minimize damage to the natural environment; and private property rights shall be preserved in accord with the Constitution of this State and of the United States." § 113A-102

13.24 (b) 7 days' right of rescission following the execution of a contract.
Purchaser's right to cancel: "No conveyance pursuant to the contract to purchase may occur until seven calendar days following the execution of the contract and a purchaser has the absolute right to cancel the contract at any time during this seven calendar period. Cancellation is without penalty, and all payments made by the purchaser before cancellation shall be refunded promptly." § 47C-4-108

13.25 (c) 120 days.
Filing claim of lien. "(b) Time of filing. - Claims of lien may be filed at any time after the maturity of the obligation secured thereby but not later than 120 days after the last furnishing of labor or materials at the site of the improvement by the person claiming the lien." § 44A-12.

13.26 (b) give buyer prospects a statement of monthly fees and assessments.
Resale of units: "except in the case of a sale where delivery of a public offering statement is required, or unless exempt under G.S. 47C-4- 101(b), a unit owner shall furnish to a prospective purchaser before conveyance a statement setting forth the monthly common expense assessment and any other fees payable by unit owners." § 47C-4-109.

13.27 (c) must receive a public offering statement prior to executing a contract.
"Any declarant or other person in the business of selling real estate who offers a unit for his own account to a purchaser shall deliver a public offering statement in the manner prescribed in G.S. 47C-4-108(a)." Also, "a person required to deliver a public offering statement pursuant to G.S. 47C-4-102(c) shall provide a purchaser of a unit or the spouse of such purchaser with a copy of the public offering statement and all amendments thereto before a contract to purchase the unit is executed. § 47C-4-102(c); § 47C-4-108.

13.28 (c) Government Survey System.
Definitions; description of boundaries: "(b) Whenever this Article requires that the boundaries of an area be described, it shall be sufficient if the boundaries are described in a manner which conveys an understanding of the location of the land and may be (1) by reference to a map, (2) by metes and bounds, (3) by general description referring to natural boundaries, boundaries of political subdivisions, existing water or sewer districts, or portions thereof, or boundaries of particular tracts or parcels of land, or (4) any combination of the foregoing." § 162A-32.

13.29 (c) twenty years.
"No action for the recovery or possession of real property, or the issues and profits thereof, shall be maintained when the person in possession thereof, or defendant in the action, or those under whom he claims, has possessed the property under known and visible lines and boundaries adversely to all other persons for 20 years; and such possession so held gives a title in fee to the possessor, in such property, against all persons not under disability." § 1-40.

13.30 (b) Non-judicial foreclosure.
A non-judicial foreclosure is one in which the sale of a liened property can be forced without a foreclosure suit due to a "power of sale" clause in the trust deed or mortgage document. A judicial foreclosure requires a foreclosure suit to force sale. Strict foreclosure, in which a lender obtains title directly by court order is not practiced in North Carolina.

13.31 (c) expenses specifically relating to a tenancy, if justified.
"Security deposits for residential dwelling units shall be permitted only for the tenant's possible nonpayment of rent and costs for water or sewer services provided pursuant to G.S. 62-110(g), damage to the premises, nonfulfillment of rental period, any unpaid bills that become a lien against the demised property due to the tenant's occupancy, costs of re-renting the premises after breach by the tenant..." G.S. 42-51.

13.32 (b) the Residential Rental Agreements article of the NC Landlord and Tenant statute.
NC Chapter 42, Article 5 ("Residential Rental Agreements"), regulates the rights, obligations and remedies for residential landlords and tenants in North Carolina. G.S. 42-38.

13.33 (a) must be in writing and recorded to be valid.
"...all leases and contracts for leasing land for the purpose of digging for gold or other minerals, or for mining generally, of whatever duration... shall be void unless said contract, or some memorandum or note thereof, be put in writing and signed by the party to be charged therewith, or by some other person by him thereto lawfully authorized." G.S. § 22-2.

13.34 (d) Vacation Rental Act
"Rental transactions conducted by the owners of these residences or licensed real estate brokers acting on their behalf present unique situations not normally found in the rental of primary residences for long terms, and therefore make it necessary for the General Assembly to enact laws regulating the competing interests

of landlords, real estate brokers, and tenants." G.S. 42A-2

13.35 (d) damages caused to the interior of an apartment that is above and beyond wear and tear.
" The tenant shall ...Be responsible for all damage, defacement, or removal of any property inside a dwelling unit in the tenant's exclusive control unless the damage, defacement or removal was due to ordinary wear and tear, acts of the landlord or the landlord's agent, defective products supplied or repairs authorized by the landlord, acts of third parties not invitees of the tenant, or natural forces." G.S. 42-43

13.36 (a) has grounds to evict the tenant.
A tenant may not unilaterally withhold rent under a lease obligation. If the tenant feels the landlord has failed to maintain the property, the tenant may stop paying rent, but must also vacate the premises. G.S. 42-26, 42-37.1, 42-44

13.37 (c) two month's rent for rentals exceeding month-to-month.
"The security deposit shall not exceed an amount equal to two weeks' rent if a tenancy is week to week, one and one-half months' rent if a tenancy is month to month, and two months' rent for terms greater than month to month." G.S. 42-51

13.38 (a) must be in writing to be valid.
"All contracts to sell or convey any lands, tenements or hereditaments, or any interest in or concerning them, and all leases and contracts for leasing land for the purpose of digging for gold or other minerals, or for mining generally, of whatever duration; and all other leases and contracts for leasing lands exceeding in duration three years from the making thereof, shall be void unless said contract, or some memorandum or note thereof, be put in writing and signed by the party to be charged therewith, or by some other person by him thereto lawfully authorized." G.S. § 22-2.

13.39 (b) landlords and brokers of vacation properties.
"The provisions of this Chapter shall apply to any person, partnership, corporation, limited liability company, association, or other business entity who acts as a landlord or real estate broker engaged in the rental or management of residential property for vacation rental as defined in this Chapter." G.S. 42A-3a

13.40 (c) need not be licensed.
Exemptions to NC license law: "any salaried person employed by a licensed real estate broker, for and on behalf of the owner of any real estate or the improvements thereon, which the licensed broker has contracted to manage for the owner, if the salaried employee's employment is limited to: exhibiting units on the real estate to prospective tenants; providing the prospective tenants with information about the lease of the units; accepting applications for lease of the units; completing and executing preprinted form leases; and accepting security deposits and rental payments for the units only when the deposits and rental payments are made payable to the owner or the broker employed by the owner." § 93A-2(c)(6).

13.41 (d) all of the above.
Vacation agreements in North Carolina must be in writing and accepted by the renter via a signature, payment of monies, or possession of the property. The agreement also contains specific language as to how the renter's monies will be handled prior to occupancy.

13.42 (c) exceed three years.
"...all other leases and contracts for leasing lands exceeding in duration three years from the making thereof, shall be void unless said contract, or some memorandum or note thereof, be put in writing and signed by the party to be charged therewith, or by some other person by him thereto lawfully authorized." G.S. 22-2

13.43 (c) Obtain a real estate license and a securities license before engaging in any sales.
"...it shall be unlawful for any person in this State to engage or assume to engage in the business of a time share agent without first obtaining a real estate broker issued by the North Carolina Real Estate Commission... " §93A-40(a)

13.44 (b) registering the time share project with the NC Real Estate Commission.
"A person ... who intentionally acts as a time share developer, allowing the offering of sale or the sale of time shares to a purchaser, without first obtaining registration of the time share project under this Article shall be guilty of a Class I felony." §93A-40(b)

13.45 (b) The time share developer.
"Each developer shall fully and conspicuously disclose in a public offering statement... " with the information required. §93A-44

13.46 (c) The project broker
"The broker designated by the developer of a time share project to be project broker shall assume responsibility for:... the proper maintenance of accurate records at the project including all records relating to the handling of trust monies at the project, records relating to time share sales and rental transactions and the project registration and renewal." Subchapter 58B §602(a)

13.47 (c) the heirs of the deceased.
Survivorship in joint tenancy defined: "except as otherwise provided herein, in all estates, real or personal, held in joint tenancy, the part or share of any tenant dying shall not descend or go to the surviving tenant, but shall descend or be vested in the heirs, executors, or administrators, respectively, of the tenant so dying, in the same manner as estates held by tenancy in common..." G.S.§ 41-2.

13.48 (a) promote the marketability and transferability of North Carolina real estate.
"It is hereby declared as a matter of public policy by the General Assembly of the State of North Carolina that: (1) Land is a basic resource of the people of the State of North Carolina and should be made freely alienable and marketable so far as is practicable.. " G.S.§ 47B-1.

13.49 (c) A limited service agency agreement
With limited service agency agreements, each item the agent will do for the client is listed and compensation listed. Typical services include MLS participation, open houses, showing, and contract negotiations. Open and full service agency agreements do not do this.

13.50 (b) The agreements do not create an agency relationship.
Protections agreements are typically used in FSBO transactions to ensure the broker receives compensation for procuring a buyer. However, they do not create an agency relationship even though the seller must be given the Working with Agents brochure.

13.51 (b) To help low-income agricultural homeowners with affordable financing.
Rural Development Loans are issued by the US Department of Agriculture for low-income rural residents for principal residences.

13.52 (b) Every 8 years
Listed, taxable North Carolina property is assessed every 8 years or more often. The tax rate is set by the jurisdiction's budget.

SAMPLE TEST: North Carolina License Examination Sample Test

S 1. (b) Trade fixtures that are personal property.
Trade fixtures are items of a tenant's personal property that the tenant has temporarily affixed to a landlord's real property in order to conduct business. Trade fixtures may be detached and removed before or upon surrender of the leased premises. Should the tenant fail to remove a trade fixture, it may become the property of the landlord through accession. Thereafter, the fixture is considered real property.

S 2. (c) Severance and affixing.
Severance is the conversion of real property to personal property by detaching it from the real estate; affixing, or attachment, is the act of converting personal property to real property by attaching it to the real estate, such as by assembling a pile of bricks into a barbecue pit, or constructing a boat dock from wood planks.

S 3. (d) absolute fee simple estate.
The fee simple freehold estate is the highest form of ownership interest one can acquire in real estate. It includes the complete bundle of rights, and the tenancy is unlimited, with certain exceptions. The fee simple absolute estate is a perpetual estate that is not conditioned by stipulated or restricted uses.

S 4. (c) the estate may revert to a grantor or heirs if the prescribed use changes.
The defeasible fee estate is perpetual, provided the usage conforms to stated conditions. Essential characteristics are: the property must be used for a certain purpose or under certain conditions; and, if the use changes or if prohibited conditions are present, the estate reverts to the previous grantor of the estate.

S 5. (a) conventional life estate.
A conventional life estate is a freehold estate that is limited in duration to the life of the owner or other named person. Upon the death of the owner or other named individual, the estate passes to the original owner or another named party. A legal life estate is created by law as opposed to a property owner's choice.

S 6. (a) a condominium owner owns a unit of air space whereas the co-op owner owns a proprietary lease.
The owner of a condominium has a fee-simple ownership interest in his/her unit and its air space. Whereas, a co-op owner has a leasehold, not fee-simple, interest with the property's corporation. Since the corporation owns an undivided interest in the cooperative property, debts and financial obligations apply to the property as a whole, not to individual units as in a condominium.

S 7. (d) Trustor, trustee and beneficiary.
In an estate in trust, a fee owner-- the grantor or trustor-- transfers legal title to a fiduciary-- the trustee-- who holds and manages the estate for the benefit of another party, the beneficiary.

S 8. (c) fee simple ownership of the airspace in a unit and an undivided share of the entire property's common areas.
A condominium is a hybrid form of ownership of multi-unit residential or commercial properties. It combines ownership of a fee simple interest in the airspace within a unit with ownership of an undivided share, as a tenant in common, of the entire property's common elements, such as lobbies, swimming pools, and hallways.

S 9. (a) the date of recordation.
Among junior liens, date of recording determines priority. The rule is: the earlier the recording date of the lien, the higher its priority. For example, if a judgment lien is recorded against a property on Friday, and a mortgage lien is recorded on the following Tuesday, the judgment lien has priority and must be satisfied in a foreclosure ahead of the mortgage lien.

S 10. (b) A state in which a mortgagor retains title to the property when a mortgage lien is created.
In lien-theory states, laws give a lender on a mortgaged property equitable title rather than legal title. The mortgagor in a lien theory state retains legal title.

S 11. (b) transfers with the property.
The term appurtenant means "attaching to." An easement appurtenant attaches to the estate and transfers with it unless specifically stated otherwise in the transaction documents.

S 12. (c) Giving constructive notice of one's rights and interests in the property.
Recorded instruments may include deeds, mortgages, liens, easements, sale contracts, and marriage, probate and tax records. The primary purpose of recording and maintaining records of these instruments is to provide constructive notice of the conditions of a property's title-- who owns it, who maintains claims against it.

S 13. (c) A chronology of successive owners of record of a parcel of real estate.
Chain of title refers to the succession of owners of record dating back to the original grant of title from the state to a private party. It is thus more than a mere list; it is a chronological list as reflected in title records.

S 14. (c) Title insurance.
A title insurance policy indemnifies the policy holder against losses arising from defects in the title and is thus generally accepted as the best evidence of marketability after a Torrens certificate, which is not available in every jurisdiction. A signed deed is no evidence of marketability, only of an intent to convey title. An attorney's opinion and a title certificate, while forms of evidence of marketability, do not guarantee

clear title or offer any protection against a defective title.

S 15. (c) percentage lease A percentage lease allows the landlord to share in the income generated from the use of the property. A tenant pays percentage rent, or an amount of rent equal to a percentage of the tenant's periodic gross sales.

S 16. (d) net lease.
A net lease requires a tenant to pay for utilities, internal repairs, and a proportionate share of taxes, insurance, and operating expenses in addition to rent.

S 17. (b) The leased property is foreclosed.
A foreclosure extinguishes all prior interests in a property, including a leasehold.

S 18. (c) the construction conforms with applicable building codes.
Building inspectors inspect a new development or improvement for code compliance. If the work complies, the municipality or county issues a certificate of occupancy which officially clears the property for occupation and use.

S 19. (b) takes title subject to the same restriction.
Deed restrictions attach to the title of the property. Therefore, the restriction passes to the new buyer.

S 20. (a) She has the right to re-possess the property because the grantee has violated the condition.
A deed condition may restrict certain uses of a property, much like a deed restriction. However, violation of a deed condition gives the grantor the right to re-take possession of the property and file suit for legal title.

S 21. (a) To create a consistent, unchanging standard for identifying a property's unique location.
A legal description of real property is one which accurately locates and identifies the boundaries of the subject parcel to a degree acceptable by courts of law in the state where the property is located. The general criterion for a legal description is that it alone provides sufficient data for a surveyor to locate the parcel. A legal description identifies the property as unique and distinct from all other properties.

S 22. (b) They identify an enclosed area, beginning and ending at the same point.
The metes and bounds description always identifies an enclosed area by starting at an origination point, called point of beginning, or POB, and returning to the POB at the end of the description.

S 23. (a) is void.
By changing any of the terms of an offer, the offeree creates a counteroffer, and the original offer is void. At this point, the offeree becomes the offeror, and the new offeree gains the right of acceptance. If accepted, the counteroffer becomes a valid contract provided all other requirements are met.

S 24. (a) may be assigned.
A real estate contract that is not a personal contract for services can be assigned to another party unless the terms of the agreement specifically prohibit assignment. Listing agreements, for example, are not assignable, since they are personal service agreements between agent and principal. Sales contracts, however, are assignable, because they involve the purchase of real property rather than a personal service.

S 25. (c) A two-year lease.
A contract may be in writing or it may be an oral, or parol, contract. Certain oral contracts are valid and enforceable, others are not enforceable, even if valid. For example, most states require listing agreements, sales contracts, and leases exceeding one year to be in writing to be enforceable.

S 26. (b) a dual agent.
Dual agency occurs whenever a single broker represents both principal parties to a transaction. Here, since Bob and Sue work for Bill, Bill is the dual agent.

S 27. (a) upon first substantive communication.
The agent must provide written notice to all parties or their agents as soon as substantive communication occurs, which can include initial face-to-face contact.

S 28. (d) neither seller nor buyer.
In recent years, the brokerage industry has striven to clear up the question of who works for whom, and who owes fiduciary duties to whom. One solution allows a broker to represent no one in a transaction. That is, the broker acts as a transaction broker, or facilitator, and has no allegiance to buyer or seller.

S 29. (b) the principal has proposed an illegal act, which should not be obeyed.
An agent must comply with the client's directions and instructions, provided they are legal. If the directive is illegal, the agent must also immediately withdraw.

S 30. (b) negotiated with clients.
The amount of a broker's commission is whatever amount the client and broker have agreed to.

S 31. (b) the client may be liable for a commission and marketing expenses.
With an exclusive right-to-sell listing, if the property sells during the term of the revoked listing, the client is liable for the commission. If the property does not sell, the client is liable for the broker's actual costs.

S 32. (b) the agent has a claim to a commission if the owner sells or leases to a party within a certain time following the listing's expiration.
Many listings include a protection clause stating that, for a certain period after expiration, the owner is liable for the commission if the property sells to a party that the broker procured, unless the seller has since listed the property with another broker.

S 33. (c) the advertising must not be deceptive.
Advertising may not be misleading or deceptive in promoting the brokerage or listed properties. Blind ads are also prohibited without exception. Salespersons, moreover, must identify their employer.

S 34. (a) collusion.
Collusion is the illegal practice of two or more businesses joining forces or making joint decisions which have the effect of putting another business at a competitive disadvantage.

S 35. (b) The brokers have illegally fixed prices.
Price fixing is the practice of two or more brokers agreeing to charge certain commission rates or fees for their services, regardless of market conditions or competitors.

S 36. (a) The seller may cancel the contract, since it can be ruled invalid.
A contingency that is too broad, vague, or excessive in duration may invalidate the entire contract on the grounds of insufficiency of mutual agreement. To avoid problems, the statement of a contingency should be explicit and clear, have an expiration date, and expressly require diligence in the effort to fulfill the requirement.

S 37. (d) claim the deposit as compensated damages for the buyer's failure to perform.
If a buyer fails to perform under the terms of a sale contract, the breach entitles the seller to legal recourse for damages. The usual remedy is forfeiture of the buyer's deposit as liquidated damages, provided the deposit is not grossly in excess of the seller's actual damages.

S 38. (b) The optionor must perform if the optionee takes the option, but the optionee is under no obligation to do so.
An option-to-buy places the optionee under no obligation to purchase the property. However, the seller must perform under the terms of the contract if the buyer exercises the option. An option is thus a unilateral agreement. Exercise of the option creates a bilateral sale contract where both parties are bound to perform.

S 39. (b) a decline in demand for all types of real estate in the real estate market.
Businesses that support the departing company will lay off or fire new employees, causing some to leave town in search of work. Some of these businesses may also have to cease operations. Hence the demand for residential real estate, as well as for commercial and industrial, will decline, and new construction will probably also halt until some other factor increases demand again.

S 40. (b). rental prices in that market will rise
An undersupply of commercial properties in relation to demand will most likely increase prices, as renters

have fewer choices and less bargaining power.

S 41. (b) absorption.
Absorption is the amount of available property that becomes occupied over a period of time, usually measured in square feet.

S 42. (b) $17,000.
First derive the annual depreciation, which is the cost divided by the economic life. Then multiply annual depreciation times the number of years to identify total depreciation. Remember to subtract depreciation from the original cost if the question asks for the ending value. Thus, ($20,000 ÷ 20 years x 3 years) = $3,000 total depreciation. The ending value is $20,000 – 3,000, or $17,000.

S 43. (b) Apartment buildings.
The income capitalization approach, or income approach, is used for income properties and sometimes for other properties in a rental market where the appraiser can find rental data. The approach is based on the principle of anticipation: the expected future income stream of a property underlies what an investor will pay for the property.

S 44. (c) estimates net income and applies a capitalization rate to it.
The steps are: estimate potential gross income; estimate effective gross income (potential minus vacancy and credit losses); estimate net operating income (effective minus total operating expenses); select a capitalization rate; and apply the capitalization rate. Use the formula: income ÷ cap rate = value.

S 45. (c) potential gross income minus vacancy and credit loss minus expenses.
Net operating income, or NOI, is always income after vacancy, credit loss and expenses. It does not, however, include debt service.

S 46. (b) $400,000.
Value = Income ÷ Cap rate. Thus, V= $40,000 ÷ .10 = $400,000.

S 47. (a) the interest rate may vary.
Adjustable rate mortgages (ARMs) allow the lender to change the interest rate at specified intervals and by a specified amount. Federal regulations place limits on incremental interest rate increases and on the total amount by which the rate may be increased over the loan term.

S 48. (b) A wraparound lender can profit when the interest rate of the wraparound exceeds that of the underlying mortgage.
In a wraparound loan arrangement, the seller receives a junior mortgage from the buyer, and uses the buyer's payments to make the payments on the original first mortgage. This potentially enables the seller to profit from any difference between a lower interest rate on the senior loan and a higher rate on the wraparound loan.

S 49. (b) a blanket mortgage loan.
A blanket mortgage is secured by more than one property, such as multiple parcels of real estate in a development.

S 50. (b) Payments are not sufficient to retire the loan.
Negative amortization causes the loan balance to increase over the term. This occurs if the borrower's periodic payment is insufficient to cover the interest owed for the period. The lender adds the amount of unpaid interest to the borrower's loan balance.

S 51. (b) the loan amount needs to be less than the property's value.
Lenders must have a margin of borrower equity to protect against falling real estate values which increase the risk of the loan. Without this margin, a lender can incur a loan loss in a foreclosure sale since the proceeds may be less than the loan amount.

S 52. (b) Truth-in-Lending laws
Truth-in-Lending Laws, implemented by the Federal Reserve's Regulation Z, regulate the disclosure of costs, the right to rescind the credit transaction, advertising credit offers, and penalties for non-compliance with the act.

S 53. (d) Participants sell mortgage-backed securities in order to buy pools of loans.
Secondary mortgage market organizations buy pools of mortgages from primary lenders and sell securities backed by these pooled mortgages to investors. By selling securities, the secondary market brings investor money into the mortgage market. By purchasing loans from primary lenders, the secondary market returns funds to the primary lenders, thereby enabling the primary lender to originate more mortgage loans.

S 54. (a) cost recovery expense.
Cash flow is the difference between the amount of actual cash flowing into the investment as revenue and out of the investment for expenses, debt service, and all other items. Cash flow concerns cash items only, and therefore excludes depreciation (cost recovery), which is not a cash expense.

S 55. (c) dividing net income by the price paid for the property.
The investment return measure known as return on investment (ROI) is calculated by dividing net income by the value of the investment. This yields a rate of return on investment.

S 56. (a) Installing a higher capacity air conditioning and purifying system.
Basis is increased by the cost of capital improvements made to the property. Examples of capital improvements are: putting on an addition, paving a driveway, replacing a roof, adding central air conditioning, and rewiring the home. Repairs, maintenance, and redecorating are not generally considered capital improvements.

S 57. (c) There are no federal ad valorem taxes on real property.
There are no federal taxes on real property. The Constitution of the United States specifically prohibits such taxes. The federal government does, however, tax income derived from real property and gains realized on the sale of real property.

S 58. (b) the assessed value of property.
General property taxes are levied on an ad valorem basis, meaning that they are based on the assessed value of the property. Assessed value is determined according to state law, usually by a county or township assessor or appraiser.

S 59. (d) The prohibition may be legal if performed correctly.
The condominium association may be exempt from fair housing prohibitions against age discrimination if it is established as a retirement community in which 80 % of the dwellings have one person who is 55 years of age or older and it has amenities for elderly residents.

S 60. (c) The agent and the owner.
The owner has illegally discriminated, and the agent, by going along with the owner, is equally guilty of violating fair housing laws.

S 61. (b) Inspection fees.
Prorated items are expenses that both parties must share. Non-prorated items are one-time individual charges such as sale commissions, recording fees, and title insurance.

S 62. (d) A lender paying a fee to a broker for referring a borrower to the lender.
RESPA prohibits the payment of fees as part of a real estate settlement when no services are actually rendered. This prohibition includes referral fees for such services as title searches, title insurance, mortgage loans, appraisals, credit reports, inspections, surveys, and legal services.

S 63. (b) Copies of required communications to principals.
Some communications with transaction parties are good and necessary for business. Others are required by law, and records of them must be maintained for a statutory period. Required records typically include listing agreements, offers, contracts, closing statements, agency agreements, disclosure documents, correspondence and other communication records, notes and any other relevant information.

S 64. (a) refuse to use terms that refer to or describe any of the classes of persons protected by the laws.
Before entering into a listing agreement, a licensee should explain that it is necessary to comply with fair housing laws and obtain the potential client's acknowledgment and agreement. The agent should make it

clear that the agent will reject the use of terms indicating race, religion, creed, color, national origin, sex, handicap, age or familial status to describe prospective buyers. Such terms should be avoided in conversation as well as in advertising.

S 65. (a) Alterations to a rental space made to fit a particular tenant
Alterations made specifically for certain tenants are called build-outs or tenant improvements. The work may involve merely painting and re-carpeting a rental space, or erecting new walls and installing special electrical or other systems.

S 66. (c) maintain a special trust account in a qualified financial depository.
State laws and real estate commission rules specify how a property manager is to manage trust funds. In general, the agent is to maintain a separate bank account for these funds, with special accounting, in a qualified depository institution. The rules for how long an agent may hold trust funds before depositing them, and how the funds are to be disbursed, are spelled out. The fundamental requirements are that the owners of all funds must be identified, and there must be no commingling or conversion of client funds and agent funds.

S 67. (c) 3
The total area of the living room is (8' x 14' + 8' x 18' + 8' x 16' + 8' x 18') = 528 SF. They will therefore need 528 / 200 SF, or 3 whole gallons.

S 68. (d) 218'
Since the investor paid $100,000 total, and that equals $250 per frontage foot, there are 400 frontage feet (100,000 / 250). If the property is two acres, it totals 87,120 SF. Dividing this by 400 produces a lot depth of 217.8'.

S 69. (c) Yes with $360 left over.
The loan she can get amounts to ($240,000 x 80%), or $192,000. The points charge is ($192,000 x .02), or $3,840. Total closing costs are then $3,840 + 800, or $4640. Thus she has $360 to spare.

S 70. (c) $90,000
First, the sale price is 115% of the appraised value, so the appraised value is $230,000 / 115%, or $200,000. The lender will lend $140,000 (70% of appraised value), so the investor will have to come up with $90,000 ($230,000 – 140,000).

S 71. (c) $96,000.
Since the comparable has an extra half-bath, it is adjusted downward to equalize with the subject. Conversely, since it has no patio, the appraiser adds value to the comparable. Thus, $100,000 minus $5,000 plus $1,000 equals $96,000.

S 72. (c) $508
The total assessed value is ($84,550 + 235,000), or $319,550. The annual tax is based on ($319,550 / 100) = 3195.5 100's. Round up to 3196. To derive the annual tax, multiply 3,196 x 1.91, or $6,104.36. Divide this by 12 for the monthly escrow: ($6,104 / 12) = $508.

S 73. (d) $92,000
The formula for equity is (current value – indebtedness). The current value is ($180,000 + 25% x 180,000), or ($180,000 x 125%), or $225,000. The current debt is ($180,000 x 80%) - $11,000, or $133,000. Their equity is therefore $92,000.

S 74. (b) $166,150
Use the formula: Gain = (Net selling price – adjusted basis) where adjusted basis = (beginning cost – depreciation). The selling price is $240,000 x 5% annual appreciation x 10 years, or ($240,000 + 50% x 240,000), or $360,000. Since land cannot be depreciated, the depreciable basis is ($240,000 total cost – 60,000 land value), or $180,000 (land = 25% total value). Annual depreciation = ($180,000 / 39 years), or $4,615. Thus total depreciation is ($4,615 x 10 years), or $46,150. The adjusted basis is therefore ($240,000 – 46,150), or $193,850. The total gain is therefore ($360,000 – 193,850), or $166,150.

S 75. (c) $80,000
Applying the formula (percent of insurable property value carried / 80% replacement cost) x claim = recovery), divide the amount of coverage carried ($160,000) by 80% of the insurable property value ($250,000) to get the percent of the claim the company will pay (80%). Multiply this percentage by the claim amount to get $80,000, what the company will pay.

S 76. (d)   Albert violates license law if he pays Barbara a referral fee.
Licensees may not pay referral fees to unlicensed parties. NCREC's License Law and Rule Comments on 93A-2(6)

S 77. (b)   be at least 18 years old; pass a 75-hour prelicense class; pass the state examination; and demonstrate sufficient moral character.
"Each applicant for a license as a real estate broker shall, within three years preceding the date the application is made, have satisfactorily completed, at a school approved by the Commission, an education program consisting of at least 75 hours of classroom instruction." §93A-4(a)

S 78. (a)   The NCREC will discipline the broker.
"Following a hearing, the Commission shall also have power to suspend or revoke any license issued under the provisions of this Chapter or to reprimand or censure any licensee when:... (4) the broker's unlicensed employee, who is exempt from the provisions of this Chapter under G.S. 93A-2(c)(6), has committed, in the regular course of business, any act which, if committed by the broker, would constitute a violation of G.S. 93A-6(a) for which the broker could be disciplined." 93A-6(b)(4)

S 79. (a)   notify the Real Estate Commission in writing within 10 days.
"Upon initial licensure and at all times thereafter, every licensee shall assure that the Commission has on record the licensee's current personal name, firm name, trade name, residence address and firm address. Every licensee shall notify the Commission in writing of each change of personal name, firm name, trade name, residence address and firm address within 10 days of said change." Subchapter 58A Section A.0103

S 80. (c)   for any of the three year's requirements.
 A provisional broker as described in G.S. 93A-4(a1) or G.S. 93A-4.3(d) may request and be granted an extension of time to satisfy the postlicensing education requirement for any of the first three years following the date of his or her initial licensure as a broker if the licensee provides evidence satisfactory to the Commission that he or she was unable to obtain the necessary education due to an incapacitating illness or other circumstance which existed for a substantial portion of the year in question and which constituted a severe and verifiable hardship such that to comply with the education requirement would have been impossible or unreasonably burdensome. 58A.1903

S 81. (c)   a broker who must be supervised by a broker-in-charge until the provisional status is removed.
"The term provisional broker within the meaning of this Chapter means a real estate broker who, pending acquisition and documentation to the Commission of the education or experience prescribed by either G.S. 93A-4(a1) or G.S. 93A-4.3, must be supervised by a broker-in-charge when performing any act for which a real estate license is required." §93A-2(a2).

S 82. (c)   before her second renewal.
"In order to renew a broker license on active status, the person requesting renewal of a license shall, upon the second renewal of such license following initial licensure, and upon each subsequent annual renewal, have completed, within one year preceding license expiration, eight classroom hours of real estate continuing education." 21 NCAC 58A .1702

S 83. (d)   Negotiating the amount of the security deposits or rents.
"...the salaried employee's employment is limited to: exhibiting units on the real estate to prospective tenants; providing the prospective tenants with information about the lease of the units; accepting applications for lease of the units; completing and executing preprinted form leases; and accepting security deposits and rental payments for the units only when the deposits and rental payments are made payable to the owner or the broker employed by the owner. The salaried employee shall not negotiate the amount of security deposits or rental payments and shall not negotiate leases or any rental agreements on behalf of the owner or broker. §93A-2

S 84. (a) The employing broker or broker-in-charge.
Provisional brokers may only receive compensation for performance of real estate services by the agent's broker or broker-in-charge. Chapter 93A-6

S 85. (d) new home sales.
Generally, the law applies to resales of all 1-4 unit residential dwellings. However, a transfer involving the first sale of a dwelling that was never inhabited is exempt. G.S. 47E-2

S 86. (b) cancel the contract within three days following the execution of the sales contract.
"If the disclosure statement is not delivered to the purchaser prior to or at the time the purchaser makes an offer, the purchaser may cancel any resulting real estate contract. The purchaser's right to cancel shall expire if not exercised prior to the following, whichever occurs first: 1) The end of the third calendar day following the purchaser's receipt of the disclosure statement; (2) The end of the third calendar day following the date the contract was made; (3) Settlement or occupancy by the purchaser in the case of a sale or exchange; or (4) Settlement in the case of a purchase pursuant to a lease with option to purchase." GS 47E-5(b)

S 87. (d) a buyer or seller begins to disclose his or her specific property needs, wants or desires.
The NCREC has generally defined first substantial contact as the point where a communication occurs regarding the real estate needs of a buyer or seller prospect. "For the purposes of this rule, 'first substantial contact' shall include contacts between a broker and a consumer where the consumer or broker begins to act as though an agency relationship exists and the consumer begins to disclose to the broker personal or confidential information." 58A.0104(c).

S 88. (d) has failed to identify his brokerage in violation of NC license laws.
"A licensee shall not advertise the sale, purchase, exchange, rent or lease of real estate, for another or others, in a manner indicating the offer to sell, purchase, exchange, rent, or lease is being made by the licensee's principal only. Every such advertisement shall conspicuously indicate that it is the advertisement of a broker or brokerage firm..." Subchapter 58A.0105(a)

S 89. (c) settle the dispute with their broker.
"The Commission shall not act as a board of arbitration and shall not compel parties to settle disputes concerning such matters as the rate of commissions, the division of commissions, pay of provisional brokers, and similar matters." Subchapter 58A.0109(f)

S 90 (a) Immediately
"Every agreement for brokerage services between a broker and a buyer or tenant shall be express and shall be reduced to writing not later than the time one of the parties makes an offer to purchase, sell, rent, lease, or exchange real estate to another. However, every agreement between a broker and a buyer or tenant which seeks to bind the buyer or tenant for a period of time or to restrict the buyer's or tenant's right to work with other agents or without an agent shall be in writing from its formation." Subchapter 58A.0104(a)

S 91. (d) to prospective buyers and sellers upon first substantial contact.
"In every real estate sales transaction, a broke shall, at first substantial contact directly with a prospective buyer or seller, provide the prospective buyer or seller with a copy of the publication "Working with Real Estate Agents," set forth the broker's name and license number thereon, review it with the buyer or seller, and determine whether the agent will act as the agent of the buyer or seller in the transaction." Subchapter 58A.0104(c)

S 92. (c) The broker must provide written disclosure confirmation on or before delivery of an offer.
"In every real estate sales transaction other than auctions, the broker shall, no later than the time of delivery of an offer to the seller or seller's agent, provide the seller or seller's agent with a written confirmation disclosing that he represents the interests of the buyer. The written confirmation may be made in the buyer's offer to purchase." Subchapter 58A.0104(f)

S 93. (c) the seller's motivations or selling terms not established by the seller, unless required by law to disclose them.
A designated seller's agent "shall not, without the seller's permission, disclose to the buyer or buyer's agent (1) that the seller may agree to a price, terms, or any conditions of sale other than those established by the

seller; (2) the seller's motivation for engaging in the transaction unless disclosure is otherwise required by statute or rule; and (3) any information about the seller which the seller has identified as confidential unless disclosure of the information is otherwise required by statute or rule." Subchapter 58A.0104(k)

S 94. (d) heated, finished, and directly accessible from other living areas.
Living area is space that is intended for human occupancy and is: (1) heated by a conventional heating system; (2) finished with walls, floors and ceilings of materials generally accepted for interior construction, and (3) directly accessible from other living area through a door or by a heated hallway or stairway.

S 95. (c) file a complaint with the North Carolina Human Relations Commission.
The filing of a complaint with the NCHRC initiates an investigative procedure followed by efforts to substantiate and remedy the violation. If the complaint cannot be resolved, the NCHRC or the complainant may sue in the courts. G.S. 41A-7(a)

S 96. (c) must disclose whether the subdivision's streets are public or private.
"Prior to entering any agreement or any conveyance with any prospective buyer, the developer and seller shall prepare and sign, and the buyer of the subject real estate shall receive and sign an acknowledgment of receipt of a separate instrument known as the subdivision streets disclosure statement. Said disclosure statement shall fully and completely disclose the status (whether public or private) of the street upon which the house or lot fronts." § 136-102.6.

S 97. (a) takes action to enforce the lien within 180 days following completion of the job.
Action to enforce lien: "(a)... An action to enforce the lien created by this Article may be instituted in any county in which the lien is filed. No such action may be commenced later than 180 days after the last furnishing of labor or materials at the site of the improvement by the person claiming the lien." § 44A-13

S 98. (c) need not be licensed.
"The provisions of this Chapter (93A) do not apply to and do not include:
(1) Any person, partnership, corporation, limited liability company, association, or other business entity who, as owner or lessor, shall perform any of the acts aforesaid with reference to property owned or leased by them, where the acts are performed in the regular course of or as incident to the management of that property and the investment therein. " G.S. 93A-2(c)

Thus, a property manager who is the owner's employee is not required to have a real estate license.

S 99. (d) The right to occupy an apartment every January for the next ten years.
"'Time share' means a right to occupy a unit or any of several units during five or more separated time periods over a period of at least five years, including renewal options, whether or not coupled with a freehold estate or an estate for years in a time share project or a specified portion thereof..." §93A-41(9)
NC - RE Time Shares 5<

S 100. (b) if a title record is free of claims for the past 30 years, the title is free and clear regardless of prior claims.
"It is the purpose of the General Assembly of the State of North Carolina to provide that if a person claims title to real property under a chain of record title for 30 years, and no other person has filed a notice of any claim of interest in the real property during the 30-year period, then all conflicting claims based upon any title transaction prior to the 30-year period shall be extinguished." G.S. § 47B-1

S 101. (d) Tyler must exclude the swing set and Sasha include the washing machine in the contract.
The swing set must be excluded and Sasha must include the washing machine in the sales contract to achieve the desired results. Personal property that is not permanently affixed to the land, can be negotiated in the sales contract.

S 102. (b) The lender and foreclosure buyer must honor the lease and all of its terms.
Foreclosing parties with recorded leases, must honor the tenancy terms. The tenant must receive advance notice and has a right to terminate the lease.

S 103. (c) subjacent support.
The right to subjacent support protects property owners from actions by abutting property owners to the subject property that would cause the land to shift, collapse or erode. This right is very similar to the right of lateral support. Riparian and littoral are water rights terms.

S 104. (a) The modular home is considered and taxed as real property once assembled.
Modular homes must be built according to state codes and are considered real property. Manufactured homes are treated as personal property until affixed to a foundation.

S 105. (b) that a new bridge is being constructed in the immediate vicinity.
A new bridge is a major change to the transportation systems and patterns of an area and must be disclosed. The fact a property may be haunted or when a tornado last impacted the area do not have to be disclosed. A possible encroachment is simply not a land use restriction issue.

Appendix: North Carolina Real Estate Licensing-Related Websites

North Carolina Real Estate Candidate Handbook
This contains crucial information regarding the PSI North Carolina Real Estate Exam. Make sure to download and read this participant booklet to fully understand the entire test taking process.
http://www.ncrec.gov/Brochures/general.pdf

Key North Carolina Contacts

North Carolina Real Estate Commission
1313 Navaho Drive, P.O. Box 17100
Raleigh, North Carolina 27619-7100
919-875-3700
ncrec@ncrec.gov
www.ncrec.state.nc.us

PSI Testing Service
(Psychological Services, Inc.)
3210 East Tropicana
Las Vegas, NV 89121
800-733-9267
https://candidate.psiexams.com/#

North Carolina Association of Realtors
4511 Weybridge Lane
Greensboro, NC 27407
800-443-9956
ncar@ncrealtors.org
www.ncrealtors.org

Made in the USA
Middletown, DE
27 July 2017